THE WORKS OF SHAKESPEARE

EDITED FOR THE SYNDICS OF THE
CAMBRIDGE UNIVERSITY PRESS

BY

JOHN DOVER WILSON

THE SONNETS

CAMBRIDGE UNIVERSITY PRESS

CAMBRIDGE

LONDON · NEW YORK · MELBOURNE

Published by the Syndics of the Cambridge University Press
The Pitt Building, Trumpington Street, Cambridge CB2 1RP
Bentley House, 200 Euston Road, London NW1 2DB
32 East 57th Street, New York, NY 10022, USA
296 Beaconsfield Parade, Middle Park, Melbourne 3206, Australia

ISBN 0 521 07555 6 hard covers
ISBN 0 521 09498 4 paperback

First published 1966
Second edition 1967
First paperback edition 1969
Reprinted 1973, 1976

First printed in Great Britain at the University Press, Cambridge
Reprinted in Great Britain by Hazell Watson & Viney Ltd,
Aylesbury, Bucks

CONTENTS

PREFACE PAGE vii

INTRODUCTION

I. The Cave and the Sun xiii

II. The Origin and Quality of the Received Text xviii

III. The Friend and the Poet xlii

IV. The Identity of Mr W.H. lxxxviii

V. Themes and Sources cviii

Appendix. Clarendon's Description of William Herbert cxx

A NOTE ON TEXT AND PUNCTUATION cxxiii

ACKNOWLEDGEMENTS cxxv

THE SONNETS

Section I: 1-126 3

Section II: 127-54 66

NOTES 81

TABLE: List of the Sonnets in Conjectured Order of Writing 267

PREFACE

I began this edition of the finest love poetry in the world in what I think must be the loveliest garden on earth. It lies in a level upland glade shut in by dark forests stretching up to jagged mountain tops, but itself containing a luxuriant orchard and stately trees dotted about it here and there, while it fearlessly exposes its grassy slopes to the midsummer heat of the southern hemisphere, being watered and cooled by running streams and deep dark pools that give teeming life to birds and flowers of many kinds and colours, while to crown all extend the sweeping curves of a stately house, dwelling-place of a great lady. Shakespeare, I fancy, had imagined just such a home of peace and delight as his Belmont. Or he may even have seen one not unlike it at Wilton. Certainly it was a happy fortune that placed me amid such surroundings when I had to set hand to my last volume in the *New Cambridge Shakespeare*, begun forty years ago. For all the plays in the canon being now published, the *Poems* and the *Sonnets* remained, the former for Professor Maxwell, the latter for myself, and I was here in South Africa sitting one morning early in 1962 under the shade of a deodar tree, with a copy of the *Sonnets* in my hand to begin what after four years would become the volume the reader has before him. In the soil I have described the work took root at once and went on steadily growing, despite unforeseen difficulties after my return to Scotland, until, when still in 1962 a second midsummer came round for me, I had already made up my mind what I wanted to say and was able before the end of the year to submit a draft introduction for approval and criticism to my friend, Mr Richard David, now also my publisher, since he had recently been appointed Secretary to the Syndics of the Cambridge University Press.

A few months later, however, my plans were suddenly complicated by a letter dated 11 June 1963 from an Oxford historian whom I had made friends with some years back when staying at All Souls. He wrote in some excitement, and no wonder, inasmuch as, he informed me, he had just completed a new Life of Shakespeare, proving all the 'literary' scholars to have misconceived the facts and giving special attention to the *Sonnets* in which he claimed to have solved all the problems. I replied that I happened at the moment to be working on the *Sonnets* myself, was intending to offer solutions to some of the problems, and sent him a typescript copy of the draft Introduction, so that he could see the lines I was following. At this in turn he courteously ordered his publisher to send me an advance copy of his book.

All this placed me, as things were, in a very awkward predicament. Like most old men I was suffering from cataract and my sight grew worse as the years went on; an unsuccessful operation early in 1963 only made matters worse. The result was that I found reading and writing increasingly difficult. I could still dictate but if I was to finish my task at all, I felt obliged to restrict my reading severely to the business of the commentary.

I told him therefore that it was impossible for me to read his book; and that unless I could read it carefully and follow the argument step by step I could not tell how far I agreed with it, if at all. It was a quandary. Yet in the end I was luckily able to effect an escape owing to an action on his part. For, some months before his biography was announced to appear, he issued a series of newspaper articles giving the gist of his case.

One of these dealt with the *Sonnets*; I had it read aloud to me; and I at once realized that I need trouble myself no more about the matter. For his conclusions differed so fundamentally from those I had come to myself that one of us must be wrong, while it was out of the question for one hampered as I was to think of answering him, still less to enter into a controversy, since a blind man is virtually cut off from access to his authorities. My only course therefore was to go forward as speedily as I could, ignoring him and letting the world judge between us when the Cambridge University Press produced my book a year or two thence.

Its Secretary, however, took a slightly different view: Let us publish the draft Introduction at once, so that the world will be able to judge, if it wishes, between the two points of view without delay. I agreed and thus it came about that when his Cornish privateer of tall building and of goodly pride put forth into the perilous main of publicity, full of 'literary' submarines, my saucy bark, dressed overall in Cambridge blue and with pennon flying inscribed *For historians and others*, was there riding alongside.

That happened towards the end of 1963; and for the next year, working with such means and such speed as a purblind man can command, I pressed forward with the preparation of a line-by-line commentary and notes. All this was based upon a thorough re-examination of the text which, I was encouraged to find, so far from leading to conclusions in conflict with those arrived at in the provisional findings of 1963, not only confirmed them in all important respects but greatly developed them.

But the issues raised by the *Sonnets* are too many and too diverse in character to be compassed by one man in a single lifetime; and being allowed but a few years, if that, by all-devouring time, I decided to limit myself to establishing if possible two matters of fact: (1) the order, and (2) the date, of the *Sonnets*, since until those two results are attained editors have no firm ground to work upon.

How true that is a glance through the documented history of *Sonnets*-criticism since the time of Malone down to 1944 is enough to show and is now shown in the monumental Variorum edition by H. E. Rollins. Without that edition, indeed, my task could not have been accomplished, for its notes comprise those of all previous editors and from these an editor of today is at liberty to select all the glosses and comments that appeal to his judgement. How salutary moreover is his Johnsonian commonsense in dealing with specious absurdities or when summing up the discussion of vexed problems that lend themselves to divergent opinions!

Apart from Rollins's, the edition from which I have learnt most is H. C. Beeching's, which is almost unknown in this country because his little book, published in America in 1904, is so rare that I know of only two copies, one at the Cambridge University Library and the other owned by Blair Leishman, who lent it me not long before his death, and which I now cherish as a bequest both for its own sake and in memory of its owner. This copy, too, reveals pencil notes here and there, in his difficult hand, many of which my secretary has been able to decipher and read for me. Beeching's outstanding value as an editor is twofold; he holds no brief for the identification of Shakespeare's Friend and his exegesis is informed with a rigid adherence to the language Shakespeare uses, or had used elsewhere, together with an unusually acute awareness of the grammar, syntax and rhetoric involved. In this respect he often has the better of the scarcely less valuable Dowden, and I found either of them useful as a check upon the other. After them I have most often availed myself of the interpretations of Tucker and Knox Pooler. What I found most interesting in Pooler was his indication of affinities between sonnets at different points of the 1609 text, which often suggested possibilities of misplacements. I cannot always agree, but at times when I do they seem to lead on to important consequences. Nor must I omit to record my debt to Martin Seymour-Smith. His thoughtful and scholarly edition appeared in 1963, too late for me to benefit from it as much as I could have wished. But it was his example which gave me courage to follow the original punctuation and if I find his commentary less pedestrian than my own, that is probably because he is a modern and I am an octogenarian. Unless, however, I am mistaken he has more still to contribute to Elizabethan and Shakespearian scholarship.

Yet when all is said the prince of Sonnet editors and commentators is one of the earliest, the great Edmund Malone. All our texts go back to his, and though an American scholar has recently called some of his readings in question, let H. E. Rollins, another American and the twentieth-century editor best qualified to judge, speak the final word:

> His effect on the text was immense: for the majority of editors before 1864[1] he left little to do except to insert (or omit) an occasional hyphen, to change a period or a comma here and there, to modernize some archaic spelling. No nineteenth-century or twentieth-century editor has done textual work at all comparable in importance to Malone's; few have surpassed him as an annotator; and dozens have

[1] The first edition of the *Cambridge Shakespeare* was published in 1863.

taken credit for details borrowed from him without acknowledgement. Truly, one knows not whether to marvel more that he in that misty time could see so clearly, or that we in this supposedly clear age walk so stumblingly after him. He will be praised of ages yet to come.[1]

J.D.W.
23 December 1964

[1] H. E. Rollins, *The Sonnets* (Variorum Shakespeare, 1944) II, 39.

POSTSCRIPT

The copy for this volume was sent to the printers shortly after the above date, but its printing and final preparation for the press was delayed by various causes for over a year: the chief cause being that by the time the first proofs were received the Editor could no longer see a line of print.

J.D.W.

SECOND EDITION 1967

I have added a table at the end of the volume, showing the order in which I conjecture the Sonnets were written; and during the interval I have found time to make a thorough revision of the notes, mostly in the form of clarification and compression.

J.D.W.

INTRODUCTION

I. The Cave and the Sun

Sir Walter Raleigh, who wrote the most human short life of William Shakespeare that we possess, began his section on the *Sonnets* as follows: 'There are many footprints around the cave of this mystery, none of them pointing in the outward direction. No one has ever attempted a solution of the problem without leaving a book behind him; and the shrine of Shakespeare is thickly hung with these votive offerings, all withered and dusty.'[1] Raleigh's cave of mystery calls another to mind, Plato's cave of illusion, in which the human race sit chained with their backs to the sun without, and are condemned to accept the passing shadows on the wall before them for the truth—the real truth being only revealed to the few who are able to break their bonds and turn to face the light of day.[2] Absorbed in our own attempts to solve the biographical puzzles that the individual sonnets offer us, we remain blind to the sun that casts these shadows but gives meaning to the whole. Begin by seeing that meaning and recognizing the whole as the greatest love-poem in the language, and the mystery of the detail becomes so unimportant as to fade away.

That this is the right approach to an understanding, apparently so obvious and so natural, has in point of fact only quite recently been realized; and realized independently and almost simultaneously by two critics, both driven by a wide study of the love-poetry of the Renaissance to admit the uniqueness of Shakespeare's.

[1] Walter Raleigh, *Shakespeare* (1907), p. 86.
[2] *The Republic*, Book VII, §§514–18.

'There is no parallel', writes J. W. Lever in a sensitive and learned book on *The Elizabethan Love Sonnet*, 'in the whole corpus of Renaissance poetry to Shakespeare's sustained exploration of the theme of friendship through more than 120 sonnets'.[1] More significant still is what he calls the Poet's 'extreme capacity for self-effacement' and emphasizes as not just an echo of the conventional sonnet lover's avowed humility. As he writes:

Sidney had always his Protestant conscience and the dignity of his rank for ultimate solace; Spenser, regarding courtship as a preliminary to the sacrament of marriage and the subordination of wife to husband, had stooped to conquer. Even Petrarch had sacrificed himself on the altar of love with a certain hauteur—*E voglio anzi un sepolcro bello e bianco*. But the self-effacement of Shakespeare as poet of the sonnets is total and unreserved. He has no place in nature or society save that accorded him by the Friend. He is in the autumn of his years, 'lame, poor, and despised', 'in disgrace with fortune and men's eyes'... he envies this man's art and that man's scope. Far from planning, like Petrarch, a memorial of white marble to commemorate his love, he pleads to be left forgotten and unmourned, lest the world should mock the man who once befriended him:

> No longer mourn for me when I am dead,
> Than you shall hear the surly sullen bell
> Give warning to the world that I am fled
> From this vile world with vilest worms to dwell:
> Nay if you read this line, remember not,
> The hand that writ it... (71)[2]

C. S. Lewis, the other critic I must quote, proclaims the *Sonnets* not only as unique in the period of the Renaissance but as the supreme love-poetry of the world.

[1] J. W. Lever, *The Elizabethan Love Sonnet* (1956). p. 165. [2] *Ibid.* pp. 185–6.

He begins by disposing of the 'cave of mystery' in these terms:

The difficulty which faces us if we try to read the sequence like a novel is that the precise mode of love which the poet declares for the Man remains obscure. His language is too lover-like for that of ordinary male friendship; and though the claims of friendship are sometimes put very high in, say, the *Arcadia*, I have found no real parallel to such language between friends in sixteenth-century literature. Yet, on the other hand, this does not seem to be the poetry of full-blown pederasty. Shakespeare, and indeed Shakespeare's age, did nothing by halves. If he had intended in these sonnets to be the poet of pederasty, I think he would have left us in no doubt; the lovely παιδικά, attended by a whole train of mythological perversities, would have blazed across the page. The incessant demand that the Man should marry and found a family would seem to be inconsistent (or so I suppose—it is a question for psychologists) with a real homosexual passion. It is not even very obviously consistent with normal friendship. It is indeed hard to think of any real situation in which it would be natural. What man in the whole world, except a father or a potential father-in-law, cares whether any other man gets married? Thus the emotion expressed in the *Sonnets* refuses to fit into our pigeon-holes....

Such is the effect of individual sonnets. But when we read the whole sequence through at a sitting (as we ought sometimes to do) we have a different experience. From its total plot, however ambiguous, however particular, there emerges something not indeed common or general like the love expressed in many individual sonnets, but yet, in a higher way, universal. The main contrast in the *Sonnets* is between the two loves, that 'of comfort' and that 'of despair'. The love 'of despair' demands all; the love 'of comfort' asks, and perhaps receives, nothing. Thus the whole sequence becomes an expanded version of Blake's 'The Clod and the Pebble'. And so it comes about that, however the whole thing began—in perversion, in convention, even (who knows?) in fiction—Shakespeare, celebrating the 'Clod' as no man has celebrated it before or since, ends by expressing simply love, the quintessence of all loves whether erotic, parental, filial, amicable, or feudal. Thus from extreme particularity there is a road to the highest universality. The love is, in the end, so simply and entirely love that our *cadres* are thrown away and we cease to ask what kind. However it may have been with Shakespeare in his daily life, the greatest of the sonnets are written from a region in which love abandons all claims and flowers into charity: after that it makes little odds what the root was like. They open a new world of love poetry; as new as Dante's and Petrarch's had been in their day. These had of course expressed humility, but it had been the humility of Eros, hungry to receive; kneeling, but kneeling to ask. They and their great successor Patmore sing a dutiful and submissive, but hardly a giving, love. They could have written, almost too easily, 'Being your slave, what should I do but tend?': they could hardly have written, 'I may not evermore acknowledge thee', or 'No longer mourn', or 'Although thou steal thee all my poverty'. The self-abnegation the 'naughting', in the *Sonnets* never rings false. This patience, this anxiety (more like a parent's than a lover's) to find excuses for the beloved, this clear-sighted and wholly unembittered resignation, this transference of the whole self into another self without the demand for a return, have hardly a précedent in profane literature. In certain senses of the word 'love', Shakespeare is not so much our best as our only love poet.[1]

There is nothing a mere editor can add to that except to quote what Keats tells us about the poet.

A Poet is the most unpoetical of any thing in existence; because he has no Identity—he is continually informing[2] and filling some other Body—The Sun, the Moon, the Sea and Men

[1] C. S. Lewis, *English Literature in the Sixteenth Century* (1954), pp. 503–5.

[2] 'Informing'—conjectural completion of 'in for—'.

and Women who are creatures of impulse are poetical and have about them an unchangeable attribute—the poet has none; no identity—he is certainly the most unpoetical of all God's creatures.[1]

As a dramatic poet, Shakespeare has no identity; as a man and a lover he is as selfless and humble as the clod in Blake's poem 'trodden with the cattle's feet'. Thus the *Sonnets* are for all time.

Yet their poet, being human, was of an age, and in order that the modern reader may not misunderstand the homage offered, I shall have to remind him, at times in many of the observations that follow, of certain Elizabethan conventions and modes of expression. There is, however, one important convention of sonnet-writers which must be set down here. To quote T. G. Tucker, one of the better editors of the *Sonnets*:

Shakespeare was the poet in 'service' or 'vassalage' to his 'lord', and in the recognized manner of sonneteers, supposed himself bound to write piece after piece to the beloved with a certain continuity of production and with as much variety of 'invention' as possible upon his adopted theme. Any intermission of greater length than usual, any omission to keep up the regular supply of offerings at the altar, would call for self-reproach and apology; it would even supply the poet with matter for the next effort.[2]

And there readers who have, like Lewis, chosen the better part of enjoying the *Sonnets* as the greatest love-poetry in the world and asking no further questions, may well leave this introduction and pass directly on to Shakespeare himself.

[1] *The Letters of John Keats*, edited by M. Buxton Forman (2nd ed., 1936), p. 228. Quoted also by Lever, *op. cit.* p. 186.

[3] *The Sonnets of Shakespeare*, edited by T. G. Tucker (1924), p. xlviii.

II. THE ORIGIN AND QUALITY OF THE RECEIVED TEXT

But there will be some whom curiosity draws back to the cave to see what, if anything, can be made of the shadows, and who would feel an editor had failed in his duty did he not hang a votive offering in the shrine. Such readers must first of all, however, pass three stationers: William Jaggard, who published two of the sonnets in 1599; Thomas Thorpe, who stands at the very threshold of the cave, since but for his enterprise the rest of the sonnets would never have been printed at all; and the later publisher John Benson, whose spurious edition held the field until the time of Wordsworth.

What was known of the 'Sonnets' before and after 1609

As far as our records go, the first public intimation that Shakespeare had written sonnets appeared in a book called *Palladis Tamia: Wits Treasury*, published in 1598 and compiled by one Francis Meres, evidently one of Shakespeare's admirers who, in a sort of comparative catalogue of English writers of his day and their Latin or Greek parallels, gives a list of Shakespeare's plays so far produced and speaks in these terms about him as a poet:

> The sweete wittie soul of *Ovid* lives in mellifluous and honey-tongued Shakespeare, witnes his *Venus and Adonis*, his *Lucrece*, his sugred Sonnets among his private friends,

and a little later names Shakespeare with other sonnet-writers as one

> most passionate among us to bewaile and bemoane the perplexities of Love.[1]

[1] See E. K. Chambers, *William Shakespeare*, II, 194–5.

Only a certain number of the sonnets now extant can here be referred to by Meres, inasmuch as some of them were in all probability composed after 1598, while others, as we shall see, are of too intimate a nature for their author to have allowed their inclusion in any selection that Meres can have heard of. But quite a large proportion of these might have been read by anyone, and from among them it would have been easy for Shakespeare or one of his 'private friends' to make a selection for private circulation, as was done with the work of other poets of the time.[1] The sonnets, however, that first appeared in print were numbers 138 and 144, and they belong to just that section of the whole collection which Shakespeare, I believe, would have been most reluctant to see published.

The name of Jaggard (William and Isaac) is famous today as that of the printers and part publishers of the First Folio. It is not generally remembered that the Jaggards had twice before dabbled in Shakespearean copy, after a rather shady fashion—though not one technically dishonest from the stationers' standpoint.[2] Four years, for example, before they published the Folio, though only a year before they began operations on the great work,[3] they had been issuing faked reprints of ten plays as Shakespeare's, only three of which were actually good texts of his.[4] And in 1598 or 1599 William Jaggard had been responsible for a little octavo book entitled *The Passionate Pilgrim by William Shake-*

[1] See Percy Simpson, *Studies in Elizabethan Drama*, pp. 184–5.

[2] Provided the 'copy' had been all read by the censor, the Stationers' Company usually accepted it without question.

[3] See W. W. Greg, *The Shakespeare First Folio* (1955), pp. 3–4.

[4] *Ibid.* pp. 9–12.

speare, containing some twenty lyrics, all, according to the title-page, ostensibly Shakespeare's but fifteen of them by other poets: and even of the five really his, three having been lifted from Act 4 of *Love's Labour's Lost* without any indication of the fact. Thus the only new and genuine Shakespearean poems in the volume were the two sonnets just mentioned, viz. 138 and 144; and it is characteristic of Jaggard's duplicity that these are placed first and second in the volume so as to lend an air of Shakespearean novelty to the rest. The text of neither sonnet tallies exactly with its parallel in the received text: that of number 144 has several unimportant variants and 138 seems to be a slightly different version. From whom had he got them? Clearly someone intimate with the author.

Two further points of interest to students of the *Sonnets* arise out of these petty fraudulences of Jaggard. First of all, while the publication by various pirates of bad Shakespearean quartos since the early nineties shows the existence of a public ever ready to purchase plays performed by his company, Jaggard's proceedings prove that before the end of the century the name of Shakespeare himself had become so well known and generally attractive that a stationer would make it his business to palm off spurious copy as his. And in the second place, what followed from the publication of *The Passionate Pilgrim* gives us what I believe is the only instance on record of Shakespeare, who seemed otherwise completely indifferent to the circulation of unauthorized, corrupt, and spurious editions of his writings, displaying anger with one of the pirates who preyed upon his productions. And even so the instance would probably not have been recorded had not another author, wronged at the same time, issued a public protest.

Jaggard seems to have done so well with the first two editions of *The Passionate Pilgrim* that he thought it worth while to issue a third in 1612. This he now printed under his own name, and in order to give the impression that he had secured more Shakespearean copy meanwhile he revised the title-page and added to the text eight new pieces of verse, this time extracted from Thomas Heywood's *Troia Britanica*, which he had himself printed in 1609. At this barefaced attempt to pass off more than half a dozen of his poems as another man's work, Heywood protested in his *Apology for Actors* which was printed by Nicholas Okes; at the same time informing the world that Shakespeare, of whom he speaks in terms of noticeable deference, was 'much offended with M. Jaggard that (altogether unknowne to him) presumed to make so bold with his name'. Shakespeare had probably never seen *The Passionate Pilgrim* until Heywood drew his attention to it. But once the book was in his hand he could not help seeing his two sonnets at the beginning. His displeasure therefore may well have been partly due to their publication, and it looks as if Jaggard had the displeasure conveyed directly to him, since he printed a cancel of the title-page from which the name Shakespeare had been removed.[1] It was surely some motive more compelling than a sense of decency or a desire to conciliate Heywood that induced Jaggard to rob his volume of its chief attraction, the attribution to Shakespeare. Further light on these matters is best sought in connexion with an inquiry into the origin and character of the publication of the complete text of the *Sonnets* in 1609, a publication which must have displeased Shakespeare far more.

[1] See Chambers, *William Shakespeare*, I, 547–48, II, 218–19; Greg, *The Shakespeare First Folio*, pp. 9–10.

But before actually coming to that, it will be convenient to go forward a generation and take a look at an edition that appeared in 1640 and carries on the story of the piratical treatment of the *Sonnets* begun by Jaggard. Why was it that its editor, while helping himself freely to Thorpe's collection, should have spared no pains to conceal both all knowledge of it and any connexion with it, so that he succeeded in so totally eclipsing its memory that it was not until Malone published his edition of the 1609 text in 1780 that Thorpe's production took its rightful place in the Shakespeare canon?

The 1640 edition which was published late in 1639 or early in 1640 bears the following title:

> *Poems*: written by Wil. Shakespeare Gent.
> Printed at London by Tho. Cotes, and are to be sold
> by Iohn Benson, dwelling in St Dunstan's
> Church-yard. 1640.[1]

Apart from a few pages of preliminaries, the volume contains all but eight of the *Sonnets*, a couple of songs from Shakespeare's plays, everything that Jaggard had published in his second edition of *The Passionate Pilgrim* of 1612, a reprint of *The Phoenix and the Turtle*, and a heterogeneous collection of poems by other poets including Milton, Ben Jonson, Herrick, and anyone else from whom the editor thought he could pilfer without infringing copyright. That of *Venus and Adonis* and *Lucrece* being still operative, he was not able to include them. And it is commonly assumed, perhaps rightly, that it was fear of infringing Thorpe's copyright that led him to disguise his wholesale borrowing from that collection, although Thorpe's copyright cannot have been very active as he published nothing after 1625. In any case, the work Benson put into the pre-

[1] See Rollins, II, 18–36, for a full account of this edition.

paration of the volume seems in excess of anything such fears demanded. He laid hands upon most of the sonnets of 1609 but he rearranged them under various headings and in other respects took elaborate pains to cover up his traces. It is sometimes stated that he altered the sex of the Friend. Blair Leishman told me he made a careful check of the text throughout some years ago but beyond one or two changes of personal pronouns, possibly misprints, he found no evidence of deliberate falsification of this sort.

There is something very odd about the make-up of Benson's volume. It is printed, as it were, like two books, each with a title-page identical in layout and obviously struck off from the same forme, the only difference being that the one standing first bears the date 1640. Yet this first part contains not more than five leaves and consists of preliminaries only, while it is clear from the printer's signatures that it was printed after the rest of the volume, which runs to ninety-two leaves and contains the material detailed above. It seems pretty clear therefore that the material in the first or preliminary part must have come to the publisher's hands after the main book was already in print. Nor is it difficult to see that this first material was a long commendatory poem of sixty-eight lines by Leonard Digges, a poem which was itself merely a longer version of the poem twenty-two lines in length which he contributed to the First Folio; both versions, indeed, refer to the quarrel between Brutus and Cassius in *Julius Caesar* as a 'half-sword parley'. And, this being so, it seems probable that the longer version had been originally intended for the First Folio but was found excessive when it came to press. Anyhow, as it deals exclusively with the plays and never mentions Shakespeare's poems at all, it was quite inappropriate to the 1640 volume. Yet Benson the publisher does his best to make it *seem* appropriate by giving it the following heading:

Upon Master William Shakespeare, the Deceased Authour, and his Poems.

Furthermore, he fills up one of the blank pages with an 'Address to the Reader' which begins thus:

I here presume (under favour) to present to your view, some excellent and sweetely composed Poems, of Master William Shakespeare, Which in themselves appeare of the same purity, the Authour himselfe then living avouched; they had not the fortune by reason of their Infancie in his death, to have the due accommodation of proportionable glory, with the rest of his everliving Workes, yet the lines of themselves will afford you a more authentick approbation than my assurance any way can, to invite your allowance....[1]

This rigmarole suggests to the reader that the following volume was being prepared for publication by Shakespeare himself just before he died and that he had been able to guarantee the purity of the text it contains while he was still living. Considering that what it contains included the whole of Jaggard's spurious collection of 1612, together with a number of other pseudo-Shakespearean poems, this Address is nothing but fraudulent blurb, and what the writer has to say about Shakespeare's avouching the purity of the verse—the most shameless part of it—was precisely what Master Benson was chiefly anxious to impress upon his public. And the long poem by Digges falling into his hands, we must suppose by chance, he seized it as an opportunity of publishing a collection of Shakespearean verse complementary to the Folio collection of his plays. For he engaged a skilful engraver to make a reproduction of the Droeshout

[1] Chambers, *William Shakespeare*, I, 557.

portrait of the First Folio as a frontispiece to face the title-page, printing scraps of Ben Jonson's verse from the same volume to stand beneath the portrait in the lower half of the plate, and introduced other minor features to the same end, so that the whole when rounded off with this additional preliminary matter made a very pretty little book. 'I have beene somewhat solicitus', says Benson towards the end of his Address, 'to bring this forth to the perfect view of all men.' He had indeed! And the enterprise was so successful that his edition of the *Sonnets* was accepted as authentic throughout the eighteenth century, perhaps even by Wordsworth himself, while as recently as 1944 Edmund Chambers was sufficiently impressed by Benson's declaration that Shakespeare had vouched for the purity of the *Poems* to observe that 'it is at least possible that Benson knew of some statement by Shakespeare, which has not come down to us'.[1] Nothing, however, that Benson says deserves any credence. His game, apart from selling his book, was to conceal its connexion with Thorpe's publication thirty years before, to a consideration of which we must now turn.

The order of the sonnets in Thorpe's text of 1609

The copy for the 1609 sonnets was entered in the Stationers' Register for Thomas Thorpe on 20 May. According to Rollins eleven copies survive, their title-pages all beginning:

SHAKE-SPEARES
SONNETS
Neuer before Imprinted.
AT LONDON
By *G. Eld* for *T. T.* and are

[1] *Shakespearean Gleanings* (1944), p. 111.

seven of them concluding

to be solde by *Iohn Wright*, dwelling
at Christ Church gate.
1609

while the other four end simply

to be sold by William Aspley. 1609

—the difference implying that Thorpe or Eld had engaged two booksellers to distribute the copies to the public.[1]

No serious student now questions the authorship of the *Sonnets*. But the authenticity of the text, that is to say how far the author was himself responsible for the copy then printed, is a different matter and one upon which critical opinion has been sharply divided; though I think most scholars would nowadays agree that the edition of 1640 has no prior claim at all, and that if we were speaking of a dramatic text the 1609 publication would be classed as a Good Quarto, which means that the copy Thorpe handed to the printer, if not Shakespeare's autograph, was a transcript, perhaps in his own hand; and there is no reason why it should not have been, since it is commonsense to suppose that Shakespeare kept copies of a sonnet before sending them on to his Friend. Anyhow, if not an autograph it must have been a tolerably competent transcript, perhaps copied out by more than one transcriber. This contingency has seemed likely to many because of the error of *their* for *thy*, first noticed by Malone, which occurs fourteen times between sonnets 26 and 70 and only once later, in 128. Wyndham lists these among the corruptions of the 1609 text. But Beeching notes that they only go to show that Shakespeare did not correct his proofs since,

[1] See Lee, Facsimile of the *Sonnets*, pp. 31–4.

while the two words are much alike in script, they would look very different in print (p. lx Introduction); and I am reminded by Professor Kenneth Muir that an author might commit an error like this when copying out his own composition, as might any other copyist.

Apart from this, the text offers one criterion of authenticity normally absent from books of playhouse origin. Consisting as it does of 154 sonnets, that is to say of a series of separate poems, or stanzas, on the same or related themes, our decision as to its proximity to Shakespeare's manuscript or manuscripts must be influenced by the order in which the sonnets appear. In other words, if upon examination of their contents we come to the conclusion that certain sonnets or groups of sonnets are in what obviously or probably is their wrong order or their wrong place in the whole collection, we are bound to assume that Thorpe or some other person had originally procured them on separate leaves or in separate bundles which he was unable to sort out correctly; unless, indeed, Shakespeare himself had disarranged them deliberately for purposes of concealment. Most readers, however, will not be disposed to deny authority to one feature of Thorpe's arrangement, namely its division into two sections, the first (numbers 1–126) being written to or about a young man, and most of those in the second (numbers 127–54) being written to or about a dark woman. It is obvious, also, that numbers 1–17 were written to persuade the young man to marry and beget heirs, while many readers would agree further to regard the twelve-line sonnet 126, which brings Thorpe's first section to an end, as an Envoy intended as its conclusion. Thus there seems to be at least the elements of arrangement in the printed text of Section 1, concerned with the young man. The same cannot, however, be said of the sonnets which follow in Section II. No one, in fact, had been able to detect any order in this second section, which Mackail described as 'a miscellaneous and disorderly appendix'[1] —until an article by Professor Brents Stirling[2] revealed not only that they were originally well-arranged but also a bibliographical reason to account for the printers going astray (see my Notes on Section II). Further, I shall assume, what is sometimes questioned, that the woman to whom they are mainly addressed is the same as the woman referred to in Section I, as having had an intrigue with the young man; just as I shall assume that practically all the sonnets of Section I were written to the same young man. The problem of sequence here, then, is that of Section I.

Now, that some sonnets in this section are not in their right order is, I believe, certain, though it is often doubted. Dowden, for example, made a brave attempt[3] to justify the 1609 order by claiming to discover points of connexion between successive sonnets, often with illuminating results; and though at times misguided even then he may be instructive. But Sidney Lee was able to demonstrate without difficulty the over-subtlety[4] of many of these links; and Dowden himself admitted that they may have been pressed too far. On the other hand, Lee while allowing the existence of certain well-marked sequences in the 1609 collection

[1] J. W. Mackail, *The Approach to Shakespeare* (1930), p. 116.

[2] *Shakespeare 1564–1964*, ed. E. A. Bloom (1964); see below, pp. 242 ff.

[3] *The Sonnets of Shakespeare*, edited by Edward Dowden (1883).

[4] Sir Sidney Lee, *Life of William Shakespeare* (1916), pp. 165 ff.

was certainly wrong in his belief that the order Thorpe gives us was in the main his own. As against this there is the impression, shared, I think, by most students today, of the existence of a general framework, embracing in particular the initial sequence 1–17 upon marriage, together with traces of several other sequences which appear at different parts of Thorpe's collection: for example, the group concerning the Rival Poet and the group (97–126), though not I think a sequence, that concludes section I as a whole.

The only order the text has in fact is 'an autobiographical one, following the ups and downs of an emotional relationship'. So it was put by Edmund Chambers in a notable essay[1] replying to an ingenious rearrangement by Denys Bray, and at the same time he indicates in Thorpe's text pairs, triplets, or at times even longer groups of contiguous sonnets linked in sense-content and often, too, by stylistic devices such as repetition of significant words or a recurrence of rhyme-sounds; links that Bray's rearrangement often ignored. Samples of such linked sonnets as Chambers cites are 27 and 28, 44 and 45, 57 and 58, 63, 64 and 65, 97, 98 and 99—and I have added 36–39, which Chambers did not mention. I shall be making use of some of these later on; for the moment it is sufficient to observe that these links still further strengthen our belief in the general correctness of Thorpe's order.

Yet while Thorpe seems to have usually followed the sequence he found in his copy (for without urgent reasons to do otherwise that would be his natural course), he did not always do so, and one of the main problems of the text is to discover what his reasons were for such departures and how the consequent operations

[1] 'The Order of the Sonnets', pp. 111–24 of *Shakespearean Gleanings.*

affected the sonnets of his framework. But let me begin by calling to witness H. C. Beeching, who was the friend of A. C. Bradley, and whom, with E. K. Chambers[1] and Blair Leishman[2], I regard as one of the best and most cautious of modern editors of this text. He writes:

Although we may, speaking generally, defend the order in which the first section of the Sonnets are given in the Quarto, it may very well be the case that some few are misplaced; 36–39, if they are rightly placed, do not explain their position; 75 would come better after 52; 77 and 81 interrupt the series on the Rival Poet; and Professor Herford notes that 'the three *Absence* sonnets 97–99 betray a frank and joyous confidence hard to reconcile with the desolate "farewell" note of the previous group and with the silence which follows'. In the main, however, the order justifies itself to an attentive reader.[3]

One attentive reader at any rate finds himself so well in agreement with what Beeching here says that he proposes to open his inquiry into the causes of Thorpe's departures from what was obviously originally the right order by following up the first of Beeching's clues. All students agree that the Quarto contains a number of sonnets referring to a liaison between the Poet's mistress and his Friend. Now sonnets 36–9, Beeching's first illustration, are mixed up with a group of sonnets (33–5, 40–2) obviously dealing with the Friend's intrigue, while 36 confesses to a 'bewailed guilt' or certain 'blots' on the Poet's own reputation which might bring shame upon the Friend if their intimacy were too well known to the world, and so can only refer

[1] *Shakespearean Gleanings*, p. 112.

[2] J. B. Leishman, *Themes and Variations in Shakespeare's Sonnets* (1961), p. 15, n.

[3] Beeching, *The Sonnets of Shakespeare*, pp. lxv–lxvi.

to quite a different set of circumstances, as Beeching also insists in a note on 36 which must be quoted as well, since it not only throws light on the join between 35 and 36 but explains how Dowden helps even when he is wrong.

'Professor Dowden', the note runs, 'who shows infinite ingenuity in connecting every sonnet with its predecessor, introduces this with the sentence: "According to the announcement made in 35, Shakespeare proceeds to make himself out the guilty party". But [Beeching objects] the poet has made no such announcement. He has called himself an "accessary," more to blame than the principal because he defends his action by arguments of reason. But that is a long way from "making himself out the guilty party". The sonnets from 36 to 39 must refer to a different topic; 36 refers to some "blots" upon the poet, and 37 to the friend's "truth" [= loyalty] as atoning for the spite of fortune. The subject of the friend's wrong to the poet is resumed in 40.'

It follows from the facts Beeching has here observed, that Thorpe or his agent has seen in sonnets 36–9 a convenient opportunity to slip liaison sonnets into the main text, relying on the apparent connexion between 'accessary' in 35 and 'guilt' in 36, to cover up his traces; and with Dowden he succeeded. Nor is this the only point in this context at which he led Dowden astray. The sonnets 36–9 were indeed peculiarly apt to Thorpe's purpose. As a reference to my Notes will explain, these four sonnets constitute one of those stylistically connected groups described by Chambers and being so were, one may surmise, written by Shakespeare on a single sheet or half-sheet of paper. In any case Thorpe wanted the quartet as a whole, because he saw that 39, the last of the four, provided another convenient hook for the insertion of three other liaison sonnets, viz. 40–2. For, as the sharp-eyed Beeching had already seen, these sonnets deal with an intrigue; and I explain 40 as an outburst written almost immediately after Shakespeare had found out what his mistress and the young man were up to. But first, listen to Dowden's note on 40 and mark him falling once again into the trap Thorpe laid:

In 39 Shakespeare desires that his love and his friend's may be separated, in order that he may give his friend what otherwise he must give also to himself. Now, separated, he gives his beloved all his loves, yet knows that, before the gift, all his was his friend's by right.

Had Thorpe been able to look into the seeds of time he might have rubbed his hands over that. And indeed this interpolation which twice hoodwinked the professor is so ingenious that I am persuaded the interpolator was no other than Thorpe himself, for by means of the quartet 36–9 he contrived to rid himself of 6 out of the 9 or 10 liaison sonnets he had to deal with.

Before leaving 36–9, however, there is more to be said about the situation glanced at above which they refer to, a situation which has not been rightly understood, because to suit his purposes Thorpe has moved them from their original position. Beeching considers the group misplaced, as does Pooler who suggests that it may be a continuation of 29 and the 'blots' (l. 3) be the 'disgrace with Fortune and men's eyes' (29. 1), because he has to earn his living as a player. This is my view also, except that I should trace the prelude to 36 further back, viz. to sonnet 25 in which Dowden rightly observes that we first hear Shakespeare complaining against fortune and his low condition.

Now sonnet 36 marks a crisis in Shakespeare's affairs at this time, since it takes leave of the Friend on the eve of a journey which a number of later sonnets written in absence seem to show must have been a tour in the country. As to the occasion and duration of this tour I have more to say in my note on 36 and on pp. lxxx ff. of the Introduction. At the moment it is sufficient to point out (1) that so large a number of sonnets written in absence implies a separation of the two friends lasting for several weeks; (2) that if we extract the interpolated liaison sonnets (and Thorpe had not many left) there is not the slightest suggestion of any treachery on the Friend's part. On the contrary, his 'constant heart' is more than once gratefully acknowledged. Most interesting of all, in sonnets 69 and 70 Shakespeare, evidently disturbed by rumours that his young Friend is making himself too cheap in London, offers a little avuncular advice, in the course of which occur lines which have been the stumbling-block of all critics attempting to determine the order of the sonnets:

> So thou be good, slander doth but approve,
> Thy worth the greater being wooed of time,
> For canker vice the sweetest buds doth love,
> *And thou present'st a pure unstainéd prime.*
> *Thou hast passed by the ambush of young days,*
> *Either not assailed, or victor being charged...*

These lines, as all have seen, cannot have been written after Shakespeare had come to know of the liaison. They were not: they were written while Shakespeare was still on tour and it was not until he got back to London that he discovered what Friend and Mistress had been doing in his absence. Such I believe is the solution of the chief puzzle of the 1609 text. Beeching, speaking of the apparent inconsistency between the sonnets 33–5 which charge the Friend with paying court to the poet's mistress and what appears to be a subsequent sonnet

(70) which credits him with a 'pure unstained prime', remarks 'The point is one that must strike every reader of the sonnets, and the reconciliation would possibly be simple if we knew all the facts'.[1] So it proves to be, and if we have had to go a long way round to arrive at it, it was by laying his finger upon the anomalous position of the mysterious 36 that Beeching first led us to discover what the facts were.

We shall have to note other possible misplacements. Yet if the assumption of a basic framework of sonnets Shakespeare allowed, or did not disallow, be correct, the bulk of the 1609 collection would presumably have been found within its confines, perhaps those of a kind of portfolio, the initial sequence on marriage, as now, standing first. It looks, too, as if the almost continuous sequence concerning the Rival Poet was also part of it.

On the other hand, among the detached sonnets there might of course be some, apart from the liaison sonnets, that were never intended to belong to the main series, or, as I think is the case of 77, even intended for the Friend. Another example would be that of duplicates, since Shakespeare might well write two sonnets on the same theme, or making the same point, and then decide which he wished to send forward; and this is what seems to have happened in the case of 153 and 154, if these are his. Or, again, there might be, though I doubt it, some of his early sonnets, love-poems, in the portfolio, written even before he ever saw his Friend at all.

I must leave to the commentary a discussion of such matters and the record of Thorpe's operations to effect the interpolation of the other unauthorized sonnets in his possession. It suffices here to note that there were in my judgement another six besides those already dealt

[1] Beeching, p. lxiv.

with. The numbers Thorpe assigns to these dozen are 33, 34, 35, 40, 41, 42, 48, 57, 58, 61, 92, 93; and if I were asked to arrange them in autobiographical order it would run 48, 57, 58, 61, 40, 41, 42, 33, 34, 35, 92, 93. Before going further some readers may be interested to read these sonnets in that order and decide for themselves whether they make an intelligible story.

One word of caution, however, in conclusion. Shakespeare's Friend was, as his Poet twice remarked, a lascivious young fellow, and is likely to have laid siege to other women besides the 'black beauty' celebrated in Section II, while the publication of sonnets alluding to such incidents could hardly have been more authorized than the others. We must look out for sonnets of the kind. A reference to my comments on 95 and 96, both almost certainly interpolated, will give the reader an example.

To sum up: Thorpe, I suggest, had to deal with two distinct classes of sonnets: (*a*) what we may call framework sonnets, namely the 'sugred sonnets' known in part to Meres by 1598, and probably including many written later; and (*b*) what we may call secret or private sonnets, namely those connected with the young man's sexual adventures, presumably sent to him but which we can feel confident Shakespeare did not release for circulation among his friends, however 'private' these friends might be. But Thorpe's real problem was to keep the framework intact with its concluding Envoy, while inserting the secret sonnets at convenient places within it.

Thomas Thorpe and the origin of his text

What has been said so far should make it clear that the copy Eld handled in 1609 was not a text that Shakespeare intended. Incidentally, its disorderly state cannot be attributed to a desire on his part to conceal the intrigue business. He might best have attained that end by simply destroying the sonnets alluding to it, whereas, things being as they are, nothing is hidden and curiosity the more stimulated. We may be certain, too, I think, that he had no hand at all in, or responsibility of any kind for, Thorpe's publication. Such at least is the considered opinion of most of the best modern critics and editors: Edward Dowden,[1] for example, and H. C. Beeching,[2] E. K. Chambers,[3] and G. L. Kittredge.[4] Only George Wyndham[5] among nineteenth-century critics of importance sought to defend the 1609 text, and the excellent Beeching to some extent turned the tables upon him by pointing out that whereas in the 1194 lines of the *Venus and Adonis* of 1593, which Shakespeare himself is generally assumed to have seen through the press, only three slight faults can be found, in the 2155 lines of the *Sonnets* of 1609 there are no fewer than three dozen. Yet all Beeching's figures show is that Shakespeare had not read the proofs of the *Sonnets* as he assuredly had those of *Venus*. The original copy may nevertheless have been Shakespeare's manuscript and I think very probably was. Yet the punctuation remains a problem; and what we think of that rather depends on what we think of Thorpe.

The absence of the dedicatory epistle commonly found in printed poems at this period seems a suspicious circumstance in the eyes of some. For myself, an early seventeenth-century title-page set out thus baldly,

[1] Dowden, *op. cit.* p. xxvii.

[2] Beeching, *op. cit.* pp. lix–lxiii.

[3] Chambers, *William Shakespeare*, I, 559.

[4] Kittredge, *The Poems of Shakespeare* (1938), p. 49.

[5] Wyndham, *The Poems of Shakespeare* (1898), p. 109.

as if it were an item in a bookseller's catalogue or broadsheet,

SHAKE-SPEARES
SONNETS
Neuer before Imprinted

proclaims itself on the face of it a publisher's 'catch', even had the publisher not called himself in the dedication 'the adventurer in setting forth'. A prime 'catch' indeed!—but not necessarily stolen goods. The entry in the Stationers' Register is quite regular:

Thomas Thorpe Entred for his copie vnder thandes of master Wilson and master Lownes Warden, a Booke called Shakespeares *sonnettes* vj[d].

Clearly, honest Masters Wilson and Lownes found nothing suspicious about the copy; nothing, that is to say, which might get the Company into trouble with the authorities, for censorship was strict and the stationers were under very stringent regulations. Further, Shakespeare's name by 1609 was a well-known one. Was he not the leading dramatist for His Majesty's players? Not that that much mattered, for at this period the author normally retained no copyright in his own productions; that belonged to the stationer, and if he had purchased his copy honestly from the author or someone else, no one asked any questions. Yet I cannot help suspecting that this innocent transaction was attended with more serious consequences than the honest stationers expected.

Sidney Lee does his best to blacken Thorpe's character and conjures up as his fellow-pirate one William Hall, a London printer in 1609, whom he casts for the part of 'Mr W. H.' in Thorpe's dedication.[1] But he can adduce no evidence that the two men

[1] Lee, *Life* (1916), pp. 159–63, 672–85.

even knew each other, and Edmund Chambers dismisses the whole theory as a mare's nest.[1] In point of fact there is no evidence either that Thorpe was anything but an honest stationer. He even seems to have had something of a literary gift. He was a friend of Edward Blount, perhaps one of the leading, certainly one of the most interesting, stationers of the day, who published Florio's *Montaigne* and was probably the principal publisher, as distinct from printer, of the First Folio. Apart from this, Blount's chief title to fame to-day is his publication of the first edition (1598) of Marlowe's *Hero and Leander*. He had been a friend of Marlowe's and 'regarded himself as in some sense his literary executor',[2] introducing *Hero* with a charming dedicatory epistle to Walsingham, the patron of his unhappily deceased friend, which is not unworthy to be mentioned in the same breath as Heminge and Condell's dedicatory epistle to the First Folio. Two years later appeared Marlowe's *First Book of Lucan translated*,[3] this time published by Thorpe, who wrote for it an even more interesting dedicatory epistle, *To his kind and true friend, Edward Blunt*, from which it appears that Blount had helped his young friend by passing on to him this piece of Marlowe copy. The epistle begins:

Blount: I purpose to be blunt with you, and, out of my dulness, to encounter you with a Dedication in the memory of that pure elemental wit, Chr. Marlowe, whose ghost or genius is to be seen walk the Churchyard in, at the least,

[1] Chambers, *William Shakespeare*, I, 566.

[2] Greg, *The Shakespeare First Folio*, p. 18.

[3] I.e. Lucan's *Pharsalia*, Book I. This was apparently Thorpe's first publication as he had just become a freeman of the Stationers' Company. The account of Thorpe in McKerrow's *Dictionary of Printers and Booksellers, 1557–1640*, is both defective and misleading.

three or four sheets. Methinks you should presently look wild now, and grow humorously frantic upon the taste of it. Well, lest you should, let me tell you, this spirit was sometime a familiar of your own, *Lucan's First Book translated*; which, in regard of your old right in it, I have raised in the circle of your patronage.

The point of all this will be clearer when we remember the 'cellarage scene' in which Hamlet became 'wild' and 'frantic' after an encounter with the 'ghost or genius' of his father, clad, however, in armour, not

> Lapt in some foul sheet or a leather pilch

like the traditional ghost.[1] It was the same sprightly pen which Thorpe gave play to again in the famous dedication that follows:

TO. THE. ONLIE. BEGETTER. OF.
THESE. INSVING. SONNETS.
MR. W. H. ALL. HAPPINESSE.
AND. THAT. ETERNITIE.
PROMISED.
BY.
OVR. EVER-LIVING. POET.
WISHETH.
THE. WELL-WISHING.
ADVENTURER. IN.
SETTING.
FORTH.
T.T.

For the meaning of this we are left guessing. My guess, based upon one by Edmund Chambers,[2] is that Thorpe

[1] See my *What Happens in Hamlet*, pp. 55 ff.

[2] Cf. Chambers, *Shakespearean Gleanings*, p. 129: 'As for Thomas Thorpe in 1609, I doubt whether he had anything before him but "To W.H." on a manuscript.'

procured his collection from a person or persons he had discovered possessed them and that he found 'To W.H.' at the head of the portfolio or chief manuscript. In any case, whether he found it there or invented it himself, it served his purpose well—better, perhaps, than he bargained for. If the initials stood, as many now believe, for William Herbert, later Earl of Pembroke, and Thorpe knew this all along, why did he not dedicate the volume to the Earl of Pembroke? Would not that have greatly increased the sales? Undoubtedly, yet Thorpe had a compelling reason as a publisher against it. Had he done so, the censor and the Court of Stationers would not have allowed it without the express permission of the earl, by 1609 one of the leading noblemen of the land. And Pembroke, of course, never could have allowed the publication of the 'private' sonnets and never did. Yet 'To Mr W.H.', if not Thorpe's device, was undoubtedly written by someone who very well knew who it was.

In other words, we must ask: From whom did Thorpe buy or borrow his collection? That, surprisingly enough, seems the easiest question to answer. For, as I figure it out, it must have been one of three persons: and, since it is incredible that either Shakespeare or the Friend could ever have countenanced the publication of the liaison sonnets or those of Section II, which would have exposed them both far more nakedly than the decent framework sonnets, I am left with the Dark Woman herself, unless some pirate unknown had been at work. All or most of the sonnets in Section II presumably belonged to her, for if she was the woman I take her for she would have enjoyed the hating sonnets as much as the tender-amorous ones, for they were an even greater testimony to her power; while as the lover of both men she should have had, following the precedent of Delilah, plenty of opportunity of getting hold of the rest, if they were not already at her house. It looks, too, as if she had come to realize some years earlier that these poems of her elder lover might become a source of profit, since the only sonnets to appear in print before 1609 were those Jaggard used to lend an air of genuineness to the spurious *Passionate Pilgrim by William Shakespeare* in 1599; and they were numbers 138 and 144, both in section II which *ex hypothesi* she alone possessed. Thus, either because she was in want of money in 1609 or because she had been got at by the smart young stationer Thorpe who somehow learned of her hoard, a bargain was struck, and he was allowed to beg, borrow or transcribe the *Sonnets*, together with *A Lover's Complaint* which was also presumably among her papers. That Thorpe engaged two booksellers to unload his 'catch' on to the public suggests that he anticipated a brisk sale. Yet no second edition was called for. The usual explanation given is that by 1609 the poetry-reading public had grown tired of sonnets: the sonnet craze, dating from the appearance in 1591 of Sidney's *Astrophel and Stella*, being supposedly exhausted eighteen years later. It was declining, no doubt, but Drayton's *Idea's Mirror* had been reprinted six times since its appearance in 1590 and was reprinted three times after 1609; and I find it very difficult to believe that Thorpe was not justified in looking for a public eager to buy a volume of hitherto unpublished poems by the very popular author of *Venus and Adonis* and *The Rape of Lucrece*, both still being reprinted at regular intervals, who was also the creator of Falstaff and Hamlet. What happened? By 1609 Shakespeare was not only a popular poet but had powerful friends at court, among them the brilliant Earl of Pembroke, to whom with his brother the Earl of Montgomery the First Folio was dedicated, and who, as just stated, perhaps had special reasons for disliking this publication. I suggest, in short, that no sooner did it appear in the bookshops and its contents become known than the printer was ordered by authority to discontinue further issues.[1] For different reasons the same thing had happened to the 1591 text of *Astrophel and Stella*. Thorpe's volume was probably long dead before Benson surreptitiously pillaged the grave a generation later, and apart from the publication in 1711 by Bernard Lintott of a collection of Shakespeare's poems containing *One Hundred and Fifty-Four Sonnets, all of them in Praise of his Mistress*, which despite this title is said to be a good text, there was no genuine resurrection until Malone reprinted the 1609 text in 1780.

III. The Friend and the Poet

The nature of the friendship and the character of the Friend

We can now leave Thomas Thorpe for the time and pass on to consider the two leading characters in his copy. We know the name of one already, and the sonnets to the Friend when seen in the sunlight tell us much for certain about the other, though assuredly without the help of C. S. Lewis we could not otherwise have guessed so much; while the sonnets to the Dark Woman leave questions in our mind about him that will have to be faced at a later stage. But at the outset the

[1] Cf. F. Mathew, *Image of Shakespeare* (1922), p. 114: 'the neglect of the Sonnets of 1609 can only be explained by concluding that they were quickly suppressed' (cited Rollins, II, 326).

Friend's name and personality are among the shadows of the cave, and if we would learn about them, all we have are those scattered hints which the Poet's love has given us.

The 'love' in question is of course the affectionate admiration—perhaps adoration would at times not be too strong a term—of a man of mature years for another man much younger than himself, in this case perhaps fifteen to seventeen years younger. Such affection, though not unusual, especially with men of an imaginative or poetical temperament, may seem strange or even repellent to most ordinary people. And as many readers nowadays, when all matters of sex are openly debated, will be ready to assume without question that Shakespeare was writing about homosexuality, something had better be said about that at once. Though a brief reference to it by C. S. Lewis has already been quoted, and I agree with him, I do so on rather more explicit grounds.

Whatever, then, psychologists may postulate about the love that inspires these sonnets, it is certain that Shakespeare was not a conscious paederast, and for two good reasons. First of all in sonnet 20, which is perhaps the most intimate of the series, he expressly dissociates his passionate admiration from sexual desire, and does so with a frankness characteristically Elizabethan, in such terms as to suggest that the sonnet was written partly in order to make this point unmistakably clear. That the love was passionate on both sides can hardly be denied by anyone who has read the reference to 'hungry eyes' in sonnet 56 or the couplet of 110. And the second reason is even more cogent, namely that a major theme of the sonnets is the Poet's infatuation for a woman which holds him in its grip and with which he not infrequently contrasts the humble and selfless adoration he feels for his young friend. The affection is so absolute that he is ready to forgive his adored anything except such actions as injure the adored himself. And there is much to forgive, for it becomes evident as the sonnets go forward that the young man is amusing himself by making love to the Poet's mistress; behaviour that, as the Poet is really deeply in love with the woman, causes him such distress, at times agony, as to introduce a note of tragedy into the series, compared with which the supplications for pity and the lamentations that are the stock-in-trade of the conventional sonneteers sound very hollow and insincere.

A genuine friendship such as that celebrated by Shakespeare is nearly always based upon reciprocal admiration, together with a readiness to make allowance on the part of the elder for the younger. When Samuel Johnson, as he often did, declared to James Boswell that he loved him, there was much to admire on both sides, but the great doctor must have known that there were aspects of Bos's character he could not admire. The relationship between the poet Gray and his young Swiss friend Bonstetten seems to have been of much the same character. And Beeching,[1] who cites it as a striking parallel to the friendship revealed in the *Sonnets*, gives extracts from Gray's letters which express Shakespeare's attitude with truly astonishing similarity. For example, 'It is impossible with me to dissemble with you; such as I am I expose my heart to your view, nor wish to conceal a single thought from your penetrating eyes'. And when in absence he writes, 'My life now is but a conversation with your shadow', he persuades us that Shakespeare spoke the simple truth when he wrote the letter we label sonnet 43.

[1] Beeching, *The Sonnets of Shakespeare*, pp. xv, xvi.

But the young Friend had his faults, and the fault that gave most trouble to the Poet was wantonness; a fault to which young men are prone, as Boswell certainly was and Bonstetten also, to judge from Gray's warning against the temptations his good looks laid him open to. But a young gentleman at the time of Elizabeth and James was conscious of fewer inhibitions than a Swiss Protestant, or a Scot having to behave more or less respectably in Georgian England (whatever he might do in the streets after dark). And the word 'lascivious' as noted above is twice used of the Friend in the *Sonnets*, while the trouble it led Shakespeare into will have to be considered later when we come to deal with the problem of the Dark Woman.

But had the boy not been admirable in other respects, Shakespeare could not have continued to praise him in 126 sonnets. Nor is it likely the Friend would have accepted this iteration of praise had he not enjoyed receiving it.

> Being fond on praise, which makes your praises worse

says the Poet at 84. 14, reproaching him for enjoying the flattery of others. That he gave his Poet a portrait of himself is sufficient indication that he was fond. Is it not probable, also, if not certain, that he was proud to claim the friendship of a leading poet and dramatist of the day? The whole tenour of the *Sonnets* goes to prove that, at any rate for most of the period they cover, they celebrate 'the marriage of true [i.e. mutually affectionate] minds'.

Yet there are two features in this particular friendship which differentiate it from the parallels just cited. In the first place both partners to it were Elizabethans. Perhaps the best thing said upon this aspect comes from the most learned of eighteenth-century editors of

Shakespeare, Edmond Malone, who in reply to a stupid note by Steevens upon sonnet 20 wrote:

> Such addresses to men, however indelicate,[1] were customary in our author's time, and neither imported criminality, nor were esteemed indecorous. To regulate our judgement of Shakespeare's poems by the modes of modern times, is surely as unreasonable as to try his plays by the rules of Aristotle.

That leaves nothing more to be said on this topic, certainly not by a modern critic less learned in Elizabethan manners than Malone.

The other feature which distinguishes this pair of friends from any other known to history is the extent of the gap between their personalities. I am not thinking at the moment of differences of rank or of the difference, spoken of in Section II, between the pebble and the clod, so much as of the gulf that divides one of the greatest of human imaginations from his young Friend who, whatever intellectual gifts he possessed, must have been intellectually and emotionally quite commonplace in comparison. How much did his adored Bonstetten understand or enter into the mind of the poet Gray? Still less could the Friend have fathomed the far greater spirit that brooded over him. Such spiritual disparities are often fraught with tragic issues. The love which a Shakespeare or a Beethoven lavishes upon the object of his devotion is accepted by the beloved as a matter of course, as a tribute due to the value of his personality, though that value is largely if not wholly the creation of the worshipper's imagination. And tragedy comes when the youth gets tired of adulation, or finds another adorer, or—as happened, I believe, in this case at the end—just grows up while the worshipper grows old.

[1] It should be explained that in Malone's day 'indelicate' meant unrefined and 'indecorous' indecent.

Turn now for a time from the relations between Poet and Friend to what we can otherwise glean about the personality and status of the latter. First of all he was, of course, very handsome; it is a theme upon which the Poet plays a hundred variations, and the *Sonnets* show that it seemed no less astonishing to others than to Shakespeare. Such beauty is as rare in men as genius, and when I try and imagine what the Friend must have looked like in the eyes of London at the beginning of the seventeenth century, my mind goes back to the impact of Rupert Brooke's radiant loveliness upon Cambridge, especially the women of Cambridge, at the beginning of the twentieth. Shakespeare gives us few details, so that there is little to get hold of if one is seeking to identify him. From sonnet 20 we learn that his beauty was of a feminine cast and elsewhere that, in keeping with this, he was endowed with a delicate complexion. This is specially insisted upon in 99 which also compares his breath to the scent first of violets and then of roses. That same sonnet has, too, the line

> And buds of marjoram had stol'n thy hair.

This is generally understood as a reference to colour, and Beeching with a bunch of half-opened marjoram blooms before him defines the colour as that of the pigment 'brown madder'. But, as l. 14 of the sonnet makes clear, it is scent ('sweet') as well as colour that Shakespeare has in mind throughout, and since marjoram is noted especially as an aromatic herb, used in the making of scents of various kinds, H. C. Hart was surely right in thinking that Shakespeare was speaking of perfume. Yet he may well have been thinking of colour, too. If, for example, the boy was William Herbert, he may have resembled his uncle Sir Philip Sidney whom Aubrey describes as 'extremely beautifull' with hair 'a darke ambor colour'.[1] Finally, 'buds', while an apt description of the close curls shown in all the representtions of Herbert we possess, seems ill-suited to the long ringlets of Southampton. Beyond these hints there is little else to help us in the way of personal description.

More can, I think, be gathered about the youth's rank or social status. That he belonged to a much higher class than the Poet's can hardly be reasonably denied, though many critics have denied it. The importance attached to the young man's perpetuating his stock by begetting an heir is almost enough by itself to indicate high rank. And when Shakespeare writes in 10

Be as thy presence is gracious and kind

he is assuredly speaking of a nobleman. We do not normally describe the bearing of a commoner as 'gracious' or refer to his company as his 'presence', a word particularly associated with persons who hold court and are besieged by suitors. On the other hand, 111. 3–4:

That did not better for my life provide, Than public means which public manners breeds

seems to suggest that a player does not know how to behave in society. Sonnets 36 and 37 again cannot be rightly understood unless we assume a considerable difference in rank between the two persons concerned. In 36 the Poet confesses to some fault, which he feels will make it awkward for the young man to admit acquaintance with him publicly. He therefore humbly suggests that they shall part company for a while, and pretend not to know each other if they chance to meet:

I may not ever more [any longer] acknowledge thee,
Lest my bewailed guilt should do thee shame,
Nor thou with public kindness honour me,
Unless thou take that honour from thy name.

[1] Aubrey, *Brief Lives*, edited by O. Lawson Dick (1949), p. 278.

And in the next sonnet he takes comfort in the thought that, even if separated from his Friend, the love they bear each other, or at least he bears him, enables him to imagine himself sharing in the Friend's 'glory':

> For whether beauty, birth, or wealth, or wit,
> Or any of these all, or all, or more
> Entitled in thy parts, do crowned sit,
> I make my love engrafted to this store:
> So then I am not lame, poor, nor despised...

The sense of social inferiority, general throughout the *Sonnets*, is here very evident; and beauty, birth, wealth, and wit[1] make an almost complete catalogue of the advantages of being born a handsome young nobleman.

A number of other terms or references point in the same direction. Sonnet 96, for instance, warning the young man against his besetting sin, exclaims:

> How many gazers mightst thou lead away [i.e. seduce],
> If thou wouldst use the strength of all thy state!

Sonnet 101, again, claims that the Poet's praise will 'much outlive a gilded tomb', which I take to be an allusion to the painted monuments beneath which Elizabethans of distinguished families lay after death. And from 16 and 47 we learn, as already noted, that the young man had had his portrait painted to give away to his friend as persons of fashion were wont, as young Sir Philip Sidney had his painted by Paul Veronese to give away to Hubert Languet. Incidentally, Languet's ecstasies over the portrait were very much in the manner of Shakespeare's in sonnet 46.[2] Then there is the Rival Poet who was clearly courting

[1] I.e. a trained intelligence or (perhaps) culture.
[2] See Dowden, *op. cit.* p. xxii.

the Friend not as a lover but as a client for his patronage. Who this other poet may have been and how far he seems to have succeeded will be discussed later. Enough at the moment to remark that it was only noblemen or persons of like distinction who were usually courted for patronage in Shakespeare's day.

When pouring forth these passionate addresses to a handsome young nobleman was Shakespeare, then, only fawning upon him in the hopes of patronage himself? Keats, the poet who is recognized as nearest to Shakespeare in spirit and of all poets understood him best, would have rejected such a notion with scorn, if not with laughter. And a charming book on the *Sonnets* by his friend Charles Armitage Brown[1] devotes a whole chapter to the persuasive thesis 'He was never a flatterer'. A. C. Bradley, again, Shakespeare's most penetrating modern critic, finds it quite impossible to take the language of many of the sonnets as that of interested flattery.[2] Equally positive on the other side was the official biographer of a generation ago who informs us that 'the sole biographical inference which is deducible with full confidence from the *Sonnets* is that at one time in his career Shakespeare, like the majority of his craft, disdained few weapons of flattery in an endeavour to monopolize the bountiful patronage of a young man of rank'.[3] To me it is a sufficient reply to Lee's aspersion to point out that a poet who rebukes, however gently, a young man for loose living (95, 96), for making himself cheap (69), for his love of flattery

[1] *Shakespeare's Autobiographical Poems* (1838). Though published fifteen years after Keats's death we may assume it owes much to conversation with him.

[2] A. C. Bradley, *Oxford Lectures on Poetry* (1909), p. 332. Cf. his reply to Lee, *ibid.* pp. 312–14.

[3] Sidney Lee, *The Life of Shakespeare* (1916), p. 230.

(84. 14), for self-satisfaction (67. 2), for keeping the said poet up for hours waiting for an appointment he fails to observe (57, 58), is going a queer way about to curry his favour. And we are led to ask whether his biographer, for all his learning in the conceits and sources of these poems, had ever troubled to sit down and think out what Shakespeare was trying to say. For what an attentive reader hears is the voice not of a client craving patronage but of an ardently affectionate uncle or guardian who, while loving the young man for his beauty and grace, both in mind and person, keeps an eye open for his faults, while he has no hesitation in offering advice when he feels it serviceable to do so; much as the humanist Languet does in his affectionate letters to the young and beautiful Philip Sidney: as indeed in that age, when the government of nations rested upon the shoulders of princes and nobles, all men of learning and art who were admitted to their friendship felt it a public duty to do.

But the friendship of Languet and Sidney differed in two important respects from that of Shakespeare and his young Friend. The humanist-diplomatist, well known in all the courts of Europe, was not likely to labour under any great sense of inferiority in company with a young English knight, even though he were the nephew of the Earl of Leicester. Shakespeare, on the other hand, was a common player, by statute classed with rogues and vagabonds, and it is impossible for us to imagine the social gulf that separated him from anyone of noble rank. A nobleman might honour a famous player with his acquaintance, or even his friendship. Burbadge was so honoured.[1] But neither party would or could ever forget that the one was conferring an

[1] See E. K. Chambers, *The Elizabethan Stage* (1923), II, 308.

honour upon the other; the difference of rank was so absolute that nothing could bridge it. One cannot read the *Sonnets* attentively without realising that the friendship between player and nobleman was nevertheless very real, came indeed to be very intimate. Yet Shakespeare is always aware of the social gulf and not infrequently bewails it, reminds himself of it or is even reminded of it by the Friend. One striking example has already been quoted from sonnets 36 and 37. Still more explicit are the following lines from 87:

> My bonds in thee are all determinate.
> For how do I hold thee but by thy granting,
> And for that riches where is my deserving?

But this consciousness, I feel sure, is what lies behind most of the passages in which the Poet dwells upon his condition: for example,

> Let those who are in favour with their stars,
> Of public honour and proud titles boast,
> Whilst I whom fortune of such triumph bars... (25)

> When in disgrace with Fortune and men's eyes,
> I all alone beweep my outcast state... (29)

> ...made lame by Fortune's dearest spite... (37. 3)

> Some glory in their birth...
> But these particulars are not my measure...
> [i.e. are not granted me by fortune] (91)

> Alas 'tis true, I have gone here and there,
> And made my self a motley to the view... (110)

Beeching glosses 'motley to the view' as 'a public jester', and asserts 'there is no reference to the poet's profession' and that 'the sonnet gives the confession of a favourite of society'. He may be right and Bradley agrees with him,[1] but he rather wilfully holds that Shake-

[1] *Oxford Lectures*, p. 322 n. 2.

speare never refers to himself as a player. Of the next line in the same sonnet Tucker writes: 'One does not by that profession [i.e. the profession of an actor] "gore his own thoughts", still less does he "make old offences of affection new".'[1] Yet Shakespeare was playwright as well as actor, and may not these words tell us what a dramatist might confess to if he drew upon his own experiences or the characters of those about him in creating his plays? Surely, too, there cannot be any doubt about this in the very next sonnet:

O for my sake do you with Fortune chide,
The guilty goddess of my harmful deeds,
That did not better for my life provide,
Than public means which public manners breeds.
Thence comes it that my name receives a brand... (111)

Even Edmund Chambers, who finds attempts to interpret the *Sonnets* as 'largely interpreting the obscure by the obscurer still' takes 'brand' to be an allusion to the old tradition of 'the infamous *histrio* of the early Fathers'.[2] And this suggestion is supported by 112, which begins:

Your love and pity doth th' impression fill,
Which vulgar scandal stamped upon my brow,

and so carries on the reference to 'brand' in 111. 5.

No situation, then, would more naturally give rise to such utterances as we find in these sonnets than this humble adoration of an Elizabethan player for a handsome boy of high rank. Yet the adoration is assuredly

[1] Tucker, *op. cit.* p. xxxv.

[2] *Shakespearean Gleanings*, p. 49. See *Cambridge History of English Literature* VI, 'The Puritan Attack upon the Stage', on the practice by puritan writers of quotation from the early fathers when attacking the stage.

even humbler than this situation demanded. One cannot imagine the boisterous Burbadge, for instance, assuming, still less genuinely possessing, that selflessness, self-abnegation, self-effacement, call it what you will,[1] which both Lever and Lewis find as the unique quality of Shakespeare's *Sonnets*. It was natural, not to the man, but to the poet, and to that particular kind of poet who has no identity apart from the objects he is continually informing and filling, objects that thus become the creatures of his imagination, one of them being in this case the young Friend. To use an expression too often debased as a cliché, he idealized him.[2]

The Treachery of the Friend and the Mistress

But out alack, he was but one hour mine.

It is evident from sonnet 33 in which these words occur that the sun soon became clouded for the Poet, not long indeed after his first meeting with the Friend: for 'one hour mine' and 'one early morn' can hardly point to any length of time. The cause of this change of climate is also evident from the sonnet that follows: the young man has come to know the mistress whom the Poet had loved dearly, and the two had betrayed him.

The *Sonnets* give us two accounts of this incident, neither very explicit because conveyed by hints or oblique references, but telling us enough to reveal the essence of the affair—telling it, however, in two very

[1] Bradley (*op. cit.* p. 334) uses the term 'prostration' but rightly rejects 'humiliation'.

[2] Cf. above p. xliv and Rupert Brooke on the Birmingham businessman, contemplating whom 'when the mood was on' him, he found 'splendid and immortal and desirable' (*The Collected Poems of Rupert Brooke* (1918), p. liii).

different moods, one being conveyed by sonnets addressed to the Friend and the other by those belonging to Section II concerned with the Dark Woman who was the mistress; and yet because they give us these two sides, either is misleading without the other. It has indeed only quite recently been possible to bring the two together, because until 1964 when Professor Brents Stirling published his article on Sonnets 127–54[1], which placed them in their right order, arranged in three groups, no one could make sense of them as a whole. In one sonnet (144), however, Shakespeare summed up that whole as he saw it, and as it represents both sides we do well to begin with it.

Two loves I have of comfort and despair,
Which like two spirits do suggest me still,
The better angel is a man right fair:
The worser spirit a woman coloured ill.
To win me soon to hell my female evil,
Tempteth my better angel from my side,
And would corrupt my saint to be a devil:
Wooing his purity with her foul pride.
And whether that my angel be turned fiend,
Suspect I may, yet not directly tell,
But being both from me both to each friend,
I guess one angel in another's hell.
  Yet this shall I ne'er know but live in doubt,
  Till my bad angel fire my good one out.

What I wish to stress at the moment is line 8:

Wooing his purity with her foul pride.

This, which depicts the woman as having made the first advance, agrees with 41.7, which implies the same thing, while 143 which represents a very early stage in the relation between Mistress and Friend depicts the

[1] In *Shakespeare 1564–1964*, ed. E. A. Bloom.

latter running from her as she turns away from Shakespeare to chase after him. The sonnet has been generally misunderstood. Anyhow, it seems to me that when he wrote it the Poet had sufficient confidence in the loyalty of his Friend to assume the Mistress had small chance of catching him so that he could jest about it. For sonnets 126–54, now arranged in order, show the affair developing, and to understand what happened we must grasp two essential points at the outset: (1) that one of the chief attractions in the Friend for Shakespeare was the boy's radiant purity, which he took (mistakenly) as an essential quality of his incomparable loveliness; and (2) another of the boy's qualities in which he placed an absolute trust until the Mistress proved him wrong, was his 'truth' or 'constant heart'. Furthermore, these last sonnets reveal something about Shakespeare himself which many modern readers will find it difficult to accept and I must confess took me by surprise. Yet I do not see how anyone can read sonnets 147, 129, 146, in that order, which is Stirling's, without realizing that Shakespeare not only believed in sin and repentance, but had come to feel that the Mistress who had by his means, we are not told how, come to know the beloved Friend, was dragging them both down to hell.

So much for the general situation. Let us now consider the two sides in turn. The liaison-sonnets, as I call them, in Section 1 of Thorpe's collection, can hardly belong to the 'sugred sonnets' mentioned by Meres in 1598, and intended for circulation among his 'private friends', but came to Thorpe's hands some other way and in no particular order, so that he had to fit them into his collection at any points that might seem not inappropriate.[1] We may expect therefore to find them

[1] See above, pp. xxx ff.

at various points in the Quarto. I reckon the group comprises twelve sonnets, viz. 33, 34, 35, 40, 41, 42, 48, 57, 58, 61, 92 and 93, which I now propose to rearrange and comment upon with a view to bringing out if I can the outlines of the story (see p. xxxv).

It begins, I take it, with numbers 48, 57, 58 and 61 (a yoked pair plus two of Thorpe's stray cattle). The second ('Being your slave') is one of the most beautiful love-poems when read in isolation; but taken with 58 and 61 it gives us a vivid picture, steeped in irony, of the unhappy player-poet, waiting into the night for a meeting with this young noble who fails to keep his appointment, and does so because, as the player comes to realize, his lordship is engaged in bed with the player's mistress. Giving it up at last the Poet goes off to his own bed, but not to sleep, for there follows the night described in 61, the bitter irony of which reveals the true nature of the personal tragedy of the greatest of tragic poets and does more than any other passage in the *Sonnets* to convince one reader at any rate of his incontestable love for the Friend, who was at that moment robbing him of the mistress dearly loved after another fashion. And when we, who today see the whole world united in proclaiming him the greatest of human poets, read these lines:

> Being your slave what should I do but tend,
> Upon the hours, and times of your desire?
> I have no precious time at all to spend;
> Nor services to do till you require.

what can we do but cry out with the greatest of his tragic heroes, 'The pity of it, O, the pity of it!'

One must suppose that the agonizing 57, 58, 61, being letters, were sent to the Friend, and that hearing shortly afterwards, from a servant perhaps, that his suspicions were all too well founded, Shakespeare followed up 57, 58 and 61 almost immediately with the passionate outburst of 40, 41 and 42, in which he no longer attempts to conceal the depth of his feelings, declares himself grievously wronged in being robbed of the woman he loves, yet, still prepared to find every excuse he can for the boy himself, knowing the mistress only too well, puts the blame on to her, even accuses himself, and actually stoops to the 'sweet flattery' of 42 and the pitiful couplet of 40:

> Lascivious grace, in whom all ill well shows,
> Kill me with spites yet we must not be foes.

Believing as one must that the young aristocrat was genuinely fond of his player-poet, who went on sending him all these charming and flattering sonnets, and had begun to realize, perhaps for the first time—for a person like him would have attached very small importance to going to bed with a woman—that the poor fellow was what was called 'in love' and really terribly hurt, he became rather sorry for what had happened, made a clean breast of the whole thing with tears in his eyes. Such, at least to judge from 33, 34 and 35, was the next scene in the story which passes on to a calmer, less hysterical mood in which the Poet finds more excuses for the sinner, this time in the natural order of things, gives his repentant Friend plenary absolution and perhaps is optimistic enough to hope the whole affair is now at an end. But it was not for, as we shall find later, sonnets 92–3 show him still racked with suspicion and tasting the bitterness of Eve's apple; nor was it likely that the Dark Woman, having entangled a handsome young nobleman, would let him go until he tired of her, which last contingency the Poet must have realized was a more likely termination to the liaison than that the bad angel would fire the good one out. Of how it does end we learn nothing in the *Sonnets* though we must infer that the savage or frenzied addresses to the mistress in Section II were written after Shakespeare had discovered the liaison or while he was still suspecting that it was going on. Even these, however, ceased, it appears, after a time. Anyhow in 1599 Jaggard was printing two of the sonnets belonging to Section II, and if he procured them from her, it suggests she was beginning to realize that she could make money out of her elder lover's poems, and one wonders whether she would have ventured to do so had she not been pretty sure by then that he had left her for good.

The Dark Woman and the lascivious Friend

But it is time to scrutinize this Dark Woman more closely. Beyond the fact that she was Shakespeare's mistress, that she had black hair and black eyes and that Shakespeare wrote a playful mocking sonnet to her beauty, nothing is known about her appearance. Nor has anybody ever made an even probable guess of her identity; for Mary Fitton,[1] the one-time favourite with Tyler and other critics, was dismissed with laughter when an unearthed portrait proved her a blonde. And if it be argued, as I believe is now the fashion, that she was after all a 'black beauty', Shakespeare's mistress was a married woman who had her 'bed-vow broke' (152), while Mistress Fitton, maid of honour, was not. The only other guess that looked possible at first sight was Mistress Davenant, wife of a vintner in Oxford and mother of Sir William Davenant the dramatist who, according to Aubrey,[2] used to hint in his cups that he

[1] See below, p. lxi.

[2] *Brief Lives*, edited O. Lawson Dick (1949), p. 85.

might be Shakespeare's son, since his mother was a very beautiful woman, and Shakespeare used to lodge at the inn on his way between Warwick and London. But Sir William was born in 1606, while it appears that the vintner did not obtain a licence in Oxford before 1605,[1] which is too late for the affair referred to in the *Sonnets*.

All we can know about the Poet's mistress must therefore be gleaned from the *Sonnets* themselves. Number 42 of Section I informs us that Shakespeare at one time 'loved her dearly', and among the sonnets of Section II we have a charming poem in which he makes love to her (or so I think)[2] as she sits at the virginals playing and perhaps singing to him (128), and another, the octosyllabic sonnet 145, perhaps a song, which seems to mark the conclusion of a lovers' quarrel. In 127, again, her black beauty is acclaimed as lovelier than all the fair beauties of the world and that, be it noted, in terms almost exactly those Berowne employs in praising his Rosaline in *Love's Labour's Lost* 4. 3. 255–61. As with Berowne, too, it is her black eyes that fascinate him (132). Some critics see her as the original of the gipsy Cleopatra and the fickle Cressida; and we may surmise from what Shakespeare writes about her that what the eyes tell him is what Berowne again hints at as he describes Rosaline elsewhere:

> A whitely wanton with a velvet brow,
> With two pitch-balls stuck in her face for eyes,
> Ay and, by heaven, one that will do the deed,
> Though Argus were her eunuch and her guard!
>
> (III. i. 195–8)

Rosaline, Cleopatra and Cressida are all ladies, but ladies in a play, and it by no means follows that the

[1] Chambers, *William Shakespeare*, I, 576.

[2] But see note. Mackail found this and 145 'trivial and undistinguished'.

mistress in the *Sonnets* was one too. Shakespeare never speaks of her as a lady and the probability is that she was a woman of his own class and, one fancies, of much about his age. She was a married woman, and there is more than a hint that she had not only broken her 'bed-vow' for Shakespeare's sake (152. 3) but was at times open to the charge of promiscuity (135. 5; 137. 6; 142. 8). Yet she was certainly no common courtesan. If sonnet 128 be not mere flattery, she could play, as we saw, and probably sing charmingly. And her lover must have credited her with an appreciation of poetry or he would never have troubled to compose some two dozen sonnets for her, or, if about her, surely intended for her eyes. On the other hand, though the shameless playfulness of 151 suggests how their meetings usually ended, we can hardly doubt that, Shakespeare being Shakespeare, what first engaged his attention and could hold it for hours at a time was witty, it may be brilliant, conversation, and more than a little grace of mind. Indeed, though Sir William Davenant probably knew he had small ground for his half-serious claim to have been Shakespeare's son, his description of his mother, the Oxford vintner's wife, as 'a very good witt, and of conversation extremely agreable'[1] shows us what a London citizen's wife might have been.

Such, I suggest, was the dark-eyed woman who held the greatest of all poets in thrall, much as Cleopatra held Antony; and who can tell for how many years it had been going on when the sonnets to the Friend opened? But there came a moment when the woman he loved thus passionately and possessively met the Friend he adored humbly, selflessly, demanding nothing. How they met we do not know. It was probably inevitable,

[1] Aubrey, *op. cit.* p. 85.

once the Friend reached London; but one cannot believe that Shakespeare deliberately arranged it, knowing both partners as he did. And when it took place catastrophe followed; his love for the woman grew rancid, a Nessus shirt that tortured him yet could not be cast off because she continued to hold him by her physical attraction:

> My love is as a fever longing still,
> For that which longer nurseth the disease,
> Feeding on that which doth preserve the ill,
> Th' uncertain sickly appetite to please. (147)

And his love for the Friend, once the sun in his heaven, became overcast with suspicion, suspicion that thickened into agonizing anxiety and jealousy until in the end, it seemed, total eclipse followed for a time.

And here I pause for a moment to ask myself and fellow-students of the *Sonnets* a question. Does his picture of Othello tell us anything about himself? If Cleopatra be—as many suppose—in some sense a portrait of the Dark Woman, I have often thought that Shakespeare's account of Antony's rapid fluctuations of mood between demanding passion and violent jealousy might be in some sense a piece of self-portraiture. The sonnets to the Dark Woman seem to support this; now tender, now savage, and at times torn between hatred and physical desire. Was his love for the Friend again in some sense, like Othello's very different love for Desdemona, now worshipping her 'not wisely but too well', with a love as selfless and as absolute as the music and motion of the spheres, and yet 'being wrought', so 'perplexed in the extreme' that he was ready to 'chop her into messes'? If he ever became furiously jealous of the Friend, it could hardly appear in the *Sonnets*, though the agony of it does and the possibility of hatred peeps out, I fancy, in the wry 'yet we must not be foes' of the pitiable couplet of 40.

The pitiful story of the clash between these loves of comfort and despair can be further traced in a series of sonnets to be considered later, after dealing with an altogether different matter which was troubling Shakespeare at the same time.

The Rival Poet and the Farewell sonnets

How far does Shakespeare's self-effacement and self-abasement help us to solve the Rival Poet puzzle? I reckon the sonnets clearly relating to this matter to be 76, 78, 79, 80 and 82–86, a virtually unbroken series which suggests that they belong to the authorised framework. In the first four, Shakespeare seems to grieve that he lags behind the fashion in verse-making, that the Friend who had previously taught his 'ignorance aloft to fly' was now adding 'feathers to the learned's wing', that his 'sick Muse doth give another place', and so on. In all this he seems to be voicing the same humility as before, and Lever, quoting 85. 5 ('I think good thoughts, whilst others write good words') and 76.1 ('Why is my verse so barren of new pride'), interprets the lines as confessions of *artistic* failure.[1] But perhaps the humblest of the series, number 80, which begins:

> O how I faint when I of you do write,
> Knowing a better spirit doth use your name,

is a confession rather of inferiority than of failure to live up to his own standards. And critics have searched in vain among his contemporaries for a poet whom Shakespeare could possibly have feared as a rival. That

[1] Lever, *op. cit.* pp. 185–6.

he felt him more learned than himself (87. 7) is not surprising, since he must have been keenly conscious of that 'small Latin, and less Greek' which was all the learning a curtailed grammar school education had furnished him with. But to what Elizabethan poet, they ask, was the compliment to the 'proud full sail of his great verse' (86. 1) appropriate except to Marlowe—and he had been stabbed in a Deptford tavern on 30 May 1593 and is therefore out of question unless the majority of students are altogether astray in their dating of the *Sonnets*.[1] Was Shakespeare then so unconscious of the value of his own work as to be prepared to eat humble pie to poets like Chapman, or Daniel, or Constable, or any other of the various candidates suggested for the position of Rival Poet? Or so uncritical of their work as to credit them with verse like Marlowe's?

There is really only one escape from this dilemma. Suppose the whole Rival Poet group was meant to be satirical?

In 1960, shortly before I set my hand to this edition, Mr Gittings, who had made notable additions to our knowledge of Keats's life, published a little book[2] in which he claimed that the Rival Poet sonnets are satirical and proposed a candidate for the rivalry whom I was inclined for long to accept as the most probable yet put forward. He began by noting that the sonnets in question form a progressive sequence which tell 'a remarkably coherent and understandable story without our trying to identify any character in it'. For example: the first two or three sonnets show a half-playful awareness that new fashions in poetic technique are abroad which Shakespeare finds he cannot imitate by changing his style because he cannot do that without

[1] See below, p. lxix.

[2] Robert Gittings, *Shakespeare's Rival* (1960).

changing his subject—the beloved Friend. It is in sonnet 79 that he first begins to speak of a particular rival in whom the Friend is becoming interested; in 80 he calls the rival a 'better spirit', yet protests that there is room both for his 'tall ship' and his own 'saucy bark' in the boundless ocean of the patron's favour. Sonnet 81 reiterates once again that the Friend's surest hopes of immortality lie in the immortality of the Poet's 'gentle verse'. Sonnets 82, 83, 84, 85 develop the theme of the Friend's limitless 'worth', while at the same time slyly criticising the rival's pen by hinting how far it came short of its subject, and more than hinting that if the Friend were not so greedy for praise he would not receive it in such bad verse.

The author of the bad verse that Gittings selects is Gervase Markham, a well-known member of the Essex entourage, a prolific writer of books on horsemanship and country pursuits generally and also of two bombastic epical poems in execrable verse, one dealing with Sir Richard Grenville's fight in the *Revenge*, and the other with the expedition by Essex and his brother to Normandy in 1591.

Gittings works out his thesis persuasively as far as the first eight sonnets are concerned, since it is not difficult to discover lines apparently satirising or ridiculing characteristic passages in Markham. But the evidence altogether breaks down when he comes to sonnet 86. So far Shakespeare had been mildly ridiculing the general characteristics of his rival's style. But in 86 the button is off the foil. He now turns upon the man directly and begins satirising his personal pretensions and way of life, outstanding features which one supposes would have been recognizable not only by the Friend addressed but by other contemporary readers. Yet Gittings was unable to relate any of these features to Markham. The rival must be a poet who was known or at least supposed to have dealings with spirits at night. The author of *Dr Faustus* might have been made to fit this, or Thomas Nashe who wrote *The Terrors of the Night*. But not a suspicion of this kind of thing seems to hang about Markham. Chapman had been the rival generally favoured by critics hitherto. Could it be George Chapman after all? I asked myself. I turned back to see what William Minto had written on the matter in 1874 when he first put forward Chapman's name.[1]

His theory had fallen into some discredit because it was later taken up and exaggerated by Arthur Acheson[2] and others. But I recollected that the identification was mainly based on a passage in Chapman about familiar spirits, and when I looked at it I found the argument more cogent than I had remembered. After rejecting Marlowe, who had previously been conjectured but had died too early, Minto points out that the first line in the sonnet

Was it the proud full sail of his great verse

which seemed to point directly to Marlowe, 'applies with almost too literal exactness to the Alexandrines of Chapman's Homer' which, though none of it appeared before 1598, must have been known of and generally talked about in literary circles long before. Minto also noted that Chapman's chief patron was Sir Francis Walsingham whose daughter Sir Philip Sidney had married; and suggested that nothing could have been more natural than for Walsingham to have introduced his favourite to the Countess of Pembroke or her son.

[1] William Minto, *Characteristics of English Poetry from Chaucer to Shirley* (1874), pp. 290–2.

[2] *Shakespeare and the Rival Poet* (1903).

But what struck many good critics when Minto first published his book was his quotation from the dedicatory epistle to Chapman's *Shadow of Night* (1594) which claims that the true poet cannot succeed 'but with invocation, fasting, watching; yea, not without having drops of their souls like an heavenly familiar'. It is all very obscure, as Chapman usually is, but it does imply a claim to inspiration from a 'heavenly familiar'—whatever that might mean.

Having got so far, I remembered further that my friend the late J. A. K. Thomson, who gave us that admirable book called *Shakespeare and the Classics*, had devoted many paragraphs therein to the relations between Shakespeare and George Chapman—relations which he confessed can only be inferred from their writings, since Shakespeare never mentions Chapman by name nor Chapman Shakespeare. A good deal of the argument is concerned with Chapman's persuasion that his spirit and the spirit of Homer were connected in a manner more intimate than can be described as inspiration—after the manner, in fact, that a Greek felt himself associated with his *daemon*, or a Roman with his *genius*. The chief evidence for this belief is to be found in a poem by Chapman entitled *The Tears of Peace*, not printed until 1609 and therefore neglected by previous theorists, but describing something like a vision the young Chapman had received before coming to London—a vision in which the spirit of Homer appeared to him and spoke as follows:

> 'I am', said he 'that spirit Elysian,
> That (in thy native air, and on the hill
> Next Hitchin's left hand) did thy bosom fill
> With such a flood of soul, that thou wert fain
> (With acclamations of her rapture then)

To vent it to the echoes of the vale;
When (meditating of me) a sweet gale
Brought me upon thee, and thou didst inherit
My true sense, for the time then, in my spirit;
And I, invisibly, went prompting thee
To those fair greens where thou didst English me.[1]

Upon this Thomson comments:

I cannot attach any other meaning to these words than this—that Chapman claims to have been directly inspired in his translation of Homer's poems by Homer himself or (what amounts to the same thing) Homer's *anima* which came to him from Elysium....Have we not got now a very probable explanation of the famous couplet in sonnet 86?

He nor that affable familiar ghost
Which nightly gulls him with intelligence.[2]

Among other things Chapman affected was to be a Stoic and Thomson aptly quotes the following from Burton's *Anatomy of Melancholy* (Pt. I, sec. II, mem. I, subs. 2):

Cardan...out of the doctrine of Stoics, will have some of these genii (for so he calls them) to be desirous of men's company, very affable and familiar with them.

Jerome Cardan,[3] one of the greatest and most widely read 'philosophers' of the age, was undoubtedly known to Shakespeare, so that the correspondence between his words and Burton's is no accident. Both are quoting as from Cardan a demonological cliché of the age. But Shakespeare is of course slyly suggesting, as Thomson

[1] Quoted by J. A. K. Thomson, *Shakespeare and the Classics* (1952), p. 169.
[2] *Op. cit.* pp. 169–72.
[3] His popular *Cardanus Comforte* was translated in 1573, and in a 'corrected' text in 1576.

observes, that Chapman's visitant, so far from being his good 'angel' or 'heavenly familiar', is a lying spirit, a devil, who 'gulls' his dupe.

In face of all this it looks as if we need have no further doubts about the identity of the Rival Poet. Nevertheless, as so often with Shakespearean biography, there is no documentary evidence to support the circumstantial. If Chapman courted the Friend in verse, no such verses have survived, while, as stated above, Shakespeare never mentions Chapman or Chapman Shakespeare.

Is there anything in the *Sonnets* which might throw light upon this? I think there is if we now round off the case for Chapman as the Rival Poet. First of all notice that if Shakespeare wrote sonnet 86 in mockery, as I believe he did, he had two reasons for deliberately recalling Marlowe when he spoke of 'the proud full sail of his great verse'. First, he knew that, as Minto says, the words might in Chapman's imagination seem to apply 'with almost too literal exactness' to the Alexandrines of his Homer; and second, by the publication of his continuation of Marlowe's *Hero and Leander*, entered in the Stationer's Register on 2 March 1598, Chapman had just proclaimed himself the heir of Marlowe's genius. Indeed, I incline to think that the appearance of this book together with that of *Seven Books of the Iliad*, the first instalment of Chapman's Homer which was entered in the Register a month later, on 10 April, accounts for the Rival Poet sonnets as a whole. In any case these can hardly have been written until Shakespeare read them. Before the spring of 1598, all he knew of Chapman were the early poems, and he was poking fun at them in sonnet 21. But the new *Hero* and the Homer translation revealed the absurd, abstruse, pedantic author of *The Shadow of Night* as capable of really great poetry in whose presence Shakespeare's 'tongue-tied muse in manners holds her still'.

Further, though in view of the relations between the two men it is not likely that Shakespeare can have read the new Chapman before the publication of his two latest books, potential patrons like Herbert or Southampton may well have received advance copies which, as the custom was in such cases, would be beautifully written manuscript copies, prefaced by dedicatory poems, probably sonnets. And if so, may it not be that Shakespeare is referring to these copies when he alludes in 82 to

> The dedicated words which writers use
> Of their fair subject, blessing every book

or more pointedly in 85, when after declaring in mock-humility to be tongue-tied, he goes on:

> While comments of your praise richly compiled,
> Reserve their character with golden quill,
> And precious phrase by all the Muses filed.

And if no poems by Chapman which can be traced as addressed to Shakespeare's Friend have come down to us, may they not have been those 'dedicated words' which were inscribed with 'golden quill' upon the manuscripts presented to him?

But neither Shakespeare nor, I think, Thomson, fully understood Chapman. For the lines quoted above come from a long dedicatory Induction to Prince Henry which reveal the poet as a mystic, much as Wordsworth was, though of course of a very different variety. In any case one cannot read them without allowing that the vision of Homer vouchsafed to the young scholar Chapman at his native Hitchin was as real to him as was the 'serene and blessed mood' which as a young man often came to Wordsworth and enabled him to 'see into the life of things'.

Shakespeare might laugh at Chapman, but in this affair the rival laughed last, for the couplet that concludes sonnet 86—

> But when your countenance filled up his line,
> Then lacked I matter, that enfeebled mine—

may be paraphrased: When you showed that you liked his verse I was left with nothing to say, was left speechless. We must suppose therefore that the Friend had given some indication that he was willing to extend his patronage to Chapman. This did not, or did not need to, imply a break with Shakespeare. Indeed, sonnets 92 and 93 seem to say that he remained to all appearances 'gracious and kind', which is what one might expect of a great gentleman.

The Farewell Sonnets

Yet the sonnets that follow, the eight 'Farewell' sonnets 87–94, represent the supreme expression of that 'unembittered resignation' which Lewis finds the peculiar mark of Shakespeare's love-poetry. In other words, they exhibit the Poet in a mood of extreme depression, so that it is clear he had felt the Friend's approval of Chapman as a kind of desertion.

Sonnet 87, after a touch of spleen, not entirely 'unembittered', in the first two lines, declares that the Friend's love was never more than a free gift on his part which he had every right to take back again, since the Poet had done nothing to deserve it. Speak slightingly, scornfully, of me, says the Poet in sonnet 88, and I will speak even more scornfully of myself, being ready for my love to bear false witness against myself to prove you right. And in 89 he goes still further: if you need an excuse for breaking off our friendship, he declares, I will invent faults in myself. Moreover, I will take care you never meet me; and—here he touches the lowest note—

in my tongue,
Thy sweet beloved name no more shall dwell,
Lest I (too much profane) should do it wrong:
And haply of our old acquaintance tell.

As for 90, those critics who refuse to accept the *Sonnets* as sincere could perhaps argue that all this self-depreciation might be put on: they could scarcely disbelieve in the genuineness of the misery this sonnet reveals. But first of all he turned aside in 91 to try another line of appeal. Imagine, he says in effect to this splendid young gentleman, yourself robbed of every-everything Fortune has assigned to you (your 'measure'[1]), namely, wealth, strength, skill, fine clothes, hawks, hounds and horses—all that gives value to your life—and think how wretched you would be. Your love is worth more to me than any or all of these and you threaten to rob me of it!

All 92 but its couplet follows quite naturally on the wretchedness of 91. 'But do thy worst to steal thy self away' shows the desertion is expected, though for the time the Poet consoles himself with the thought that whatever the Friend can do he is his friend while life lasts, because life would leave him if the Friend left him. A pretty conceit, but obviously resorted to for the sake of the couplet, the meaning of which is made clear in 93. One of the woes that make him 'wretched' in 90 is a horrible suspicion that in spite of the young man's repentance and precious tears that 'ransom all

[1] Cf. *As You Like It*, 5. 4. 172, 'According to the measure of their states'.

ill deeds' as depicted in sonnet 34, the liaison with the Dark Woman was still being carried on without his knowing it. What else can be the meaning of

> Thou mayst be false, and yet I know it not (92)

and

> So shall I live, supposing thou art true,
> Like a deceived husband, so love's face,
> May still seem love to me, though altered new:
> Thy looks with me, thy heart in other place (93)

and above all perhaps the couplet

> How like Eve's apple doth thy beauty grow,
> If thy sweet virtue answer not thy show

which is a development of 41. 13, 'thy beauty tempting her to thee'? Eve's apple is, of course, 'the fruit of the tree in the midst of the garden' with which the Devil tempted Eve. It was at this point of agonizing suspicion that, one may imagine, Shakespeare wrote the most famous of all the sonnets, 'Two loves I have of comfort and despair'. It was at this point too, it seems, that he suffered a double loss of his 'beauteous and lovely youth', (i) to the pedant Chapman whose verse was preferred, (ii) to the Dark Woman. And it was at this point, I think, that for a time he stopped writing sonnets, at any rate to his better angel. And when we come to 97 it seems to refer to some kind of break, the cause and duration of which constitute one of the major problems of the *Sonnets*.

We left the Poet bidding the Friend farewell in the series of sonnets that culminated with the bitter reference to 'Eve's apple' of 93. There follows one of the sections of the 1609 text most difficult to understand, which indeed can be understood only when we discover the person to whom they were addressed. For instance, the sonnets that succeed 'Eve's apple', viz.

95 and 96, seem to refer to some incident of a lascivious character, quite distinct from the liaison with the Dark Woman.

What the Sonnets tell us about the Poet's life 1597–98

But before discussing all these matters, there is one major problem to be faced. When were the *Sonnets* begun? The answer to this is closely bound up with the problem of the identity of the Friend. But it can, I think, be solved independently, and it will be of great advantage to have it solved first, since if solved satisfactorily it narrows our field of choice in dealing with this identification.

(i) *Beeching's date for the first* 94 *sonnets*

In his edition of 1904, Beeching offers striking evidence on this matter, which has been strangely overlooked, largely I suspect because it has been regarded as one aspect of another kind of evidence (though he expressly warned against this). He calls this evidence 'the argument from repeated expressions' and declares:

> This argument must not be confused with an argument from what are called 'parallel passages'. It is primarily an argument from the *use of identical words*, only secondarily from *similar ideas*....Of course it must be used with discretion. The repeated phrase of which notice is taken must be striking and individual. It would not do, for instance, to suggest that sonnet 29 is of the same date as *Cymbeline* because in both the poet speaks of the lark as singing 'at heaven's gate'.[1]

Perhaps the best way of bringing out the significance and true character of Beeching's method of dating is to compare his results with those of a critic who uses the

[1] Beeching, p. xxiv, n. 3 (my italics).

ordinary method of parallel passages. That method, a complex of verbal parallels, parallelisms of thought and ideas, and metrical tests of various kinds, is elaborately discussed by Edmund Chambers, and forms to a large extent the basis of his well-known chronological table of the plays which is now widely accepted by scholars.[1] I myself find it more reliable for the plays after 1597 than before; it is demonstrably wrong, for example, in the placing of *Love's Labour's Lost* (which was certainly revised in part after the appearance of Gerard's *Herbal* in 1597).[2] And a chronology based upon tests applicable to dramas mainly in blank verse is manifestly unreliable for the dating of sonnets. Chambers admits this to a certain extent, for he writes 'Of the plays, it is naturally only those with a strong love-interest which are relevant'.[3] But since love is the element in which practically every sonnet of Section I moves, it would be strange indeed if the parallel passages were not very numerous, or if Chambers did not discover about 150 parallels in plays like *The Two Gentlemen*, *Love's Labour's Lost*, *Romeo and Juliet*, and *A Midsummer Night's Dream*. What is needed for dating purposes in the *Sonnets* is plays with little or no love interest. The truth is that the ordinary parallel-passage tests in plays are largely irrelevant to the *Sonnets*. We must look for a new kind of touchstone altogether. And this Beeching discovered in repeated expression, which he thus expounds:

> Every writer knows the perverse facility with which a phrase once used presents itself again; and Shakespeare seems to have been not a little liable to this literary habit.

[1] Chambers, *William Shakespeare*, I, 254 ff.

[2] See note on *Love's Labour's Lost* 5. 2. 890 (*New Cambridge Shakespeare*, 2nd edition, 1962).

[3] *William Shakespeare*, I, 564.

It is not uncommon for him to use a word or phrase twice in a single play, and never afterwards. There is a strong probability, therefore, if a remarkable phrase or figure of speech occurs both in a sonnet and in a play, that the play and the sonnet belong to the same period. Now the greater number of the parallel passages hitherto recognized are to be found in *Henry IV*, in *Love's Labour's Lost*, and in *Hamlet*; and it is certain that *Henry IV* was written in 1597, that *Love's Labour's Lost* was revised in that same year, and that *Hamlet* is later still. To take an example: the phrase 'world-without-end' makes a sufficiently remarkable epithet; but it is so used only in Sonnet 57 and in *Love's Labour's Lost* (5. 2. 785). But as it is open to any one to reply that this and other phrases may have occurred in the original draft of the play, written several years earlier, it will be best to confine the parallels to *Henry IV*, the date of which is beyond dispute.

Compare, then, Sonnet 33—

> Anon *permit* the *basest* clouds to ride,
> With ugly rack on his celestial face—

with *1 Henry IV*, 1. 2. 189—

> the sun,
> Who doth *permit* the *base* contagious clouds
> To smother up his beauty from the world.

Again, compare Sonnet 52—

> Therefore are *feasts* so *solemn* and so *rare*,
> Since *seldom* coming in the long year set
> ....
> So is the time that keeps you as my chest,
> Or as the wardrobe which the *robe* doth hide,
> To make some special instant special blest—

with *1 Henry IV*, 3. 2. 56—

> My presence like a *robe* pontifical,
> Ne'er seen but wond'red at, and so my state,
> *Seldom* but sumptuous, showed like a *feast*,
> And won by *rareness* such *solemnity*—

where the concurrence of the images of a feast and a robe is very noticeable. Compare also Sonnet 64 with *2 Henry IV*, 3. 1. 45, where the revolution of states is compared with the sea gaining on the land, and the land on the sea,—an idea not found in the famous description of the works of Time in *Lucrece* (939–59).[1] Compare also the epithet 'sullen', applied to a bell in Sonnet 71 and *2 Henry IV*, 1. 1. 102, and in the same sonnet the phrase 'compounded with clay' or 'dust', found in *2 Henry IV*, 4. 5. 115, and *Hamlet*, 4. 2. 6. The contrast between the canker or wild rose and the cultivated rose, used so admirably in Sonnet 54, is found again in *1 Henry IV*, 1. 3. 176, and also in *Much Ado About Nothing* 1. 3. 25, a play written probably a year or two years later. The very remarkable use of the word 'blazon', a technical term in heraldry, of the limbs of the human body, is found twice, once in Sonnet 106, and once in *Twelfth Night*, 1. 5. 297, the date of which is probably 1600. Again, the idea expressed in the phrases 'sick of welfare' or 'rank of goodness' in Sonnet 118 is paralleled in *2 Henry IV*, 4. 1. 64, 'sick of happiness', and in *Hamlet*, 4. 7. 116, 'goodness growing to a plurisy', and in these plays only. The comparison of the eye in its socket to a star moving in its 'sphere' is found only in Sonnets 119 and in *Hamlet*, 1. 5. 17. In Sonnet 125 and in *Othello*, 1, 1. 62, there is a conjunction of the word 'outward' with the curious synonym 'extern' which occurs only in these two places. I do not wish to press this argument further than it will go, but it must be allowed that its force accumulates with every instance adduced; and, in my opinion, it is strong enough to dispose of the hypothesis that the main body of the sonnets was written in 1593 or 1594.[2]

(ii) *Further evidence for 1597–98*:

Prince Hal and the disloyal Friend

Soon after the foregoing paragraphs were published some two years ago, my attention was drawn to an

[1] See below, pp. 169 ff.

[2] Beeching, *op. cit.* Introduction, pp. xxiv–xxvii.

important article by Professor M. M. Mahood[1] which but for my half-blindness I should have known before, an article which, apparently independently of Beeching, and for quite different reasons, corroborates his dating while emphasizing the close emotional links between the *Sonnets* and the plays of the middle period, *Henry IV* in particular. Before going further, then, it will be well to have a list of these plays, which I take from the chronological table by Chambers mentioned above.

The plays of Shakespeare's Middle Period

1596–7 *King John. The Merchant of Venice.*
1597–8 The Two Parts of *Henry IV.*
1598–9 *Much Ado. Henry V.*
1599–1600 *Julius Caesar. As You Like It. Twelfth Night.*
1600–1 *Hamlet. Merry Wives.*
1601–2 *Troilus and Cressida.*
1602–3 *All's Well That Ends Well.*
1603–4 Blank.
1604–5 *Measure for Measure. Othello.*
1605–6 *King Lear. Macbeth.*

It is a list that students of the *Sonnets* who have accepted Beeching's date of 1597–8 for their commencement should keep before their eyes, a striking feature being the comparative meagreness of the output after *Hamlet* in 1601, culminating in the complete blank in the last year of the Queen's reign, which seems to correspond closely with the obvious break in the sonnet sequence marked by the contrast between the desolate 87–94 and the tender composure of 97–9, written in absence, and the more self-assured sonnets of the last phase, 100–26.

[1] *Shakespeare Survey,* 15 (1962).

Returning, then, to the date at which the *Sonnets* began, I have first to report that since the original draft of this Introduction was completed in 1963 I have been able to review all the problems in the light of a much fuller and more searching examination of the significance and occasion of the sonnets individually, the results of which are given in the commentary and notes below, results I was happy to find appeared to confirm—and what was better to amplify—Beeching's conclusions about the date.

To take one instance as an illustration. As one of the links with *Henry IV*, which all agree belongs to 1597–8, Beeching quotes the image of the sun being hidden in cloud, an image that occurs both in sonnet 33 and in Prince Hal's famous (to many readers infamous) soliloquy, announcing his intention of dropping his boon companions after he has amused himself with them for a while. Here I owe the amplification of the parallel to Miss Mahood who, while pointing out that the sun and cloud metaphor is elaborated in much the same way in soliloquy and sonnet and exhibits other verbal and stylistic resemblances so close that it is hard to believe the two were not composed at approximately the same time, goes on to observe that nevertheless they reflect the two sides of the same relationship and express the points of view of persons at opposite ends of the social scale. But sonnet 33 in which the poet of humble birth speaks obliquely of a wrong done to him by a friend of lofty rank, is one of the liaison sonnets. We can feel pretty certain, then, that this sonnet and the painful episode it alluded to belong like 1 *Henry IV* to the years 1597–8.

And the Rival Poet affair can be assigned to a slightly later date with equal confidence, if, as I hope my readers now agree, the rival was George Chapman, seeing that the series 78–86 can hardly have been written before the early summer of 1598, inasmuch as until Chapman had published his Second Part of *Hero and Leander* and the *Seven Books of the Iliad* in March and April of that year, Shakespeare had no evidence that he could be a dangerous rival. It was indeed a very different Chapman who came before the world in 1594–5 with *The Shadow of Night* in verse at once so absurd and obscure that Shakespeare dismissed it in sonnet 21 with the good-humoured banter of a skit upon his *Amorous Zodiac*.

Sonnet 21 belongs to the halcyon period of Shakespeare's friendship, and was probably written soon after its commencement in the spring of 1597, for which we shall find evidence for a more precise date in a later sonnet. But—

...out alack, he was but one hour mine

as we learn from 33, and not long after 21 something took place that led to separation of at least two months. The sonnet which begins

Let me confess that we two must be twain

is listed 36 by Thorpe but probably preceded sonnet 25. In any case here is another date, for unless I am all astray in my interpretation of the whole run of sonnets 25–76, Shakespeare was forced to leave London at the end of July 1597 and travel like other actors as the result of an injunction by the Privy Council ordering the closing down of all the theatres, after the production of a 'seditious' play, *The Isle of Dogs*. Playing was resumed early in October and presumably Shakespeare returned about that time to produce *Henry IV*, the success of Falstaff therein no doubt going far to mollify the wrath which *The Isle of Dogs* had aroused. But something less pleasant than plaudits of London audiences met him on his return. From the fact that there is no hint whatever of treachery on the part of his Friend in the fifteen or more sonnets written in absence during the tour in the autumn of 1597 I infer that he first discovered it later. I therefore assign the earlier sonnets in the liaison series to the winter of 1597–8, with the Rival Poet series following close after, as we have just seen, in the summer of 1598. The double disaster of this six months, when he lost the loyalty of his Friend twice over, as it were, is more than sufficient to account for the blend of bitterness and desolation that marks the eight Farewell sonnets (87–94) that follow sonnets in which Shakespeare concedes victory to the learned Chapman. And after that comes a silence that all critics have perceived but the duration of which none has determined.

It will be obvious that the composition of *Henry IV* must have been more or less contemporaneous with the writing of the sonnets, roughly 25–90. And Miss Mahood who tightened up for us the intimate links between Prince Hal's soliloquy in 1 *Henry IV* and sonnet 33 establishes an equally close connexion between the rejection of Falstaff in the last scene of 2 *Henry IV* and the Farewell sonnets. Yet if the promise of his rejection in Part I and its enactment in Part II are both paralleled with the relation between Poet and Friend in the *Sonnets*, we are left with the astonishing paradox of a Shakespeare = Falstaff equation which Miss Mahood attempts to explain by suggesting that the dramatist sought relief in a kind of exorcism from the Poet's haunting fear of the Friend's disloyalty, by presenting the similar disloyalty of Hal towards Falstaff as an act of prudence required of persons moving on the higher social levels. And that this is not a mere piece of critical ingenuity is demonstrated by the parallelism between the misplaced sonnet 49 and act 5 scene 5 of 2 *Henry IV*, a parallelism which includes verbal resemblance, a particularly striking one being pointed out by Professor Maxwell in a review of Miss Mahood's article, viz.

> (Sonnet 49. 7) When love converted from the thing it was
> (*2 Henry IV*, 5. 5. 57) Presume not that I am the thing I was.

Date-clues and subject-matter in 94–9

Assuredly the connexion between the *Sonnets* and the two parts of *Henry IV* is an extremely intimate one, so intimate that we can feel tolerably certain that 25–94 were all written during the years 1597–8. How long the silence that followed the heartbroken farewell of 87–94 continued we do not know. But it is significant that the period 1599–1603 when, but for the big exception of *Hamlet*, Shakespeare's dramatic muse seemed least prolific, yields the fewest number of sonnets, while the confidence and comparative maturity of everything in Section I from sonnet 100 onwards seems to coincide with the inspiration which gave us the supreme tragedies *Othello*, *King Lear*, *Macbeth*. Is there anything wrong with a biographical reconstruction that shows a genius producing his greatest comic character at his gloomiest period and his greatest tragedies when he has found happiness again?

But political events must not be forgotten. For it was probably no accident that the years of comparative silence, roughly 1599–1603, are the years of trouble that brought to an end the reign of the Great Queen.

Yet the silence of the Poet between 94, when he said

what he clearly imagined to be his final farewell, and 100 with its question

> Where art thou, Muse, that thou forget'st so long,

is not entirely unbroken. For it gave utterance to two little groups of sonnets, both I think belonging to 1600, though unconnected in theme, viz. (i) 95–6, and (ii) a linked triplet 97–9. The first, which Leishman persuaded me was probably concerned with the Mary Fitton scandal, must be left for consideration until we can decide which of the Queen's young courtiers is most likely to have been Shakespeare's Friend, though, if Leishman be right, 1600 must be the year of composition with the summer its probable season.

Sonnets in absence: 97, 98, 99 [104]

The other group, which is one of the triplets observed by Chambers[1] as linked together by rhymes and repetitions, records two consecutive seasons of memorable beauty: in 97 an autumn so early that it seemed late summer, which was quite unusually rich in crops and fruit, and in 98–9 which was being written in the month the Poet describes, an exceptional April. The year of composition is uncertain, but 98 contains an astrological reference which thanks to Wyndham[2] can, I believe, be dated almost to the day. The spring spoken of is one of peculiar beauty and luxuriance with an early April resplendent with colour, scent and song. But, so the poet concludes,

> Yet seemed it winter still, and you away.

Now one of the wonders of this glorious spring, the Poet relates, was the rēmarkable appearance of Saturn

[1] *Shakespearean Gleanings*, pp. 117–18.

[2] Wyndham, *op. cit.* pp. 244 ff.

in the April sky. This planet, usually considered slow, melancholy, sullen, unfavourable, even malevolent, seemed to appear leaping and laughing when he became visible in the brilliant heaven. Assuming that Shakespeare was, like most serious people of that age, interested in astrology and is here speaking of the real planet, Wyndham, after citing an astronomer at the Royal Observatory, Edinburgh, as his authority, notes that Saturn was seen 'in opposition' in the night sky in only three Aprils between 1592 and 1609, viz. on 4 April 1600, 17 April 1601, and 29 April 1602. He is himself inclined to favour the third of these years because Saturn then rose gradually, after crossing the horizon, reached a greater height when in opposition, and became a most conspicuous object. But gradualness was surely not in Shakespeare's mind. On the contrary, 'leaped and laughed' implies at once suddenness and an ascent so unusual as to suggest sauciness. In other words, Saturn was clearly visible immediately after sunset, leaping above the horizon in mockery of the sun which had only just disappeared into the underworld from which he had come. A brilliantly clear sky and the relative positions of Saturn and his royal master the sun on 4 April 1600, accounts for it all. If this date be correct, it may prove to be of biographical importance, were our chosen candidate for the honour of being Shakespeare's Friend to be William Herbert, who became Earl of Pembroke in 1601. For he was born on 8 April 1580, so that the spring day sonnet 98 speaks of would be somewhere near the Friend's 20th birthday; celebrated, however, in his absence. In any case, the group was probably never sent since, as Beeching shows, the third remains unfinished.

That was roughly the point which I reached in my survey of the Sonnets for the original draft. But as

I was nearing the end of this second draft I came upon a matter not of theory but of fact which put a fresh complexion on the group as a whole. Sonnet 104, which Thorpe placed as fifth in the final series 100–26, a series preceded in the opinion of nearly all serious students by a break of one or more years, proclaims itself as being written three years after the two friends first met, i.e. in 1600, unless my dating of the sonnets had hitherto gone all astray, while to my mind the sonnet had clearly been intended to wish the young man many happy returns on his 20th birthday; in other words it was written for the same occasion as 97–9. It was all very puzzling until a searching scrutiny of 104 revealed the fact, one which could not be questioned, that it was linked with 97–9 by rhyme and repetition in the same fashion as they were linked: sonnets 97, 98, 99, 104 formed in fact a linked quartet. Yet 104 was in one way different from the others. They were written in absence and the fact that the beloved is 'away' makes the splendour of the autumn and the spring seem like winter. In 104 there is nothing of this: on the contrary, the Poet seems to be addressing the Friend directly, to be gazing at him, delighting to be once again in the light of 'that sun' his eye. It looks as if the jolly Saturn had reminded him that 8 April was the Friend's birthday, and that 99 was left unfinished because he put away gloomy thoughts and hastened to lay his birthday offering at the boy's feet. This is of course surmise, as so much of one's interpretation of the sonnets must be. Yet it fits in if, as I shall presently ask readers to believe, provisionally at least, the boy actually was William Herbert. The date 8 April 1600 was, as has been said, his 20th birthday and there could be no celebrating in 1601 for he had then just been thrown into prison. And if after the misery of the Farewell sonnets Shakespeare began to crave for all the friendship meant to him, a birthday offered a fine opportunity of renewal, while the men were both busy in London so that meeting would be easy. And once intimacy were restored there might be many more meetings in 1600, as indeed seems to be shown in 95–6, provoked I imagine by rumours of the visit of Mary Fitton to the young man's bedroom after the Masque on 16 June.

And then, in the opening weeks of 1601, three events took place, the death of Herbert's father and his succession to the earldom (19 January), the discovery of Mistress Fitton's condition and the arrest of the young earl (5 February), and the abortive rising of Essex (8 February). Fortunately the second preceded the third or the Earl of Pembroke might have been arrested upon a much more serious charge. In any case, he was either in prison or in banishment until the death of the Queen—two years. Such I believe is the main reason for the break before the final sonnets. Was there another? What was Shakespeare himself doing at that period? Why that diminuendo in his dramatic output? Had he found it wise to be absent from London for a while?

Dates and allusions in a sonnet towards the end of the first group

The group 100–26 being divided by a gap of some two years from the sonnets that were written earlier, let us now determine if we can, at any rate approximately, the beginning and the end of this last group. The frequent apologies it contains for silence or poverty of invention seem to show that the sonnets cover a fairly long period, during which Shakespeare wrote intermittently when he had time. Tyler's claim, already referred to, that the group constituted a single continuous poem may at any rate be ruled out, since it comprises two sonnets (107, 124) which contain topical allusions of different dates, allusions for which Beeching furnishes what seem to be eminently satisfactory explanations. Here is his treatment of 124 which takes us nearly to the end of the series.

Pointing out that the obvious moral of the sonnet is that Love is the only true policy, Beeching explains that the particular 'state' policy alluded to in lines 13–14 is the policy of 'the Jesuit conspirators whose object in life was to murder the king, and who when caught, posed as martyrs for the faith. Such inconstancy of principle would justify the poet in calling them "the fools of time"[1] and pointing his moral with them'.[2] And he interprets 'the blow of thralled discontent' as the Powder Plot in which the discontented 'party held down by penal enactments' planned to blow up Parliament including King, Lords and Commons. He hesitates to see in 'builded far from accident' an indirect allusion to the threatened Houses of Parliament, which were not so builded, but line 6 'in smiling pomp' seems to suit the ceremonial opening of Parliament, for which occasion the Plot was designed.

If we accept this reading, as I think we may, important results follow. First, it implies that Shakespeare went on writing sonnets after James's accession, and at least seven years after he had written those 'sugred sonnets' known to Meres in 1598; second, all serious objections to the interpretation of sonnet 107 as a reference to the death of Elizabeth fall to the ground. This sonnet will be considered in detail on p. cvi. Here it need only be observed that anyone who supposes the

[1] I.e. persons deceived by the world in which they live.

[2] Beeching, note on lines 13–14.

'mortal moon' refers to the Spanish Armada which in 1588 sailed up the Channel in crescent formation has less astronomy than Shakespeare who, like all Elizabethans well versed in astrology, was specially interested in eclipses and knew very well that the moon is only eclipsed when full.

IV. The Identity of Mr W. H.

Southampton pro and con

The time is now come to hang up a votive offering in the cave of mystery or, to vary the metaphor, to attempt to let in the light of history upon that shadow in the cave that throws all the other shadows into the shade; in a word, to answer the question, who was this

Lascivious grace in whom all ill well shows—

this youth to whom Shakespeare paid tribute with the finest love-poetry in the world, and such absolute homage that, as Valentine with Proteus, he was ready to give him the woman he dearly loved? Unless all this was mere sycophancy to catch a patron, a notion we have utterly rejected, the youth must have been an unusual person, not only beyond all measure handsome, but with intelligence and powers of appreciation—if far inferior to those of the 'mighty poet of the human heart' who lavished his adoration upon him—yet of sufficient quality to be invited to 'the marriage of true minds'. We have nothing to go upon but the *Sonnets* themselves; and the character of the Friend I have attempted to sketch from the hints they supply and they alone. And though, as any Shakespearian student must, I began with an idea as to a possible answer to the question,[1]

[1] E.g. in my *Essential Shakespeare* (1932), long before I had made a study of the Sonnets.

I had not proceeded far before coming to realize that an agnostic attitude was advisable.

Strange as it may seem, no one appears to have taken much interest in the question until Malone edited Thorpe's edition in 1780 and thus revealed for the first time the autobiographical character of the *Sonnets*. And even then it was hardly realized until Wordsworth in 1827 boldly declared

> with this key
> Shakespeare unlocked his heart;[1]

and by so doing unlocked the flood-gate through which an ever-broadening tide of speculation flowed until by 1944 it took over fifty closely-packed pages in the second volume of a monumental American edition of the *Sonnets* to record even brief extracts of the various theories about the identity of the Friend.

There they lie, the whole wilderness of them, for the inspection of curious eyes, a strange chapter in this history of human folly. In this study, however, apart from a passing reference to another 'Mr W. H.' whose claims to be 'the onlie begetter' were first put forth only the other day, I shall confine myself to the two who have divided the allegiance of most modern scholars: Henry Wriothesley (1573–1624), third Earl of Southampton, and William Herbert, who succeeded his father in 1601 as third Earl of Pembroke.

Southampton's claims were first advanced by Nathan Drake in 1817.[2] He seemed an obvious candidate. The Friend was clearly a man of high rank. Shakespeare had acknowledged Southampton as his patron by dedicating to him *Venus and Adonis* in 1593 and *The Rape of Lucrece* in 1594. Moreover, as many have observed, the general argument of sonnets 1–17,

[1] *Miscellaneous Sonnets*, Part II, 'Scorn not the Sonnet'.
[2] Nathan Drake, *Shakespeare and his Times* (1817).

namely that 'nothing 'gainst Time's scythe can make defence save breed', is anticipated or echoed in *Venus and Adonis*, lines 163–74:

Torches are made to light, jewels to wear,
Dainties to taste, fresh beauty for the use,
Herbs for their smell, and sappy plants to bear;
Things growing to themselves are growth's abuse:
  Seeds spring from seeds, and beauty breedeth beauty;
  Thou wast begot; to get it is thy duty.

Upon the earth's increase why shouldst thou feed,
Unless the earth with thy increase be fed?
By law of nature thou art bound to breed,
That thine may live when thou thyself art dead;
  And so in spite of death, thou dost survive,
  In that thy likeness still is left alive.

And it is difficult to resist the impression of E. K. Chambers that the *Sonnets* were a 'continuation of the lyrical impulse represented by *Venus and Adonis*'.[1] Yet it is equally difficult not to agree with Beeching's assertion that 'their writing is distinctly finer than anything in the *Venus*, and the thought and experience are riper. The mastery of rhythm deepened in sonnet 5 and the melancholy of that and sonnet 12 point to a later date.'[2] Speaking generally, one has only to compare any of the first half-dozen sonnets with the lines from *Venus* just quoted, and how much more elaborate, more highly wrought is their treatment. It is open to anyone to argue that the Poet had here taken up again and greatly developed subject-matter dealt with earlier, perhaps years earlier. This being so, the *Sonnets* might have been written for another nobleman altogether.

Other points have been often advanced against

[1] Chambers, *William Shakespeare*, I, 564.
[2] Beeching, p. xxiv, n. 2.

Southampton. The sonnets punning on the name Will[1] make it virtually certain that the youth's name was William like the Poet's. As for Thorpe's dedication 'to Mr W. H.'[2], whatever that may mean, it cannot possibly denote Master Henry Wriothesley. There is no evidence, again, that Southampton had any dealings with Shakespeare after 1594,[3] the absence of any reference to him in the dedicatory material of the First Folio being particularly noticeable. On the other hand, the *Sonnets* contain no conceivable allusions to his courtship of Elizabeth Vernon in 1595, to his adoration of Essex in 1597, with whom he took part in the Islands Voyage expedition, the war in Ireland, or his part in the rising of 1601 and subsequent imprisonment. Above all, if we accept 1597–8 as the year in which Shakespeare began the *Sonnets*, he was at that date too old, being then twenty-four or twenty-five, while he must have been thirty or more when Shakespeare was writing his Envoy to his 'lovely boy'.

If Southampton, then, be ruled out we are left with William Herbert. But which William Herbert? Before we cast our vote in favour of his namesake who became the Earl of Pembroke in January 1601, another William must be considered, his first cousin who indeed was raised to the peerage in 1629 as Baron Powys of Powys (or Poole or Red) Castle, Montgomeryshire. In 1609 when Thorpe was dedicating the *Sonnets* to Mr W.H., he was the only William Herbert of noble

[1] 135, 136 and 143. See Beeching, p. xxxvi–xxxvii.

[2] Southamptonites try to escape from this dilemma by conjecturing that Thorpe obtained the *Sonnets* from Sir William Hervey, widower of the Countess of Southampton.

[3] For the facts of Southampton's career see Rollins, II, 56–7.

birth who could have been so described with propriety —a fact which gives him what will seem to many quite a long lead, since to the best of our knowledge the other William was always addressed as The Lord Herbert until he became an Earl.

This new candidate for Shakespeare's friendship was first proposed in a little book with the question-begging title of *The Onlie Begetter*, published in 1936 by Ulric Nisbet. It is discursive and its argumentation has been rather roughly handled by the veteran Shakespeare scholar Professor T. W. Baldwin, while the whole matter has been judiciously summed up by Rollins (II, 227) with a somewhat reluctant verdict that 'fairness demands' that this other Herbert's 'claims to the only begettership are hardly more unsupported than those of certain better-known claimants'—which suggests that more might be made of Nisbet's case than he was able to make of it. But if the last word has not yet been said about this Red William Herbert, there is one fact that Nisbet has discovered which puts him out of court as far as I am concerned—he was born in 1572, a year before Southampton. That is to say, he was, like him, too old; and would have been, like him, a 'lovely boy' of well over thirty!

We turn then to his cousin, the young man who was under twenty-one at the beginning of 1601 when he became an earl. Reasons for his being addressed as 'Mr' by Thorpe have been suggested above (p. xl). Beeching, though no advocate of Southampton, and highly critical of Sidney Lee, could not find enough certain evidence to convince him that Herbert was the Friend. Nevertheless, there is more evidence in the *Sonnets* than he was aware of. Before coming to that, however, it will be helpful I think to look at the vivid picture we have of Herbert in later life.

Clarendon's portrait of Pembroke in his 'History of the Rebellion'

The Earl of Clarendon prefaces his famous history with an account of the chief persons at the English court immediately before the outbreak of the civil war, among whom William Herbert Earl of Pembroke stood pre-eminent. And if Shakespeare's young Friend did indeed grow up to become this great man, surely all we can learn about him is of first importance to students of the *Sonnets*. Yet the passage in Clarendon has been strangely neglected. Tyler and Leishman both give extracts but neither Beeching nor Chambers mentions it and even Rollins dismisses it with the briefest reference. It is lengthy but should be made readily accessible. I am therefore printing it as a whole in an appendix, together with passages from John Aubrey's 'brief life' of Pembroke, which supports Clarendon at all salient points.

If the child is father of the man, surely the man whom Clarendon gives us was offspring of the youth whose character we have attempted to build up or guess at from material supplied by the *Sonnets*. If ever, for instance, there was an 'Eve's apple', a lascivious grace, to tempt the young Eves at court with its beauty, it was Pembroke's. 'Immoderately given up to women', Clarendon tells us, yet never marrying except once, and then for property, since the wife was the daughter of the Earl of Shrewsbury and probably the richest heiress available—a marriage 'in which he was most unhappy'. It is noteworthy, too, that Clarendon, who knew all the court gossip, links this unhappiness with the sexual indulgence by explaining the latter as due either to 'his natural disposition or for want of his domestic content and delight'. Here the *Sonnets*, had he known them, might have taught him to leave the wife out, for the 'disposition' had been Herbert's from the age of adolescence, and sonnet 40 may well have supplied the key to it in the line

> By wilful taste of what thy self refusest,

though the paradox involved must be left to psychologists to expound.

But there is the other side of the picture, and if the bad side helps us to identify the young Friend, may not the side that both Clarendon and Aubrey cannot praise enough help us to see, if only in germ, aspects of the boy's character we should not otherwise know, and to believe that his fascination for Shakespeare was by no means confined to a poet's worship of physical beauty? What a boy it must have been who became a few years later 'the most universally loved and esteemed of that age', the man who could live in the politically and socially corrupt court of James I and not only escape this corruption but help to purify the court by his presence in it, a man of such magnanimity and integrity that all could trust him never to seek his own interests or self-advancement, never to act out of private resentment or to curry favour with the king or his favourites; a man who, himself not without learning, could appreciate it in others, 'his conversation' being 'most with men of the most pregnant parts and understanding', while he was 'very liberal' towards such persons who had been recommended for his patronage; being indeed 'the greatest Maecenas to learned men of any peer of his time, or since'; finally, a man who was 'handsome, and of an admirable presence...and delighted in poetry: and did sometimes write some sonnets and epigrams'!

After pondering these passages from Clarendon and Aubrey, many, I think, will be disposed to accept them provisionally as historical accounts of the person Shakespeare glorified in 126 sonnets.

Sonnets 1–17 *and the youth's reluctance to marry*

Let us now see, therefore, how far it is possible to trace allusions in the *Sonnets* to the events of his career as a young man. The main facts are to be found in state documents, in the shape of letters to correspondents in the country and abroad, including those from Rowland Whyte the agent of Herbert's uncle, Sir Robert Sidney, then at Flushing, and a few from Herbert himself to Cecil, and a very revealing one from Cecil to his friend Sir George Carew; and it is from these sources, or the bulk of them, that the story of the career has been told by two scholars, both Herbertists: namely Thomas Tyler in the edition of *Shakespeare's Sonnets*, 1890, and Edmund Chambers in his *William Shakespeare: A Study of Facts and Problems* (1930), together with its appendix *Shakespearean Gleanings* (1943); and more recently in 1944 by Rollins[1] (vol. II, 209–12). The account that follows attempts to combine the first two versions, which is not difficult, since one virtually begins where the other ends, according to the date they assign to the first meeting of Poet and Friend. For whereas Tyler, as we have seen, rightly assigns it to 1597–8, Chambers argues for 1595, and that for two reasons: (i), because the records show Herbert, then fifteen, paying a visit in that year to court with his parents, to arrange for a marriage with Elizabeth, daughter of Sir George Carey, granddaughter of the Lord Chamberlain, who was the patron of Shakespeare's Company; and (ii), as seen above, because Chambers regarded the *Sonnets* as a product of the same poetic afflatus as gave us *Venus*

[1] In his Variorum edition of the *Sonnets*.

and Adonis—an argument Beeching has already countered, as we have also seen.

Chambers had already suggested this date in 1930 in his *William Shakespeare*. But a few years later, the recovery of fresh letters about the negotiations for Carey's daughter showed that they were broken off not, as had earlier appeared, on account of failure to agree about the property involved, but because of young Herbert's not 'liking' the lady when it came to the point. Accordingly, Chambers felt justified in summing up as follows when he returned to the problem in 1943.[1] 'There can be no certainty, but clearly Herbert's "not liking" brings us much nearer to the situation indicated by sonnets 1–17, than any other clue, which has yet been suggested.' Yet though this seems to point towards the identification of the Friend with this youth averse to marrying, it tells us nothing about the date of the *Sonnets* themselves. These, Chambers assumed, began in 1595 and had ended by 1599; and though by way of winding up the story he goes on to mention later negotiations for Herbert's marriage, he adds 'These things lie outside the ambit of the *Sonnets*'.

Tyler missed the mark no less than Chambers but by so narrow a margin that the failure can only be set down to blindness, the scholar's blindness of an *idée fixe*. For it was Tyler who chose the right negotiation, viz. that conducted with Lord Burghley in favour of his granddaughter, and Tyler who printed the documents describing its progress. Yet though the latter are all dated 1597 he insisted upon 1598 as the year of the beginning of the *Sonnets*. What led him astray was a double illusion: (1) that sonnets 100–26 form a single continuous poem, and (2) that the two most obviously

[1] 'The "Youth" of the Sonnets' in *Shakespearean Gleanings* (1944), p. 126.

topical sonnets, 107 and 124, both referred to the same events, the unsuccessful rising of Essex, February 1601. It therefore followed for him that sonnet 104 in which the Poet speaks of having first met the Friend three years previously had been written like the rest of the group in 1601, and so by subtracting 3 from 1601 he arrived at the spring of 1598 as the date of that first meeting.[1] Yet when he came to treat of Herbert's disinclination to marry which is the *raison d'être* of sonnets 1–17, and of the fruitless negotiation that he claimed led to the writing of those sonnets, he printed letters by Herbert's parents from which one would infer (as he infers himself) that the negotiation for the hand of Burghley's granddaughter Bridget Vere had been in progress for many months in 1597 which was therefore a far more likely year for the first meeting than 1598.

To understand the negotiation it must be noted that Herbert's father was a very sick man who found it difficult to get to London, so that, though he wrote a long letter dated 16 August 1597 dealing with the business side of the affair, a letter apparently intended to bring the whole matter to a head, it is obvious that the personal aspect, viz. bringing the young people together and securing their consent, had been carried on during the summer by Lady Pembroke, who wrote on the same date as her husband informing Burghley that her son, then a boy of 17, had 'so far forth' shown 'best liking, affection and resolution to answer my desires herein as if the late interview have mutually wrought, it is sufficient'.[2] 'So far forth' does not sound very confident; but he had clearly said Yes.

[1] Tyler, *op. cit.* pp. 5, 22–7.

[2] Tyler, *op. cit.* p. 45. I am unfortunately dependent on his transcript.

After all, there was plenty of time from his point of view. The girl was only 13, and there was no question of their living together yet. Moreover, the boy's head was full of preparations for travel, as we gather from his father's letter to Burghley; travel being then a necessary phase of a young nobleman's education. On the other hand, the Countess no doubt insisted that his consent was a matter of urgency, because of the state of his father's health. They had, too, it seems, been some time in town; for, as Tyler notes, a letter dated 8 September to Burghley from Bridget's father the Earl of Oxford shows that the negotiations had by that time gone a long way.[1] It also shows that Oxford realized how necessary it was to hurry the marriage on, for he writes: 'My lord of Pembroke is a man very sickly and therefore it is to be gathered he desireth in his life time to see his son bestowed to his liking.' Yet after this the negotiations continue to drag on, until on 22 October they were reported as 'upon a sudden quite dashed, and in the opinion of the wise by great fault of Pembroke'; and Burghley, we learn, thinks he was 'not well dealt withal' by Pembroke who refused his offer.[2]

Why had the prolonged efforts of the parents, desperately anxious to give the dying father a married heir, come to nothing? On 8 October Pembroke was reported to be resolved to accept Burghley's latest offer and yet a fortnight later he was himself raising his terms; why?[3] Chambers's discovery of the negotiations over Sir George Carey's daughter in 1595 and in particular the cause of their breakdown provides the answer. To have told the great Lord Treasurer that his granddaughter after being once accepted was on further

[1] Tyler, p. 47.

[2] Chambers, *Shakespearean Gleanings*, p. 127.

[3] *Ibid.* pp. 125–6.

view 'not liked' would have been an affront to the most powerful man in England, so when the young colt jibbed, poor Pembroke had to get out of it by raising his terms, as he had to do with Carey in 1595. It was no doubt the same story with other attempts to marry him off, until Rowland Whyte was drily informing Herbert's uncle Sir Robert Sidney who was urging another attempt, that he could not 'find any disposition in this gallant young lord to marry'.[1]

How came Shakespeare into all this? From my reading of the evidence, now seen as a whole, it seems more than likely, as many others have supposed, that sonnets 1–17 were written to work upon the young gentleman's imagination. But now we have been able to date the first meeting between Poet and Friend as 8 April 1597 by dating sonnet 104, 8 April 1600, which, as it tells us, was written exactly three years later, we can go a step further than the surmises of Tyler and Beeching, by asserting categorically that the first meeting actually took place at Wilton. For 8 April 1597 was Herbert's 17th birthday which he would naturally spend at Wilton and that he did so in point of fact is as good as proved by the useful Rowland Whyte who was writing a few days later to tell Sir Robert Sidney: 'My Lord Herbert hath with much ado brought his father to consent that he live at London, yet not before the next spring.'[2] And if the lad was at Wilton when this was written, Shakespeare must have been there to meet him. Thus the notion thrown out by Tyler and Beeching takes on an air of something more than probability. The Countess had arranged it all, had secured the assistance of the poet now famous as the author of *Venus and Adonis* and well known to the boy's

[1] Chambers, p. 127.

[2] Both Tyler (p. 44, n. 1) and Beeching (p. xxxix).

tutor, Samuel Daniel, for the writing of sonnets to persuade him to marry and had asked him to meet the young lord at Wilton, on his 17th birthday. That Shakespeare wrote seventeen sonnets, neither more nor less, has excited the curiosity of some readers. Is it absurd to suggest that the number had a special meaning for all at Wilton on the heir's 17th birthday?

That Shakespeare came to be familiar with Wilton might have been borne out by a letter, now unhappily lost, but reported by William Cory as existing in 1865, in which Lady Pembroke, Sidney's sister, wrote to her son in December 1603, telling him to bring King James I, then staying at Salisbury, to Wilton to see *As You Like It*, and adding 'we have the man Shakespeare with us'.[1] And if James did come to Wilton, who more suitable to bear the canopy beneath which his royal master was ushered into the great house than the chief dramatist of the King's Men?[2]

In any case, it is unlikely that Shakespeare had not been acquainted before this with Wilton which, Aubrey tells us, was in Lady Herbert's time 'like a College, there were so many learned and ingenious persons',[3] and the qualification 'ingenious' would certainly apply to the writer for the Lord Chamberlain's company of players and author of *Venus and Adonis*. The 'man' was not of course of noble rank, scarcely indeed a gentleman; but could no doubt carry himself very agreeably in mixed company.

Sonnets 1–17 need not have been written with any particular bride in mind, but it is improbable that the Countess was not already thinking of Bridget for the negotiations with Burghley began not long after, and

[1] See Chambers, *William Shakespeare*, II, 329.

[2] See Sonnet 125.

[3] Aubrey, *op. cit.* p. 138.

they, as we have seen, brought the young lord up to London with his mother, on a visit to meet Bridget, but not yet to 'live at London', which implied setting up an establishment. In any case the friends who had come to know each other at Wilton would have further opportunities of meeting.

Herbert comes to town

Whether Shakespeare met him at Wilton or not, he was certainly doing so in London in the spring of 1598 when Herbert, leaving his sick father with his mother at Wilton, took up his residence in Baynard's Castle.

What he did in 1598 there is little in the record to show. But we may place here the two episodes of the Rival Poet and the Dark Woman which the *Sonnets* reflect and which relate, we have conjectured, especially to the Farewell series. Beeching's heading to the Farewell Sonnets runs *The Poet appeals against the Friend's Estrangement*—an estrangement, we may feel confident, not only or even perhaps mainly due to the influence of the Rival Poet, but to that of the Dark Woman. A young lord setting up house in London and wishing to cut a dash at court would have many preoccupations of greater immediate importance than keeping the friendship of his old player-poet in repair. Shakespeare gives us an idea of such preoccupations in the semi-satirical lines of sonnet 91, which reminds us of Xenophon's description of the young Alcibiades:

> Some glory in their birth, some in their skill,
> Some in their wealth, some in their body's force,
> Some in their garments though new-fangled ill:
> Some in their hawks and hounds, some in their horse.

And Rowland Whyte, Sir Robert Sidney's agent, gives us a further glimpse in his letter next year (1599), which speaks of the project of Herbert putting himself at the head of a bodyguard of two hundred horse to attend upon the Queen, and of his 'swaggering it among the men of war'.[1] We read, too, in the letters of 1600 that, his parents remaining at Wilton, he was left free to do what he wished, and the fact that he accompanied Sir Charles Danvers (who was later executed for his part in the rising of Essex) on a visit to Lady Rich and Lady Southampton at Gravesend, suggests that he was being tempted to associate with dangerous company. In fact, he yielded to a temptation of another but more characteristic sort, which was followed by a situation even more dangerous. For after making herself conspicuous as the leading lady in a masked dance before the Queen at the wedding festivities on 16 June 1600 of a cousin of Herbert's, the lovely but wanton Mary Fitton found her way late at night and disguised as a man to Herbert's private quarters,[2] with the result that on 5 February next year, a fortnight after Herbert had succeeded his father as Earl of Pembroke, we find no less a person than Sir Robert Cecil casually remarking in a letter to a friend,

> We have no news but that there is a misfortune befallen Mistress Fitton, for she is proved with child, and the Earl of Pembroke, being examined, confesseth a fact, but utterly renounceth all marriage. I fear they will both dwell in the Tower awhile, for the Queen hath vowed to send them thither.[3]

A later letter, written on 28 March, tells us that Pembroke was 'committed to the Fleet and that his cause [i.e. the woman responsible] is delivered of a boy who is dead'. It may be that Mary Fitton hoped to better

[1] See Tyler, *op. cit.* p. 51. [2] *Ibid.* p. 57.
[3] See Tyler, p. 56.

her condition by thus entangling a young and wealthy nobleman—for her visit was clearly uninvited. If so, the gamble failed utterly; she had no putative heir to offer him and he had already refused to be caught by the claims of honour and decency which her family urged upon him. He justifiably refused to marry her. Yet he, too, paid; and after serving a term in prison he was banished to the country and there, forbidden to travel, he languished so long as the Queen lived.

Now this collapse in the young Earl's fortunes just at the outset of what promised to be the loftiest of careers, together with his enforced absence from London, seems to afford a ready explanation of the supposed 'break' in the Absence Sonnets (97 etc.). In other words, I am persuaded by my friend Blair Leishman[1] that sonnets 95 and 96 are discreet, if deliberately obscure, reflexions of the Fitton affair, and I would add that they were written in 1600 when the rumours of her midnight visit to Herbert, which are known to have been current among the gossip-mongers shortly after, were reaching Shakespeare's ears. That this couple of 'licentious grace' sonnets had nothing to do with the liaison group is proved by their tone of affectionate indulgence. Shakespeare, in fact, writes like a worldly-wise uncle giving advice to a favourite nephew, almost like Lord Chesterfield writing to his son. Sonnet 93, with its reference to a deceived husband, shows he had not forgotten the youth's theft of his mistress, but we learnt in 34 and 35 that he had forgiven, and the boy had repented with tears. Yet reproof there is. In that 'mask of beauty' sonnet, 94, which is a development of the charge of 'wilful taste of what thy self refusest' in sonnet 40. 8, the young earl is told by inference that he is given to the

[1] In personal talk shortly before the accident that led to his death.

detestable practice of enjoying women out of mere curiosity, which is very much what Clarendon tells us about Pembroke.

Occasions in the final group

If all the foregoing be granted and Pembroke be accepted as the Friend, the rest of the sonnets that seem to point to definite dates or occasions fall into place. Despite his disgrace, Pembroke's friends took the opportunity of assuring him of their continued admiration. For example, Francis Davison, son of Secretary Davison, thus addressed Pembroke in dedicating *The Poetical Rhapsody* to him in 1602:

> Great earl, whose high and noble mind is higher
> And nobler than thy noble high desire;
> Whose outward shape, though it most lovely be,
> Doth in fair robes a fairer soul attire....[1]

After all, Pembroke was by no means the first of Elizabeth's courtiers to get one of her maids into trouble; his position as earl was unassailable and the disgrace could only be temporary.

If sonnet 124 makes use, as we have seen, of allusions to the Gunpowder Plot of 5 November 1605, it would seem that Shakespeare ceased writing sonnets to Pembroke about 1606. Indeed, sonnet 125 seems to hint that his praises of the Friend's beauty by this date were growing stale in men's eyes and prompted in part by self-interest—'mixed with seconds'. Thus sonnets 96 to 126 would cover the period of 1600 to 1606. Between the birthday sonnet, misplaced 104, and 100 we have the gap of about two years. So it follows that only twenty-seven sonnets were written in a period of some two to four years. In other words they were

[1] Quoted from Beeching, *op. cit.* p. xxxviii.

written intermittently and confessedly so, in contrast with the Poet's earlier activity, when

> Our love was new, and then but in the spring,
> When I was wont to greet it with my lays.[1] (102)

No doubt both men were extremely busy. During these years Shakespeare was writing and producing his greatest tragedies and Pembroke had more than enough to do if he was to pick a path of integrity and honour for himself through the muddy waters of James's court. He would wish, too, to steal sometime from court to enjoy a few months of the travel that the tyrant Queen had robbed him of, in the course of which he was bound to go to Italy and to visit Rome where, like other travellers, he would gaze in wonder at the rebuilt pyramids spoken of in sonnet 123, as Mr Hotson has reminded us. And so we get sonnets apologising for long silence, for the poverty of the poet's invention, for allowing other claims, the claims of his profession as actor-dramatist, love-affairs—all after the conventionally traditional fashion of the poet in 'service' to his lord.[2]

For in this last group (100–26) Shakespeare is no longer, as before, a guardian, as it were, watching over the boy, but a humble follower watching his own steps, apologizing and pleading for understanding of the way of life his profession involves.

Among other sonnets are some that glow with a peculiarly emotional or joyous quality. Such is the birthday greeting just noticed. Another is the splendid sonnet 116,

> Let me not to the marriage of true minds
> Admit impediments

[1] This refers, I think, to the aubade or dawn-song.

[2] See Tucker, cited p. xvii.

—one of the finest and most 'universal' love-sonnets in the whole collection. It must, nevertheless, I feel, have been composed for a special occasion, as when the young earl had conferred upon his poet some conspicuous token of his appreciation, one of those 'favours' that Heminge and Condell speak of in the dedication to the First Folio; perhaps an enthusiastic letter in praise of the performance of a play, for by this time he would have been growing increasingly proud of his beloved poet-player's triumphs. And in 112 we receive clear evidence that the young nobleman responded to Shakespeare's plea for understanding of what the actor's life involved, and one of the indications that the great man accepted the 'service' of his humble player-poet without question and with genuine affection. Thus, when rightly understood, the much-debated sonnet 107 is an example of pure joy, jubilation indeed, which they both shared. One of the results of having settled the dating of the *Sonnets* as a whole and the identity of the Poet's Friend is that it enables us to accept as certain the occasion of sonnet 107, which, though bandied about in recent years by critics in order to accord it with their own dating, has seemed obvious since Minto wrote of it in 1874. I mean the death of the aged Queen Elizabeth on 24 March 1603.

Think what that meant for Pembroke! He could return to London from his banishment, and at once take his rightful place at court with a king on the throne favourable to himself and his friends. As for Shakespeare, the last days of Elizabeth make an obscure chapter of his life. He seems not to have been held guilty for the performance of *Richard II*, with its deposition scene, on the eve of the abortive rising of Essex; but she obviously could have harboured no kindly feelings towards the author, if she knew who he was. In any case, James at once showed him much good will: the Company became His Majesty's Players, and the principal actors, Shakespeare among them, were created Grooms of the Chamber. The whole country too seemed to share a similar good fortune, for as the queen lay dying no one but Robert Cecil knew who would succeed or what fate or even what form of religion awaited England. Thus, all was in doubt, speculation ran riot, a number of possible heirs 'gaped' for the throne; so that a great fear oppressed men's hearts, while the astrologers prognosticated that terrible disasters would follow the Queen's death. A sigh, therefore, of immense relief greeted the arrival of the ungainly Scot, whose coronation settled the succession for good (or, as Shakespeare put it, 'incertainties crowned themselves assured') and whose first act was to declare that he had come to bring peace not only to England, to Britain, but to the whole of Europe—a peace that would last for ever. It was a balmy time indeed: the very season, an unusually mild spring, seemed to share in the joy and those who had prophesied evil now laughed at their own forecasts.

Such was the general sense of the sonnet in relation to the affairs of state. Meanwhile, this chapter may be appropriately rounded off with the concluding couplet of the sonnet—which combines both its public and its personal significance:

> And thou in this shalt find thy monument,
> When tyrants' crests and tombs of brass are spent.

The lines are a variation of the famous Horatian claim in the Odes, III. 30, that in his verses he has created a monument more durable than brass, a claim which Shakespeare has transferred to the eternal beauty of his Friend in several earlier sonnets. But here the loan from Horace is given a double meaning since the 'monumentum aere perennius' is that of the tyrant queen.

V. Themes and Sources

One of the tasks laid upon a competent editor of a Shakespeare play is to provide some account of its source (or sources) and a discussion of the nature and extent of the dramatist's debt to it; while 'source' in this sense should embrace not merely the books or previous dramas from which he presumably drew his material, but also (even more important, if far less easy to determine with any precision), the medieval or sixteenth-century ideas and assumptions he entertained, without some knowledge of which the play in question cannot be fully understood.

Somewhat analogous problems face an editor of the *Sonnets*, both as regards their main and recurrent themes and in connexion with points that may crop up in individual sonnets. Two questions of major relevance must be taken up at this point. The first is: What themes, etc., does Shakespeare as a sonneteer owe to earlier writers of sonnets, or other classical and Renaissance poems? There are some critics, indeed, Sidney Lee in particular, who hold that the *Sonnets* are merely imitative, a tissue of echoes and borrowings from the Italian and French sonneteers who had been celebrating their ladies or their patrons since the thirteenth century. This view has been already discussed above, and is now I believe no longer held by any reputable critic. On the other hand, poets of all periods who, like Shakespeare, propose to immortalize their beloved or even themselves in verse, inevitably have recourse to similar imagery and ideas without any question of imitation or borrowing at all. This similarity of treatment is the subject of a stimulating and learned book by Blair Leishman entitled *Themes and Variations in Shakespeare's Sonnets* (1961). His principal concern is with the theme of poetry, and of course love-poetry, as a defier of Time which devours all things, or with the kindred theme of poetry that confers immortality upon the person addressed: a theme best expressed in sonnets 18 and 19, the first of Shakespeare's real love-sonnets. For he has suddenly dropped the advice to marry, which he had been commissioned to impart, and had given in seventeen sonnets; and has turned to the adoration of the beloved. He sums it up in the couplet of sonnet 19 which, after a dozen lines exemplifying the ruthless omnipotence of devouring Time, contemptuously exclaims

> Yet do thy worst old time: despite thy wrong,
> My love shall in my verse ever live young.

Leishman's purpose being not to edit but to illustrate, he is primarily interested in parallels and affinities in the sonnets of Shakespeare's predecessors: Horace and Ovid, Petrarch, Tasso and Ronsard, Sidney and Spenser, Daniel and Drayton, to name the chief only. But when, as he could hardly have avoided doing at times, he came face to face with the question of whether Shakespeare had actually read this or that of his forerunners, the answer varies in cogency. The evidence, for example, as regards the Italian poets, even Petrarch, is so uncertain as to be virtually negative. It seems pretty conclusive, on the other hand, for Ronsard—it being clear at any rate that sonnet 74 is to some extent connected with the *Élégie à Marie*. Yet in this case both Shakespeare and Ronsard appear to go back to Ovid, a point to which we must return.

As for the English predecessors, we cannot doubt that

Shakespeare read them eagerly, without necessarily paying them the compliment of imitation. In one instance indeed he only borrowed to make fun of the writer in question. Thomas Watson was a pretentious poetaster who came early into the field with a sonnet sequence published in 1582 under the title of the ΕΚΑΤΟΜΠΑΘΙΑ or *Passionate Centurie of Love*, the seventh 'Passion' running as follows:

> Harke you that list to heare what sainte I serue:
> Her yellowe lockes exceede the beaten goulde;
> Her sparkeling eies in heau'n a place deserue;
> Her forehead high and faire of comely moulde;
>   Her wordes are musicke all of siluer sounde;
>   Her wit so sharpe as like can scarse be found:
> Each eybrowe hanges like *Iris* in the skies;
> Her *Eagles* nose is straight of stately frame;
> On either cheeke a *Rose* and *Lillie* lies;
> Her breath is sweete perfume, or hollie flame;
>   Her lips more red than any *Corall* stone;
>   Her necke more white, then aged *Swans* yat mone;
> Her brest transparent is, like *Christall* rocke;
> Her fingers long, fit for *Apolloes* Lute;
> Her slipper such as *Momus* dare not mocke;
> Her vertues all so great as make me mute:
>   What other partes she hath I neede not say,
>   Whose face alone is cause of my decaye.

Turn now to Shakespeare's description of his Dark Woman in sonnet 130, beginning 'My mistress' eyes are nothing like the sun', and it will be seen that it parodies all but one of Watson's lines.[1] And there are other signs that Shakespeare had read and marked his Watson. For instance, when Rosalind says of a lover that 'Cupid hath clapped him o'th' shoulder'[2] she seems to be echoing a line from the first 'Passion'.

[1] Pointed out by Patrick Cruttwell, *The Shakespearean Moment* (1954), p. 18.
[2] *As You Like It*, 4. 1. 46.

But Shakespeare was already eighteen when Watson's *Centurie* appeared on the book-stalls; and a volume entitled *Songes and Sonettes written by the ryght honourable Lorde Henry Howard late Earle of Surrey and other Apud Richardum Tottel*, commonly known today as *Tottel's Miscellany*, had taken London by storm in 1557, a few years before he was born, and went through eight editions before 1591, when Sidney's *Astrophel and Stella* appeared—a publication which is usually taken as the beginning of the Elizabethan sonnet craze. Knowing as they do that Wyatt and Surrey were writing sonnets in the third and fourth decades of the sixteenth century, scholars imagine a gap of a whole generation—more than a quarter of a century—between them and Sidney. Surely the immense vogue of *Tottel's Miscellany* has been strangely ignored. During these forty years it had become part of the popular literature of the country. Surrey's Geraldine had become a legendary figure, a kind of English Laura, before Nashe published his *Jack Wilton* in 1593.[1] If Shakespeare may be taken as a witness, lovers in the provinces about 1600 still took it with them when they went a-courting,[2] and the very grave-diggers sang snatches of it as they 'built houses that last till doomsday'.[3] Addressing the 'gentle reader' in his preface, the worthy Tottel claims it

> not euill doon, to publish, to the honor of the Englishe tong, and for profit of the studious of Englishe eloquence, those workes which the vngentle horders vp of such treasure haue heretofore enuied thee.[4]

[1] See *Works of Nashe*, edited by R. B. McKerrow, IV, p. 252.

[2] *The Merry Wives of Windsor*, I. I. 184.

[3] *Hamlet*, 5. I. 61 ff.

[4] *Tottel's Miscellany*, ed. H. E. Rollins, I, 3.

Who these 'ungentle hoorders' may have been is unknown, but the expression leaves us asking whether any reader, even Sidney himself, would have had access to Surrey's poems if Tottel had not printed the text three years after he was born. And one can guess with what delight the lad at Stratford, his junior by ten years, might have come upon Surrey's 'Description and praise of his loue Geraldine':

From Tuskane came my Ladies worthy race:
Faire Florence was sometyme her auncient seate:
The Western yle, whose pleasaunt shore doth face
Wilde Cambers clifs, did geue her liuely heate:
Fostered she was with milke of Irishe brest:
Her sire, an Erle: her dame, of princes blood.
From tender yeres, in Britain she doth rest,
With kinges childe, where she tasteth costly food.
Honsdon did first present her to mine yien:
Bright is her hewe, and Geraldine she hight.
Hampton me taught to wishe her first for mine:
And Windsor, alas, dothe chase me from her sight.
Her beauty of kind her vertues from aboue.
Happy is he, that can obtaine her loue.[1]

or his 'Vow to loue faithfully howsoever he be rewarded', a page or two further on:

Set me wheras the sunne doth parche the grene,
Or where his beames do not dissolue the yse:
In temperate heate where he is felt and sene:
In presence prest of people madde or wise.
Set me in hye, or yet in lowe degree:
In longest night, or in the shortest daye:
In clearest skye, or where clowdes thickest be:
In lusty youth, or when my heeres are graye.
Set me in heauen, in earth, or els in hell,
In hyll, or dale, or in the fomyng flood:
Thrall, or at large, aliue where so I dwell:

[1] *Tottel*, 1, 9, [8].

Sicke, or in health: in euyll fame, or good.
Hers will I be, and onely with this thought
Content my selfe, although my chaunce be nought.[1]

Professor Prince calls this sonnet 'conventional' but, as he shows, Surrey had achieved the form of the English sonnet by learning from the fumbling attempts by Wyatt.[2] And Shakespeare learned from Surrey and followed much the same rhetorical pattern as Surrey used in this last sonnet when he came to write his own sonnets 66 and 129.

But perhaps the most important effect of Tottel's publication is that it determined the form of the English sonnet, viz. three quatrains of ten-syllabled lines, concluding with a couplet, as opposed to the Italian form of two parts, an octave consisting of two quatrains and a sextet of two tercets. The latter was far more complicated than the one Wyatt and Surrey between them developed, and the proof that their form was the one suited to the genius of the English language[3] is shown by the fact that only one of their English successors adopted the Petrarchan sonnet. Both Sidney and Spenser were influenced by it, but the only poet to write consistently in the Italian form is Henry Constable, whose sonnet-sequence *Diana* was published in 1592. More significantly perhaps, George Gascoigne, whose *Posies* (1575) contained 'Certain Notes of Instruction concerning the Making of Verse', seems to ignore any but the English form, since he writes

Some thinke that all Poemes (being short) may be called Sonets, as in deede it is a diminutive word derived of *Sonare*,

[1] *Tottel*, I, 11, [12].

[2] F. T. Prince, 'The Sonnet from Wyatt to Shakespeare' in *Elizabethan Poetry*, Stratford-upon-Avon Studies, 2 (1960).

[3] See Matthew Black, *Elizabethan and Seventeenth Century Lyrics* (1938), pp. 40, 51–2.

but yet I can beste allowe to call those Sonets whiche are of fouretene lynes, every line conteying tenne syllables. The first twelve to ryme in staves of foure lines by crosse meetre, and the last twoo ryming togither do conclude the whole.[1]

That Shakespeare read his Sidney, his Spenser, his Daniel and his Drayton, together with other English sonnet-writers, among his elders and contemporaries, goes without saying. But though it is clear that both Daniel and Drayton learned from him, what he may have owed to them seems quite uncertain;[2] and naturally none of them offered him material for scorn as Watson had done. It is not that there were no parallels or affinities, but that, as in the case of Ronsard, it is often possible to trace them to Ovid and/or Horace from whom Shakespeare may have derived them directly—which brings us to the capital problem of Shakespeare's sources in the *Sonnets*. This is Leishman's 'main subject'[3] in his book, namely Shakespeare's relation in the *Sonnets* to Ovid and Horace, and in particular what his 'resonant promise of immortality' in defiance of devouring Time owes to the great Roman poets.

It has always been known that Ovid's *Metamorphoses* was one of the dramatist's principal source-books, in making use of which he relied chiefly but not entirely upon Golding's English translation.[4] And Leishman underlines the close connection between the great sonnets 64 and 65 and Ovid's epilogue to the final book of

[1] George Gascoigne, *Posies*, edited by J. W. Cunliffe (1907), pp. 471–2.

[2] Leishman, *Themes and Variations in Shakespeare's Sonnets*, ch. 5. See also Beeching, pp. 132 ff.

[3] Leishman, *op. cit.* p. 30.

[4] See my article on 'Shakespeare's "small Latin"—how much?' in *Shakespeare Survey*, 10, pp. 12 ff.

the *Metamorphoses*. He is, too, I think, the first to detect an unmistakable echo of Ovid in the tender 63. But though he quotes sonnet 55[1] he does not appear to notice that this, too, derives direct from Ovid, is indeed virtually a translation of earlier lines of the same final book. Nor has he observed that Sidney Lee had been before him here and driven the point firmly home.

The truth is that one of Lee's best treatments of the *Sonnets* has been generally overlooked because it was not published until after his death, in a volume of his essays edited by F. S. Boas.[2] The strength of Lee's argument lies in the close verbal parallelisms he notes between Shakespeare and Golding, which leave no doubt that the main, if not the only, source of the great sonnets on Time the devourer was the English version of Ovid. Examples are:

Golding XV, 984–95: *Ovid* XV, 871 *ff.*

Now have I brought a woork too end which neither Ioues feerce wrath,
Nor sword, nor fyre, nor freating age with all the force it hath
Are able too abolish quyght. Let comme that fatall howre
Which (saving of this brittle flesh) hath over mee no powre,
And at his pleasure make an end of myne uncerteyne tyme.
Yit shall the better part of mee assured bee too clyme
Aloft above the starry skye. And all the world shall never
Be able for to quench my name. For looke how farre so ever
The Roman Empyre by the ryght of conquest shall extend,
So farre shall all folke read this woork. And tyme without all end
(If Poets as by prophesie about the truth may ame)
My lyfe shall everlastingly bee lengthened still by fame.

[1] Leishman, *op. cit.* p. 37.

[2] *Elizabethan and other Essays* (1929).

Sonnet 55

Not marble, nor the gilded monuments
Of princes shall outlive this powerful rhyme,
But you shall shine more bright in these contents
Than unswept stone, besmeared with sluttish time.
When wasteful war shall statues overturn,
And broils root out the work of masonry,
Nor Mars his sword, nor war's quick fire shall burn:
The living record of your memory.
'Gainst death, and all-oblivious enmity
Shall you pace forth, your praise shall still find room,
Even in the eyes of all posterity
That wear this world out to the ending doom.
So till the judgment that your self arise,
You live in this, and dwell in lovers' eyes.

While Leishman refers once again to Ovid's 'impressive discourse on mutability which meant so much to Spenser and other Elizabethans', and notes that this passage from Book xv of the *Metamorphoses* (like the conclusion about Poetry as the defier of Time) must have been much in Shakespeare's memory, he has not observed how closely that memory clung to the actual words of Golding. Lee spends the rest of his remarkable essay in elaborating this matter. I content myself here with one or two instances of Shakespeare's use of Ovid's vivid physiographic proofs of his central cosmic theory. The ceaseless recurrence of natural phenomena is illustrated by Ovid from the example of the sea-waves' motion. Golding translates the passage:

As every wave drives other forth, and that that comes behind
Both thrusteth and is thrust itself: even so the times by kind
Do fly and follow both at once and evermore renew.

Shakespeare presents the argument less methodically, but he adopts the illustrative figure without much disguise. Thus he begins sonnet 60:

Like as the waves make towards the pebbled shore,
So do our minutes hasten to their end,
Each changing place with that which goes before,
In sequent toil all forwards do contend.

Even more striking is Shakespeare's reproduction of Ovid's graphic description of the constant encroachment of land on sea and sea on land, which the Latin poet adduces as fresh evidence of matter's endless variations, and fortifies by a long series of professed personal observations. In Golding's rendering the passage opens thus:

Even so have places oftentimes exchanged their estate.
For I have seen it sea which was substantial ground alate,
Again where sea was, I have seen the same become dry land.

In sonnet 64 Shakespeare assimilates these words with a literalness which makes him claim to 'have seen' with his own eyes the phenomena of Ovid's narration:

When I have seen the hungry ocean gain
Advantage on the kingdom of the shore,
And the firm soil win of the watery main,
Increasing store with loss, and loss with store.
When I have seen such interchange of state...

The driving vigour with which Ovid pursues this corroborative theme of 'interchange' or 'exchange' between earth and ocean is well reflected in the swing of Golding's ballad metre:

And in the tops of mountains high old anchors have been found.
Deep valleys have by watershot been made of level ground,
And hills by force of gulling oft have into sea been worne.
Hard gravel ground is sometime seen where marish was beforne.

With especial force does Ovid point to the subsidence of land beneath the voracious sea:

Men say that Sicil also hath been joined to Italy,
Until the sea consumed the bounds between, and did supply
The room with water. If ye go to seek for Helice
And Bury, which were cities of Achaea, you shall see
Them hidden under water, and the shipmen yet do show
The walls and steeples of the towns drowned under as they
 row.[1]

Lee discovers a reflection of what he calls 'Ovid's metaphysical or physical interpretation of the universe' in some fifteen of the *Sonnets*. He also finds the same influence in the passage of 2 *Henry IV* (3. 1. 45 ff.) already referred to on p. lxxvii. Leishman has missed a good deal of this because of his, preoccupation with Horace and more particularly with his ode 30 in Book III, which begins

exegi monumentum aere perennius.

It is an ode, as is well known, which inspired the similar vaunt with which Ovid concluded his immortal *Metamorphoses*, and Leishman sees it as the inspiration likewise of sonnet 55, which he twice refers to as echoing the 'Horatian resonance': but, as we have seen, Shakespeare caught the resonance at second hand inasmuch as the sonnet is virtually a paraphrase of Ovid's lines.

Yet though the influence of Horace may have been mainly indirect, it was certainly direct also. 'Was Shakespeare familiar with Horace's Odes?' asks Leishman. 'I can see no way of proving that he was, but, on the other hand, it seems to me almost incredible that he should not have been.'[2] In his noteworthy

[1] Lee, *Elizabethan and other Essays*, pp. 129–30.
[2] Leishman, *op. cit.* p. 36.

essay on *Shakespeare's Significances*[1] Edmund Blunden furnished the proof that Leishman sought, by demonstrating that in *Lear* 3. 4 the King is reminded of one of Horace's Epistles by the name of a fiend 'poor Tom' borrowed from Harsnett, and at 3. 6. 78–80 himself refers to the last ode of Book 1 'Persicos odi, puer, apparatus', known to any schoolboy, when he bids Edgar change his garments.[2] Thus, though it is impossible to trace the influence of Horace in the *Sonnets*, we may rest assured that Shakespeare had once read a little Horace at school.

It should be added that Thomas Tyler, who anticipated so much modern criticism in the Introduction to his edition of the *Sonnets* published in 1890, has in a sense anticipated Lee by insisting upon Shakespeare's debt to Ovid and Horace. But sharing the accepted opinion of his age, he refused to believe this influence could have been direct and threw out the ingenious suggestion that Shakespeare derived the 'small Latin' he made use of in the *Sonnets*, and especially sonnet 55, from Meres (who in dealing with Shakespeare among other poets quotes both the Horatian *exegi monumentum* and the famous vaunt of Ovid at the conclusion of the *Metamorphoses*). But in face of the far greater quantity and variety of the parallels cited by Lee it is clear that if there were any borrowing it was Meres who borrowed from the *Sonnets* and not vice versa.

[1] A lecture delivered before the Shakespeare Association in 1929, reprinted in *The Mind's Eye* (1934) and again in Bradby, *Shakespearean Criticism 1919–35*.

[2] See also *King Lear* (*New Cambridge Shakespeare*), notes on 3. 4. 144, and 3. 6, 78–80.

Appendix: Clarendon's Description of William Herbert

After describing the character of the detestable, insolent and unpopular Earl of Arundel, Clarendon continues:

William earl of Pembroke was next, a man of another mould and making, and of another fame and reputation with all men, being the most universally loved and esteemed of any man of that age; and, having a great office in the Court, [he] made the Court itself better esteemed and more reverenced in the country. And as he had a great number of friends of the best men, so no man had ever the wickedness to avow himself to be his enemy. He was a man very well bred, and of excellent parts, and a graceful speaker upon any subject, having a good proportion of learning, and a ready wit to apply it and enlarge upon it; of a pleasant and facetious humour, and a disposition affable, generous, and magnificent. He was master of a great fortune from his ancestors, and had a great addition by his wife, (another daughter and heir of the earl of Shrewsbury,) which he enjoyed during his life, she outliving him: but all served not his expense, which was only limited by his great mind and occasions to use it nobly.

He lived many years about the Court before in it, and never by it; being rather regarded and esteemed by King James than loved and favoured; and after the foul fall of the earl of Somerset, he was made Lord Chamberlain of the King's house more for the Court's sake than his own; and the Court appeared with the more lustre because he had the government of that province. As he spent and lived upon his own fortune, so he stood upon his own feet, without any other support than of his proper virtue and merit; and lived towards the favourites with that decency as would not suffer them to censure or reproach his master's judgment and election, but as with men of his own rank. He was exceedingly beloved in the Court, because he never desired to get that for himself which others laboured for, but was still ready to promote the pretences of worthy men. And he was equally celebrated in the country for having received no obligations from the Court which might corrupt or sway his affections and judgment; so that all who were displeased and unsatisfied in the Court or with the Court were always inclined to put themselves under his banner, if he would have admitted them; and yet he did not so reject them as to make them choose another shelter, but so far to depend on him that he could restrain them from breaking out beyond private resentments and murmurs.

He was a great lover of his country, and of the religion and justice which he believed could only support it; and his friendships were only with men of those principles. And as his conversation was most with men of the most pregnant parts and understanding, so towards any who needed support or encouragement, though unknown, if fairly recommended to him, he was very liberal. And sure never man was planted in a Court that was fitter for that soil, or brought better qualities with him to purify that air.

Yet his memory must not be so flattered that his virtues and good inclinations may be believed without some allay of vice, and without being clouded with great infirmities, which he had in too exorbitant a proportion. He indulged to himself the pleasures of all kinds, almost in all excesses. Whether out of his natural constitution, or for want of his domestic content and delight, (in which he was most unhappy, for he paid much too dear for his wife's fortune by taking her person into the bargain,) he was immoderately given up to women. But therein he likewise retained such a power and jurisdiction over his very appetite, that he was not so much transported with beauty and outward allurements, as with those advantages of the mind as manifested an extraordinary wit and spirit and knowledge, and administered great pleasure in the conversation. To these he sacrificed himself, his precious time, and much of his fortune. And some who were nearest his trust and friendship were not without apprehension that his natural vivacity and vigour of mind began to lessen and decline by those excessive indulgences.[1]

[1] Clarendon, *History of the Rebellion*, ed. W. Dunn Macray (Oxford, 1888), I, 71–3.

A few sentences from Aubrey's *Brief Lives* may be quoted to supplement Clarendon's account. Aubrey says that Pembroke and his brother Philip

were the most popular Peers in the West of England; but one might boldly say, in the whole Kingdome....Earle William entertained at Wilton, at his own Cost, King James the first, during the space of many moneths. King Charles 1st loved Wilton above all places: and came thither every Sommer....William Herbert, Earl of Pembroke was a most noble Person and the Glory of the Court....He was handsome, and of an admirable presence. He was the greatest Maecenas to learned Men of any Peer of his time: or since. He was very generous and open handed: He gave a noble Collection of choice Bookes, and Manuscripts to the Bodlaean Library at Oxford....He was a good Scholar, and delighted in Poetrie: and did sometimes (for his Diversion) write some Sonnets and Epigrammes, which deserve Commendation....Wilton will appeare to have been an Academie, as well as Palace, and was (as it were) the Apiarie, to which Men, that were excellent in Armes, and Arts, did resort, and were caress't; and many of them received honourable Pensions.

[1] Aubrey, *op*, *cit.* edited by O. Lawson Dick (1949), pp. 144–6.

A NOTE ON TEXT AND PUNCTUATION

The text that follows is conservative. That is to say it very rarely departs from Malone's, though it takes careful note of the criticisms recently passed upon that text by Professor Landry,[1] and when it adopts his suggested changes this is only because he has persuaded me that they bring us back to Shakespeare; for as explained in my Introduction, there is no reason for thinking that Thorpe had anything but a manuscript in Shakespeare's hand to work upon. It is all the more regrettable that the principle of modernization which I had to adopt for the *New Cambridge Shakespeare* since 1921 (including an accent on -ed pronounced), prevented me from reprinting the spelling of the Quarto, as Mr Seymour-Smith has wisely done in his edition. I say wisely, because modernization is attended with almost as many risks as emendation, of which indeed it may be called a variation.

In the matter of punctuation on the other hand he has also set editors an example which I can follow, and follow the more readily that, persuaded by Percy Simpson's *Shakespearian Punctuation* (1911), I attempted to make use of it when I began editing the *New Shakespeare* in 1921, but abandoned it in effect later on when I did not find it worked with some of the Folio texts. But Seymour-Smith is right in his contention, which I think Edmund Chambers[2] would have agreed with, that the chances are that in a poem and particularly

[1] 'Malone's Edition of Shakespeare's Sonnets' by Hilton Landry (p. 438 of *Bulletin of the New York Public Library*, September 1963).

[2] See *William Shakespeare*, I, 190 ff.

poetry of a highly emotional character like a love sonnet, Shakespeare might have used punctuation to make the meaning quite clear if otherwise in doubt, to bring out the rhythm, and that on the other hand when he wished to be ironical or ambiguous, as he often is in the *Sonnets*, the pointing might be very scanty indeed. In any case, as Seymour-Smith insists, to impose a modern punctuation upon the *Sonnets* would indubitably lead to misrepresentation. The only safe thing then, the only scholarly thing, to do is to leave the Q text virtually unchanged in this respect, on the hypothesis that the punctuation at best may be Shakespeare's, and at worst will pretty certainly be Thorpe's, when it is not palpably compositorial. Thus one must always attempt to explain punctuation that strikes the modern reader as wrong or even absurd before setting it down as a printer's error—the possibility of which of course one must reckon with. As an example, here are eight passages quoted by Beeching as instances in which he asserts the Q pointing cannot be explained on grounds advanced by Wyndham,[1] and of which a reference to my notes will provide explanations, I hope satisfactory, except the obvious compositorial misprints.

16. 10 Which this (Times pensel or my pupill pen)

39. 7, 8 That by this separation I may give:
That due to thee which thou deserv'st alone:

55. 7, 8 Nor Mars his sword, nor warres quick fire shall burne:
The living record of your memory.

99. 2–5 Sweet theefe whence didst thou steale thy sweet that smels
If not from my loves breath, the purple pride,

[1] See pp. 259 ff. of Wyndham's *The Poems of Shakespeare*.

Which on thy soft cheeke for complexion dwells?
In my loves veines thou hast too grosely died,

113. 13 Incapable of more repleat, with you,

117. 10 And on iust proofe surmise, accumilate,

118. 9, 10 Thus pollicie in love t' anticipate
The ills that were, not grew to faults assured,

126. 7, 8 She keepes thee to this purpose, that her skill.
May time disgrace, and wretched mynuit kill.

ACKNOWLEDGEMENTS

In the preparation of this edition I owe debts to so many persons that it is impossible to name them all. But I cannot omit to mention my friend Mr Charles Graves, Professor Prince, Dr W. E. Oakeshott, and above all Blair Leishman, who gave me important advice upon the interpretation of one or two sonnets.

Furthermore, a blind man has to record special thanks in their reading and correction to five helpers: of them I must first mention my secretary Miss C. A. M. Sym, who crowned the labour of typing the whole, in many places more than once, by reading the entire body of the proofs aloud to me, line by line. Next, Professor Kenneth Muir, who not only read the proofs but gave me the benefit of many valuable suggestions and was the means of drawing my attention to the essay of Brents Stirling, who discovered the true order of the Sonnets in Section II. Two other readers were Professor J. C. Maxwell, who twice read through the proofs and whose microscopic eye I felt confident would allow no error to escape, and my neighbour the Rev. David Stalker, the Hebrew scholar who, accustomed to reading proofs and not, like the rest of my team, particularly familiar with the Sonnets would therefore be the less likely to overlook a printer's departure from the copy. And lastly, Mr Richard Hamilton, once a student of mine in the English Department at Edinburgh University and at present acting as Head of the Education Department there, helped me with the Text and later, despite heavy responsibilities of his own, followed up the other readers by checking all the references and making several important suggestions about the edition as a whole.

And my very special thanks are due to the university printers for dealing so patiently with an editor suffering from defective eyesight.

SONNETS

TO. THE. ONLIE. BEGETTER. OF.
THESE. INSUING. SONNETS.
MR. W. H. ALL. HAPPINESSE.
AND. THAT. ETERNITIE.
PROMISED.
BY.
OUR. EVER-LIVING. POET.
WISHETH.
THE. WELL-WISHING.
ADVENTURER. IN.
SETTING.
FORTH.

T. T.

1

From fairest creatures we desire increase,
That thereby beauty's rose might never die,
But as the riper should by time decease,
His tender heir might bear his memory:
But thou contracted to thine own bright eyes,
Feed'st thy light's flame with self-substantial fuel,
Making a famine where abundance lies,
Thy self thy foe, to thy sweet self too cruel:
Thou that art now the world's fresh ornament,
And only herald to the gaudy spring,
Within thine own bud buriest thy content,
And tender churl mak'st waste in niggarding:
    Pity the world, or else this glutton be,
    To eat the world's due, by the grave and thee.

2

When forty winters shall besiege thy brow,
And dig deep trenches in thy beauty's field,
Thy youth's proud livery so gazed on now,
Will be a tattered weed of small worth held:
Then being asked, where all thy beauty lies,
Where all the treasure of thy lusty days;
To say within thine own deep sunken eyes,
Were an all-eating shame, and thriftless praise.
How much more praise deserved thy beauty's use,
If thou couldst answer 'This fair child of mine
Shall sum my count, and make my old excuse'
Proving his beauty by succession thine.
    This were to be new made when thou art old,
    And see thy blood warm when thou feel'st it cold.

3

Look in thy glass and tell the face thou viewest,
Now is the time that face should form another,
Whose fresh repair if now thou not renewest,
Thou dost beguile the world, unbless some mother.
For where is she so fair whose uneared womb
Disdains the tillage of thy husbandry?
Or who is he so fond will be the tomb,
Of his self-love to stop posterity?
Thou art thy mother's glass and she in thee
Calls back the lovely April of her prime,
So thou through windows of thine age shalt see,
Despite of wrinkles this thy golden time.
  But if thou live remembered not to be,
  Die single and thine image dies with thee.

4

Unthrifty loveliness why dost thou spend,
Upon thy self thy beauty's legacy?
Nature's bequest gives nothing but doth lend,
And being frank she lends to those are free:
Then beauteous niggard why dost thou abuse,
The bounteous largess given thee to give?
Profitless usurer why dost thou use
So great a sum of sums yet canst not live?
For having traffic with thy self alone,
Thou of thy self thy sweet self dost deceive,
Then how when nature calls thee to be gone,
What acceptable audit canst thou leave?
  Thy unused beauty must be tombed with thee,
  Which uséd lives th' executor to be.

5

Those hours that with gentle work did frame
The lovely gaze where every eye doth dwell
Will play the tyrants to the very same,
And that unfair which fairly doth excel:
For never-resting time leads summer on
To hideous winter and confounds him there,
Sap checked with frost and lusty leaves quite gone,
Beauty o'er-snowed and bareness every where:
Then were not summer's distillation left
A liquid prisoner pent in walls of glass,
Beauty's effect with beauty were bereft,
Nor it nor no remembrance what it was.
  But flowers distilled though they with winter meet,
  Leese but their show, their substance still lives sweet.

6

Then let not winter's raggéd hand deface,
In thee thy summer ere thou be distilled:
Make sweet some vial; treasure thou some place,
With beauty's treasure ere it be self-killed:
That use is not forbidden usury,
Which happies those that pay the willing loan;
That's for thy self to breed another thee,
Or ten times happier be it ten for one,
Ten times thy self were happier than thou art,
If ten of thine ten times refigured thee:
Then what could death do if thou shouldst depart,
Leaving thee living in posterity?
  Be not self-willed for thou art much too fair,
  To be death's conquest and make worms thine heir.

7

Lo in the orient when the gracious light
Lifts up his burning head, each under eye
Doth homage to his new-appearing sight,
Serving with looks his sacred majesty,
And having climbed the steep-up heavenly hill,
Resembling strong youth in his middle age,
Yet mortal looks adore his beauty still,
Attending on his golden pilgrimage:
But when from highmost pitch with weary car,
Like feeble age he reeleth from the day,
The eyes (fore duteous) now converted are
From his low tract and look another way:
  So thou, thy self out-going in thy noon:
  Unlooked on diest unless thou get a son.

8

Music to hear, why hear'st thou music sadly?
Sweets with sweets war not, joy delights in joy:
Why lov'st thou that which thou receiv'st not gladly,
Or else receiv'st with pleasure thine annoy?
If the true concord of well-tunéd sounds,
By unions married do offend thine ear,
They do but sweetly chide thee, who confounds
In singleness the parts that thou shouldst bear:
Mark how one string sweet husband to another,
Strikes each in each by mutual ordering;
Resembling sire, and child, and happy mother,
Who all in one, one pleasing note do sing:
  Whose speechless song being many, seeming one,
  Sings this to thee, 'Thou single wilt prove none'.

9

Is it for fear to wet a widow's eye,
That thou consum'st thy self in single life?
Ah, if thou issueless shalt hap to die,
The world will wail thee like a makeless wife,
The world will be thy widow and still weep,
That thou no form of thee hast left behind,
When every private widow well may keep,
By children's eyes, her husband's shape in mind:
Look what an unthrift in the world doth spend
Shifts but his place, for still the world enjoys it;
But beauty's waste hath in the world an end,
And kept unused the user so destroys it:
  No love toward others in that bosom sits
  That on himself such murd'rous shame commits.

10

For shame deny that thou bear'st love to any
Who for thy self art so unprovident.
Grant if thou wilt, thou art beloved of many,
But that thou none lov'st is most evident:
For thou art so possessed with murd'rous hate,
That 'gainst thy self thou stick'st not to conspire,
Seeking that beauteous roof to ruinate
Which to repair should be thy chief desire:
O change thy thought, that I may change my mind,
Shall hate be fairer lodged than gentle love?
Be as thy presence is gracious and kind,
Or to thy self at least kind-hearted prove,
  Make thee another self for love of me,
  That beauty still may live in thine or thee.

11

As fast as thou shalt wane so fast thou grow'st,
In one of thine, from that which thou departest,
And that fresh blood which youngly thou bestow'st,
Thou mayst call thine, when thou from youth convertest,
Herein lives wisdom, beauty, and increase,
Without this folly, age, and cold decay,
If all were minded so, the times should cease,
And threescore year would make the world away:
Let those whom nature hath not made for store,
Harsh, featureless, and rude, barrenly perish:
Look whom she best endowed, she gave thee more;
Which bounteous gift thou shouldst in bounty cherish:
She carved thee for her seal, and meant thereby,
Thou shouldst print more, not let that copy die.

12

When I do count the clock that tells the time,
And see the brave day sunk in hideous night,
When I behold the violet past prime,
And sable curls all silvered o'er with white:
When lofty trees I see barren of leaves,
Which erst from heat did canopy the herd
And summer's green all girded up in sheaves
Borne on the bier with white and bristly beard:
Then of thy beauty do I question make
That thou among the wastes of time must go,
Since sweets and beauties do themselves forsake,
And die as fast as they see others grow,
And nothing 'gainst Time's scythe can make defence
Save breed to brave him, when he takes thee hence.

13

O that you were your self, but love you are
No longer yours, than you your self here live,
Against this coming end you should prepare,
And your sweet semblance to some other give.
So should that beauty which you hold in lease
Find no determination, then you were
Your self again after your self's decease,
When your sweet issue your sweet form should bear.
Who lets so fair a house fall to decay,
Which husbandry in honour might uphold,
Against the stormy gusts of winter's day
And barren rage of death's eternal cold?
  O none but unthrifts, dear my love you know,
  You had a father, let your son say so.

14

Not from the stars do I my judgement pluck,
And yet methinks I have astronomy,
But not to tell of good, or evil luck,
Of plagues, of dearths, or seasons' quality,
Nor can I fortune to brief minutes tell;
Pointing to each his thunder, rain and wind,
Or say with princes if it shall go well
By oft predict that I in heaven find.
But from thine eyes my knowledge I derive,
And constant stars in them I read such art
As truth and beauty shall together thrive
If from thy self, to store thou wouldst convert:
  Or else of thee this I prognosticate,
  Thy end is truth's and beauty's doom and date.

15

When I consider every thing that grows
Holds in perfection but a little moment.
That this huge stage presenteth nought but shows
Whereon the stars in secret influence comment.
When I perceive that men as plants increase,
Cheered and checked even by the self-same sky:
Vaunt in their youthful sap, at height decrease,
And wear their brave state out of memory.
Then the conceit of this inconstant stay,
Sets you most rich in youth before my sight,
Where wasteful time debateth with decay
To change your day of youth to sullied night,
And all in war with Time for love of you,
As he takes from you, I engraft you new.

16

But wherefore do not you a mightier way
Make war upon this bloody tyrant Time?
And fortify your self in your decay
With means more blessed than my barren rhyme?
Now stand you on the top of happy hours,
And many maiden gardens yet unset,
With virtuous wish would bear you living flowers,
Much liker than your painted counterfeit:
So should the lines of life that life repair
Which this (Time's pencil) or my pupil pen
Neither in inward worth nor outward fair
Can make you live your self in eyes of men.
To give away your self, keeps your self still,
And you must live drawn by your own sweet skill.

17

Who will believe my verse in time to come
If it were filled with your most high deserts?
Though yet heaven knows it is but as a tomb
Which hides your life, and shows not half your parts:
If I could write the beauty of your eyes,
And in fresh numbers number all your graces,
The age to come would say this poet lies,
Such heavenly touches ne'er touched earthly faces.
So should my papers (yellowed with their age)
Be scorned, like old men of less truth than tongue,
And your true rights be termed a poet's rage,
And stretchéd metre of an antique song.
  But were some child of yours alive that time,
  You should live twice in it, and in my rhyme.

18

Shall I compare thee to a summer's day?
Thou art more lovely and more temperate:
Rough winds do shake the darling buds of May,
And summer's lease hath all too short a date:
Sometime too hot the eye of heaven shines,
And often is his gold complexion dimmed,
And every fair from fair sometime declines,
By chance, or nature's changing course untrimmed:
But thy eternal summer shall not fade,
Nor lose possession of that fair thou ow'st,
Nor shall death brag thou wand'rest in his shade,
When in eternal lines to time thou grow'st,
  So long as men can breathe or eyes can see,
  So long lives this, and this gives life to thee.

19

Devouring Time blunt thou the lion's paws,
And make the earth devour her own sweet brood,
Pluck the keen teeth from the fierce tiger's jaws,
And burn the long-lived phœnix in her blood,
Make glad and sorry seasons as thou fleet'st,
And do whate'er thou wilt swift-footed Time
To the wide world and all her fading sweets:
But I forbid thee one most heinous crime,
O carve not with thy hours my love's fair brow,
Nor draw no lines there with thine antique pen,
Him in thy course untainted do allow,
For beauty's pattern to succeeding men.
    Yet do thy worst old Time: despite thy wrong,
    My love shall in my verse ever live young.

20

A woman's face with nature's own hand painted,
Hast thou the master mistress of my passion,
A woman's gentle heart but not acquainted
With shifting change as is false women's fashion,
An eye more bright than theirs, less false in rolling:
Gilding the object whereupon it gazeth,
A man in hue all hues in his controlling,
Which steals men's eyes and women's souls amazeth.
And for a woman wert thou first created,
Till nature as she wrought thee fell a-doting,
And by addition me of thee defeated,
By adding one thing to my purpose nothing.
    But since she pricked thee out for women's pleasure,
    Mine be thy love and thy love's use their treasure.

21

So is it not with me as with that muse,
Stirred by a painted beauty to his verse,
Who heaven it self for ornament doth use,
And every fair with his fair doth rehearse,
Making a couplement of proud compare
With sun and moon, with earth and sea's rich gems:
With April's first-born flowers and all things rare,
That heaven's air in this huge rondure hems.
O let me true in love but truly write,
And then believe me, my love is as fair,
As any mother's child, though not so bright
As those gold candles fixed in heaven's air:
  Let them say more that like of hearsay well,
  I will not praise that purpose not to sell.

22

My glass shall not persuade me I am old,
So long as youth and thou are of one date,
But when in thee time's furrows I behold,
Then look I death my days should expiate.
For all that beauty that doth cover thee,
Is but the seemly raiment of my heart,
Which in thy breast doth live, as thine in me,
How can I then be elder than thou art?
O therefore love be of thyself so wary,
As I not for my self, but for thee will,
Bearing thy heart which I will keep so chary
As tender nurse her babe from faring ill.
  Presume not on thy heart when mine is slain,
  Thou gav'st me thine not to give back again.

23

As an unperfect actor on the stage,
Who with his fear is put beside his part,.
Or some fierce thing replete with too much rage,
Whose strength's abundance weakens his own heart;
So I for fear of trust, forget to say,
The perfect ceremony of love's rite,
And in mine own love's strength seem to decay,
O'ercharged with burthen of mine own love's might:
O let my looks be then the eloquence,
And dumb presagers of my speaking breast,
Who plead for love, and look for recompense,
More than that tongue that more hath more expressed.
O learn to read what silent love hath writ,
To hear with eyes belongs to love's fine wit.

24

Mine eye hath played the painter and hath stelled,
Thy beauty's form in table of my heart,
My body is the frame wherein 'tis held,
And perspective it is best painter's art.
For through the painter must you see his skill,
To find where your true image pictured lies,
Which in my bosom's shop is hanging still,
That hath his windows glazéd with thine eyes:
Now see what good turns eyes for eyes have done,
Mine eyes have drawn thy shape, and thine for me
Are windows to my breast, where-through the sun
Delights to peep, to gaze therein on thee;
Yet eyes this cunning want to grace their art,
They draw but what they see, know not the heart.

25

Let those who are in favour with their stars,
Of public honour and proud titles boast,
Whilst I whom fortune of such triumph bars
Unlooked for joy in that I honour most;
Great princes' favourites their fair leaves spread,
But as the marigold at the sun's eye,
And in themselves their pride lies buriéd,
For at a frown they in their glory die.
The painful warrior famouséd for fight,
After a thousand victories once foiled,
Is from the book of honour razéd quite,
And all the rest forgot for which he toiled:
  Then happy I that love and am beloved
  Where I may not remove nor be removed.

26

Lord of my love, to whom in vassalage
Thy merit hath my duty strongly knit;
To thee I send this written embassage
To witness duty, not to show my wit.
Duty so great, which wit so poor as mine
May make seem bare, in wanting words to show it;
But that I hope some good conceit of thine
In thy soul's thought (all naked) will bestow it:
Till whatsoever star that guides my moving,
Points on me graciously with fair aspect,
And puts apparel on my tattered loving,
To show me worthy of thy sweet respect,
  Then may I dare to boast how I do love thee,
  Till then, not show my head where thou mayst
    prove me.

27

Weary with toil, I haste me to my bed,
The dear respose for limbs with travel tired,
But then begins a journey in my head
To work my mind, when body's work's expired.
For then my thoughts (from far where I abide)
Intend a zealous pilgrimage to thee,
And keep my drooping eyelids open wide,
Looking on darkness which the blind do see.
Save that my soul's imaginary sight
Presents thy shadow to my sightless view,
Which like a jewel (hung in ghastly night)
Makes black night beauteous, and her old face new.
  Lo thus by day my limbs, by night my mind,
  For thee, and for my self, no quiet find.

28

How can I then return in happy plight
That am debarred the benefit of rest?
When day's oppression is not eased by night,
But day by night and night by day oppressed.
And each (though enemies to either's reign)
Do in consent shake hands to torture me,
The one by toil, the other to complain
How far I toil, still farther off from thee.
I tell the day to please him thou art bright,
And dost him grace when clouds do blot the heaven:
So flatter I the swart-complexioned night,
When sparkling stars twire not thou gild'st the even.
  But day doth daily draw my sorrows longer,
  And night doth nightly make grief's length
    seem stronger.

29

When in disgrace with Fortune and men's eyes,
I all alone beweep my outcast state,
And trouble deaf heaven with my bootless cries,
And look upon my self and curse my fate,
Wishing me like to one more rich in hope,
Featured like him, like him with friends possessed,
Desiring this man's art, and that man's scope,
With what I most enjoy contented least,
Yet in these thoughts my self almost despising,
Haply I think on thee, and then my state,
(Like to the lark at break of day arising
From sullen earth) sings hymns at heaven's gate,
  For thy sweet love remembered such wealth brings,
  That then I scorn to change my state with kings.

30

When to the sessions of sweet silent thought,
I summon up remembrance of things past,
I sigh the lack of many a thing I sought,
And with old woes new wail my dear time's waste:
Then can I drown an eye (unused to flow)
For precious friends hid in death's dateless night,
And weep afresh love's long since cancelled woe,
And moan th' expense of many a vanished sight.
Then can I grieve at grievances foregone,
And heavily from woe to woe tell o'er
The sad account of fore-bemoanéd moan,
Which I new pay as if not paid before.
  But if the while I think on thee (dear friend)
  All losses are restored, and sorrows end.

31

Thy bosom is endearéd with all hearts,
Which I by lacking have supposéd dead,
And there reigns love and all love's loving parts,
And all those friends which I thought buriéd.
How many a holy and obsequious tear
Hath dear religious love stol'n from mine eye,
As interest of the dead, which now appear,
But things removed that hidden in thee lie.
Thou art the grave where buried love doth live,
Hung with the trophies of my lovers gone,
Who all their parts of me to thee did give,
That due of many, now is thine alone.
Their images I loved, I view in thee,
And thou (all they) hast all the all of me.

32

If thou survive my well-contented day,
When that churl death my bones with dust shall cover
And shalt by fortune once more re-survey
These poor rude lines of thy deceaséd lover:
Compare them with the bett'ring of the time,
And though they be outstripped by every pen,
Reserve them for my love, not for their rhyme,
Exceeded by the height of happier men.
O then vouchsafe me but this loving thought,
'Had my friend's Muse grown with this growing age,
A dearer birth than this his love had brought
To march in ranks of better equipage:
But since he died and poets better prove,
Theirs for their style I'll read, his for his love'.

33

Full many a glorious morning have I seen,
Flatter the mountain tops with sovereign eye,
Kissing with golden face the meadows green;
Gilding pale streams with heavenly alchemy:
Anon permit the basest clouds to ride,
With ugly rack on his celestial face,
And from the forlorn world his visage hide
Stealing unseen to west with this disgrace:
Even so my sun one early morn did shine,
With all triumphant splendour on my brow,
But out alack, he was but one hour mine,
The region cloud hath masked him from me now.
  Yet him for this, my love no whit disdaineth,
  Suns of the world may stain, when heaven's
    sun staineth.

34

Why didst thou promise such a beauteous day,
And make me travel forth without my cloak,
To let base clouds o'ertake me in my way,
Hiding thy brav'ry in their rotten smoke?
'Tis not enough that through the cloud thou break,
To dry the rain on my storm-beaten face,
For no man well of such a salve can speak,
That heals the wound, and cures not the disgrace:
Nor can thy shame give physic to my grief,
Though thou repent, yet I have still the loss,
Th' offender's sorrow lends but weak relief
To him that bears the strong offence's cross.
  Ah but those tears are pearl which thy love sheds,
  And they are rich, and ransom all ill deeds.

35

No more be grieved at that which thou hast done,
Roses have thorns, and silver fountains mud,
Clouds and eclipses stain both moon and sun,
And loathsome canker lives in sweetest bud.
All men make faults, and even I in this,
Authorizing thy trespass with compare,
My self corrupting salving thy amiss,
Excusing thy sins more than thy sins are:
For to thy sensual fault I bring in sense,
Thy adverse party is thy advocate,
And 'gainst my self a lawful plea commence:
Such civil war is in my love and hate,
  That I an accessary needs must be,
  To that sweet thief which sourly robs from me.

36

Let me confess that we two must be twain,
Although our undivided loves are one:
So shall those blots that do with me remain,
Without thy help, by me be borne alone.
In our two loves there is but one respect,
Though in our lives a separable spite,
Which though it alter not love's sole effect,
Yet doth it steal sweet hours from love's delight.
I may not evermore acknowledge thee,
Lest my bewailéd guilt should do thee shame,
Nor thou with public kindness honour me,
Unless thou take that honour from thy name:
  But do not so, I love thee in such sort,
  As thou being mine, mine is thy good report.

37

As a decrepit father takes delight,
To see his active child do deeds of youth,
So I, made lame by Fortune's dearest spite
Take all my comfort of thy worth and truth.
For whether beauty, birth, or wealth, or wit,
Or any of these all, or all, or more
Entitled in thy parts, do crownéd sit,
I make my love engrafted to this store:
So then I am not lame, poor, nor despised,
Whilst that this shadow doth such substance give,
That I in thy abundance am sufficed,
And by a part of all thy glory live:
  Look what is best, that best I wish in thee,
  This wish I have, then ten times happy me.

38

How can my muse want subject to invent
While thou dost breathe that pour'st into my verse,
Thine own sweet argument, too excellent,
For every vulgar paper to rehearse?
O give thy self the thanks if aught in me,
Worthy perusal stand against thy sight,
For who's so dumb that cannot write to thee,
When thou thy self dost give invention light?
Be thou the tenth Muse, ten times more in worth
Than those old nine which rhymers invocate,
And he that calls on thee, let him bring forth
Eternal numbers to outlive long date.
  If my slight muse do please these curious days,
  The pain be mine, but thine shall be the praise.

39

O how thy worth with manners may I sing,
When thou art all the better part of me?
What can mine own praise to mine own self bring;
And what is't but mine own when I praise thee?
Even for this, let us divided live,
And our dear love lose name of single one,
That by this separation I may give:
That due to thee which thou deserv'st alone:
O absence what a torment wouldst thou prove,
Were it not thy sour leisure gave sweet leave,
To entertain the time with thoughts of love,
Which time and thoughts so sweetly doth deceive.
And that thou teachest how to make one twain,
By praising him here who doth hence remain.

40

Take all my loves, my love, yea take them all,
What hast thou then more than thou hadst before?
No love, my love, that thou mayst true love call,
All mine was thine, before thou hadst this more:
Then if for my love, thou my love receivest,
I cannot blame thee, for my love thou usest,
But yet be blamed, if thou thy self deceivest
By wilful taste of what thy self refusest.
I do forgive thy robbery gentle thief
Although thou steal thee all my poverty:
And yet love knows it is a greater grief
To bear love's wrong, than hate's known injury.
Lascivious grace, in whom all ill well shows,
Kill me with spites yet we must not be foes.

41

Those pretty wrongs that liberty commits,
When I am sometime absent from thy heart,
Thy beauty, and thy years full well befits,
For still temptation follows where thou art.
Gentle thou art, and therefore to be won,
Beauteous thou art, therefore to be assailed.
And when a woman woos, what woman's son,
Will sourly leave her till he have prevailed?
Ay me, but yet thou mightst my seat forbear,
And chide thy beauty, and thy straying youth,
Who lead thee in their riot even there
Where thou art forced to break a twofold truth:
  Hers by thy beauty tempting her to thee,
  Thine by thy beauty being false to me.

42

That thou hast her it is not all my grief,
And yet it may be said I loved her dearly,
That she hath thee is of my wailing chief,
A loss in love that touches me more nearly.
Loving offenders thus I will excuse ye,
Thou dost love her, because thou know'st I love her,
And for my sake even so doth she abuse me,
Suff'ring my friend for my sake to approve her.
If I lose thee, my loss is my love's gain,
And losing her, my friend hath found that loss,
Both find each other, and I lose both twain,
And both for my sake lay on me this cross,
  But here's the joy, my friend and I are one,
  Sweet flattery, then she loves but me alone.

43

When most I wink then do mine eyes best see,
For all the day they view things unrespected,
But when I sleep, in dreams they look on thee,
And darkly bright, are bright in dark directed.
Then thou whose shadow shadows doth make bright,
How would thy shadow's form, form happy show,
To the clear day with thy much clearer light,
When to unseeing eyes thy shade shines so!
How would (I say) mine eyes be blessèd made,
By looking on thee in the living day,
When in dead night thy fair imperfect shade,
Through heavy sleep on sightless eyes doth stay!
All days are nights to see till I see thee,
And nights bright days when dreams do show thee me.

44

If the dull substance of my flesh were thought,
Injurious distance should not stop my way,
For then despite of space I would be brought,
From limits far remote, where thou dost stay,
No matter then although my foot did stand
Upon the farthest earth removed from thee,
For nimble thought can jump both sea and land,
As soon as think the place where he would be.
But ah, thought kills me that I am not thought
To leap large lengths of miles when thou art gone,
But that so much of earth and water wrought,
I must attend, time's leisure with my moan.
Receiving nought by elements so slow,
But heavy tears, badges of either's woe.

45

The other two, slight air, and purging fire,
Are both with thee, wherever I abide,
The first my thought, the other my desire,
These present-absent with swift motion slide.
For when these quicker elements are gone
In tender embassy of love to thee,
My life being made of four, with two alone,
Sinks down to death, oppressed with melancholy.
Until life's composition be recured,
By those swift messengers returned from thee,
Who even but now come back again assured,
Of thy fair health, recounting it to me.
 This told, I joy, but then no longer glad,
 I send them back again and straight grow sad.

46

Mine eye and heart are at a mortal war,
How to divide the conquest of thy sight,
Mine eye, my heart thy picture's sight would bar,
My heart, mine eye the freedom of that right,
My heart doth plead that thou in him dost lie,
(A closet never pierced with crystal eyes)
But the defendant doth that plea deny,
And says in him thy fair appearance lies.
To side this title is impanellèd
A quest of thoughts, all tenants to the heart,
And by their verdict is determinèd
The clear eye's moiety, and the dear heart's part.
 As thus, mine eye's due is thy outward part,
 And my heart's right, thy inward love of heart.

47

Betwixt mine eye and heart a league is took,
And each doth good turns now unto the other,
When that mine eye is famished for a look,
Or heart in love with sighs himself doth smother;
With my love's picture then my eye doth feast,
And to the painted banquet bids my heart:
Another time mine eye is my heart's guest,
And in his thoughts of love doth share a part.
So either by thy picture or my love,
Thy self away, art present still with me,
For thou not farther than my thoughts canst move,
And I am still with them, and they with thee.
  Or if they sleep, thy picture in my sight
  Awakes my heart, to heart's and eye's delight.

48

How careful was I when I took my way,
Each trifle under truest bars to thrust,
That to my use it might unusèd stay
From hands of falsehood, in sure wards of trust!
But thou, to whom my jewels trifles are,
Most worthy comfort, now my greatest grief,
Thou best of dearest, and mine only care,
Art left the prey of every vulgar thief.
Thee have I not locked up in any chest,
Save where thou art not, though I feel thou art,
Within the gentle closure of my breast,
From whence at pleasure thou mayst come and part,
  And even thence thou wilt be stol'n I fear,
  For truth proves thievish for a prize so dear.

49

Against that time (if ever that time come)
When I shall see thee frown on my defects,
When as thy love hath cast his utmost sum,
Called to that audit by advised respects,
Against that time when thou shalt strangely pass,
And scarcely greet me with that sun thine eye,
When love converted from the thing it was
Shall reasons find of settled gravity;
Against that time do I ensconce me here
Within the knowledge of mine own desert,
And this my hand, against my self uprear,
To guard the lawful reasons on thy part,
  To leave poor me, thou hast the strength of laws,
  Since why to love, I can allege no cause.

50

How heavy do I journey on the way,
When what I seek (my weary travel's end)
Doth teach that ease and that repose to say
'Thus far the miles are measured from thy friend.'
The beast that bears me, tiréd with my woe,
Plods dully on, to bear that weight in me,
As if by some instinct the wretch did know
His rider loved not speed being made from thee:
The bloody spur cannot provoke him on,
That sometimes anger thrusts into his hide,
Which heavily he answers with a groan,
More sharp to me than spurring to his side,
  For that same groan doth put this in my mind,
  My grief lies onward and my joy behind.

51

Thus can my love excuse the slow offence,
Of my dull bearer, when from thee I speed,
From where thou art, why should I haste me thence?
Till I return of posting is no need.
O what excuse will my poor beast then find,
When swift extremity can seem but slow?
Then should I spur though mounted on the wind,
In wingéd speed no motion shall I know,
Then can no horse with my desire keep pace,
Therefore desire (of perfect'st love being made)
Shall neigh (no dull flesh) in his fiery race,
But love, for love, thus shall excuse my jade,
  Since from thee going, he went wilful-slow,
  Towards thee I'll run, and give him leave to go.

52

So am I as the rich whose blesséd key,
Can bring him to his sweet up-lockéd treasure,
The which he will not every hour survey,
For blunting the fine point of seldom pleasure.
Therefore are feasts so solemn and so rare,
Since seldom coming in the long year set,
Like stones of worth they thinly placed are,
Or captain jewels in the carcanet.
So is the time that keeps you as my chest,
Or as the wardrobe which the robe doth hide,
To make some special instant special-blest,
By new unfolding his imprisoned pride.
  Blesséd are you whose worthiness gives scope,
  Being had to triumph, being lacked to hope.

53

What is your substance, whereof are you made,
That millions of strange shadows on you tend?
Since every one, hath every one, one shade,
And you but one, can every shadow lend:
Describe Adonis and the counterfeit,
Is poorly imitated after you,
On Helen's cheek all art of beauty set,
And you in Grecian tires are painted new:
Speak of the spring, and foison of the year,
The one doth shadow of your beauty show,
The other as your bounty doth appear,
And you in every blessèd shape we know.
  In all external grace you have some part,
  But you like none, none you for constant heart.

54

O how much more doth beauty beauteous seem,
By that sweet ornament which truth doth give!
The rose looks fair, but fairer we it deem
For that sweet odour, which doth in it live:
The canker blooms have full as deep a dye,
As the perfumèd tincture of the roses,
Hang on such thorns, and play as wantonly,
When summer's breath their maskèd buds discloses:
But for their virtue only is their show,
They live unwooed, and unrespected fade,
Die to themselves. Sweet roses do not so,
Of their sweet deaths, are sweetest odours made:
  And so of you, beauteous and lovely youth,
  When that shall vade, by verse distills your truth.

55

Not marble, nor the gilded monuments
Of princes shall outlive this powerful rhyme,
But you shall shine more bright in these contents
Than unswept stone, besmeared with sluttish time.
When wasteful war shall statues overturn,
And broils root out the work of masonry,
Nor Mars his sword, nor war's quick fire shall burn:
The living record of your memory.
'Gainst death, and all-oblivious enmity
Shall you pace forth, your praise shall still find room,
Even in the eyes of all posterity
That wear this world out to the ending doom.
So till the judgment that your self arise,
You live in this, and dwell in lovers' eyes.

56

Sweet love renew thy force, be it not said
Thy edge should blunter be than appetite,
Which but to-day by feeding is allayed,
To-morrow sharpened in his former might.
So love be thou, although to-day thou fill
Thy hungry eyes, even till they wink with fulness,
To-morrow see again, and do not kill
The spirit of love, with a perpetual dulness:
Let this sad interim like the ocean be
Which parts the shore, where two contracted new,
Come daily to the banks, that when they see:
Return of love, more blest may be the view.
Or call it winter, which being full of care,
Makes summer's welcome, thrice more wished, more rare.

57

Being your slave what should I do but tend,
Upon the hours, and times of your desire?
I have no precious time at all to spend;
Nor services to do till you require.
Nor dare I chide the world-without-end hour,
Whilst I (my sovereign) watch the clock for you,
Nor think the bitterness of absence sour,
When you have bid your servant once adieu.
Nor dare I question with my jealous thought,
Where you may be, or your affairs suppose,
But like a sad slave stay and think of nought
Save where you are, how happy you make those.
So true a fool is love, that in your will,
(Though you do any thing) he thinks no ill.

58

That god forbid, that made me first your slave,
I should in thought control your times of pleasure,
Or at your hand th' account of hours to crave,
Being your vassal bound to stay your leisure.
O let me suffer (being at your beck)
Th' imprisoned absence of your liberty,
And patience tame to sufferance bide each check,
Without accusing you of injury.
Be where you list, your charter is so strong,
That you your self may privilege your time
To what you will, to you it doth belong,
Your self to pardon of self-doing crime.
I am to wait, though waiting so be hell,
Not blame your pleasure be it ill or well.

59

If there be nothing new, but that which is,
Hath been before, how are our brains beguiled,
Which labouring for invention bear amiss
The second burthen of a former child!
O that record could with a backward look,
Even of five hundred courses of the sun,
Show me your image in some antique book,
Since mind at first in character was done.
That I might see what the old world could say,
To this composéd wonder of your frame,
Whether we are mended, or whether better they,
Or whether revolution be the same.
  O sure I am the wits of former days,
  To subjects worse have given admiring praise.

60

Like as the waves make towards the pebbled shore,
So do our minutes hasten to their end,
Each changing place with that which goes before,
In sequent toil all forwards do contend.
Nativity once in the main of light,
Crawls to maturity, wherewith being crowned,
Crookéd eclipses 'gainst his glory fight,
And Time that gave, doth now his gift confound.
Time doth transfix the flourish set on youth,
And delves the parallels in beauty's brow,
Feeds on the rarities of nature's truth,
And nothing stands but for his scythe to mow.
  And yet to times in hope, my verse shall stand
  Praising thy worth, despite his cruel hand.

61

Is it thy will, thy image should keep open
My heavy eyelids to the weary night?
Dost thou desire my slumbers should be broken,
While shadows like to thee do mock my sight?
Is it thy spirit that thou send'st from thee
So far from home into my deeds to pry,
To find out shames and idle hours in me,
The scope and tenure of thy jealousy?
O no, thy love though much, is not so great,
It is my love that keeps mine eye awake,
Mine own true love that doth my rest defeat,
To play the watchman ever for thy sake.
  For thee watch I, whilst thou dost wake elsewhere,
  From me far off, with others all too near.

62

Sin of self-love possesseth all mine eye,
And all my soul, and all my every part;
And for this sin there is no remedy,
It is so grounded inward in my heart.
Methinks no face so gracious is as mine,
No shape so true, no truth of such account,
And for my self mine own worth do define,
As I all other in all worths surmount.
But when my glass shows me my self indeed
Beated and chopt with tanned antiquity,
Mine own self-love quite contrary I read:
Self, so self-loving were iniquity.
  'Tis thee (my self) that for my self I praise,
  Painting my age with beauty of thy days.

63

Against my love shall be as I am now
With Time's injurious hand crushed and o'erworn,
When hours have drained his blood and filled his brow
With lines and wrinkles, when his youthful morn
Hath travelled on to age's steepy night,
And all those beauties whereof now he's king
Are vanishing, or vanished out of sight,
Stealing away the treasure of his spring:
For such a time do I now fortify
Against confounding age's cruel knife,
That he shall never cut from memory
My sweet love's beauty, though my lover's life.
His beauty shall in these black lines be seen,
And they shall live, and he in them still green.

64

When I have seen by Time's fell hand defaced
The rich-proud cost of outworn buried age,
When sometime lofty towers I see down-rased,
And brass eternal slave to mortal rage.
When I have seen the hungry ocean gain
Advantage on the kingdom of the shore,
And the firm soil win of the watery main,
Increasing store with loss, and loss with store.
When I have seen such interchange of state,
Or state it self confounded, to decay,
Ruin hath taught me thus to ruminate
That Time will come and take my love away.
This thought is as a death which cannot choose
But weep to have, that which it fears to lose.

65

Since brass, nor stone, nor earth, nor boundless sea,
But sad mortality o'ersways their power,
How with this rage shall beauty hold a plea,
Whose action is no stronger than a flower?
O how shall summer's honey breath hold out,
Against the wrackful siege of batt'ring days,
When rocks impregnable are not so stout,
Nor gates of steel so strong but time decays?
O fearful meditation, where alack,
Shall Time's best jewel from Time's chest lie hid?
Or what strong hand can hold his swift foot back,
Or who his spoil of beauty can forbid?
  O none, unless this miracle have might,
  That in black ink my love may still shine bright.

66

Tired with all these for restful death I cry,
As to behold desert a beggar born,
And needy nothing trimmed in jollity,
And purest faith unhappily forsworn,
And gilded honour shamefully misplaced,
And maiden virtue rudely strumpeted,
And right perfection wrongfully disgraced,
And strength by limping sway disablèd,
And art made tongue-tied by authority,
And folly (doctor-like) controlling skill,
And simple truth miscalled simplicity,
And captive good attending captain ill.
  Tired with all these, from these would I be gone,
  Save that to die, I leave my love alone.

67

Ah wherefore with infection should he live,
And with his presence grace impiety,
That sin by him advantage should achieve,
And lace it self with his society?
Why should false painting imitate his cheek,
And steal dead seeming of his living hue?
Why should poor beauty indirectly seek,
Roses of shadow, since his rose is true?
Why should he live, now nature bankrupt is,
Beggared of blood to blush through lively veins,
For she hath no exchequer now but his,
And proud of many, lives upon his gains?
O him she stores, to show what wealth she had,
In days long since, before these last so bad.

68

Thus is his cheek the map of days outworn,
When beauty lived and died as flowers do now,
Before these bastard signs of fair were born,
Or durst inhabit on a living brow:
Before the golden tresses of the dead,
The right of sepulchres, were shorn away,
To live a second life on second head,
Ere beauty's dead fleece made another gay:
In him those holy antique hours are seen,
Without all ornament, it self and true,
Making no summer of another's green,
Robbing no old to dress his beauty new,
And him as for a map doth Nature store,
To show false Art what beauty was of yore.

69

Those parts of thee that the world's eye doth view,
Want nothing that the thought of hearts can mend:
All tongues (the voice of souls) give thee that due,
Uttering bare truth, even so as foes commend.
Thy outward thus with outward praise is crowned,
But those same tongues that give thee so thine own,
In other accents do this praise confound
By seeing farther than the eye hath shown.
They look into the beauty of thy mind,
And that in guess they measure by thy deeds,
Then churls their thoughts (although their eyes were kind)
To thy fair flower add the rank smell of weeds:
But why thy odour matcheth not thy show,
The soil is this, that thou dost common grow.

70

That thou art blamed shall not be thy defect,
For slander's mark was ever yet the fair,
The ornament of beauty is suspect,
A crow that flies in heaven's sweetest air.
So thou be good, slander doth but approve,
Thy worth the greater being wooed of time,
For canker vice the sweetest buds doth love,
And thou present'st a pure unstainéd prime.
Thou hast passed by the ambush of young days,
Either not assailed, or victor being charged,
Yet this thy praise cannot be so thy praise,
To tie up envy, evermore enlarged,
If some suspect of ill masked not thy show,
Then thou alone kingdoms of hearts shouldst owe.

71

No longer mourn for me when I am dead,
Than you shall hear the surly sullen bell
Give warning to the world that I am fled
From this vile world with vilest worms to dwell:
Nay if you read this line, remember not,
The hand that writ it, for I love you so,
That I in your sweet thoughts would be forgot,
If thinking on me then should make you woe.
O if (I say) you look upon this verse,
When I (perhaps) compounded am with clay,
Do not so much as my poor name rehearse;
But let your love even with my life decay.
Lest the wise world should look into your moan,
And mock you with me after I am gone.

72

O lest the world should task you to recite,
What merit lived in me that you should love
After my death (dear love) forget me quite,
For you in me can nothing worthy prove.
Unless you would devise some virtuous lie,
To do more for me than mine own desert,
And hang more praise upon deceasèd I,
Than niggard truth would willingly impart:
O lest your true love may seem false in this,
That you for love speak well of me untrue,
My name be buried where my body is,
And live no more to shame nor me, nor you.
For I am shamed by that which I bring forth,
And so should you, to love things nothing worth.

73

That time of year thou mayst in me behold,
When yellow leaves, or none, or few do hang
Upon those boughs which shake against the cold,
Bare ruined choirs, where late the sweet birds sang.
In me thou seest the twilight of such day,
As after sunset fadeth in the west,
Which by and by black night doth take away,
Death's second self that seals up all in rest.
In me thou seest the glowing of such fire,
That on the ashes of his youth doth lie,
As the death-bed, whereon it must expire,
Consumed with that which it was nourished by.
  This thou perceiv'st, which makes thy love more strong,
  To love that well, which thou must leave ere long.

74

But be contented when that fell arrest,
Without all bail shall carry me away,
My life hath in this line some interest,
Which for memorial still with thee shall stay.
When thou reviewest this, thou dost review,
The very part was consecrate to thee,
The earth can have but earth, which is his due,
My spirit is thine the better part of me,
So then thou hast but lost the dregs of life,
The prey of worms, my body being dead,
The coward conquest of a wretch's knife,
Too base of thee to be rememberéd,
  The worth of that, is that which it contains,
  And that is this, and this with thee remains.

75

So are you to my thoughts as food to life,
Or as sweet-seasoned showers are to the ground;
And for the peace of you I hold such strife
As 'twixt a miser and his wealth is found.
Now proud as an enjoyer, and anon
Doubting the filching age will steal his treasure,
Now counting best to be with you alone,
Then bettered that the world may see my pleasure,
Sometime all full with feasting on your sight,
And by and by clean starvéd for a look,
Possessing or pursuing no delight
Save what is had, or must from you be took.
Thus do I pine and surfeit day by day,
Or gluttoning on all, or all away.

76

Why is my verse so barren of new pride?
So far from variation or quick change?
Why with the time do I not glance aside
To new-found methods, and to compounds strange?
Why write I still all one, ever the same,
And keep invention in a noted weed,
That every word doth almost tell my name,
Showing their birth, and where they did proceed?
O know sweet love I always write of you,
And you and love are still my argument:
So all my best is dressing old words new,
Spending again what is already spent:
For as the sun is daily new and old,
So is my love still telling what is told.

77

Thy glass will show thee how thy beauties wear,
Thy dial how thy precious minutes waste,
These vacant leaves thy mind's imprint will bear,
And of this book, this learning mayst thou taste.
The wrinkles which thy glass will truly show,
Of mouthéd graves will give thee memory,
Thou by thy dial's shady stealth mayst know,
Time's thievish progress to eternity.
Look what thy memory cannot contain,
Commit to these waste blanks, and thou shalt find
Those children nursed, delivered from thy brain,
To take a new acquaintance of thy mind.
  These offices, so oft as thou wilt look,
  Shall profit thee, and much enrich thy book.

78

So oft have I invoked thee for my muse,
And found such fair assistance in my verse,
As every alien pen hath got my use,
And under thee their poesy disperse.
Thine eyes, that taught the dumb on high to sing,
And heavy ignorance aloft to fly,
Have added feathers to the learnéd's wing,
And given grace a double majesty.
Yet be most proud of that which I compile,
Whose influence is thine, and born of thee,
In others' works thou dost but mend the style,
And arts with thy sweet graces gracéd be.
  But thou art all my art, and dost advance
  As high as learning, my rude ignorance.

79

Whilst I alone did call upon thy aid,
My verse alone had all thy gentle grace,
But now my gracious numbers are decayed,
And my sick muse doth give an other place.
I grant (sweet love) thy lovely argument
Deserves the travail of a worthier pen,
Yet what of thee thy poet doth invent,
He robs thee of, and pays it thee again,
He lends thee virtue, and he stole that word,
From thy behaviour, beauty doth he give
And found it in thy cheek: he can afford
No praise to thee, but what in thee doth live.
Then thank him not for that which he doth say,
Since what he owes thee, thou thy self dost pay.

80

O how I faint when I of you do write,
Knowing a better spirit doth use your name,
And in the praise thereof spends all his might,
To make me tongue-tied speaking of your fame.
But since your worth (wide as the ocean is)
The humble as the proudest sail doth bear,
My saucy bark (inferior far to his)
On your broad main doth wilfully appear.
Your shallowest help will hold me up afloat,
Whilst he upon your soundless deep doth ride,
Or (being wrecked) I am a worthless boat,
He of tall building, and of goodly pride.
Then if he thrive and I be cast away,
The worst was this, my love was my decay.

81

Or I shall live your epitaph to make,
Or you survive when I in earth am rotten,
From hence your memory death cannot take,
Although in me each part will be forgotten.
Your name from hence immortal life shall have,
Though I (once gone) to all the world must die,
The earth can yield me but a common grave,
When you entombéd in men's eyes shall lie,
Your monument shall be my gentle verse,
Which eyes not yet created shall o'er-read,
And tongues to be, your being shall rehearse,
When all the breathers of this world are dead,
  You still shall live (such virtue hath my pen)
  Where breath most breathes, even in the mouths of men.

82

I grant thou wert not married to my muse,
And therefore mayst without attaint o'erlook
The dedicated words which writers use
Of their fair subject, blessing every book.
Thou art as fair in knowledge as in hue,
Finding thy worth a limit past my praise,
And therefore art enforced to seek anew,
Some fresher stamp of the time-bettering days.
And do so love, yet when they have devised,
What strainéd touches rhetoric can lend,
Thou truly fair, wert truly sympathized,
In true plain words, by thy true-telling friend.
  And their gross painting might be better used,
  Where cheeks need blood, in thee it is abused.

83

I never saw that you did painting need,
And therefore to your fair no painting set,
I found (or thought I found) you did exceed,
The barren tender of a poet's debt:
And therefore have I slept in your report,
That you your self being extant well might show,
How far a modern quill doth come too short,
Speaking of worth, what worth in you doth grow.
This silence for my sin you did impute,
Which shall be most my glory being dumb,
For I impair not beauty being mute,
When others would give life, and bring a tomb.
  There lives more life in one of your fair eyes,
  Than both your poets can in praise devise.

84

Who is it that says most, which can say more,
Than this rich praise, that you alone, are you?
In whose confine immurèd is the store,
Which should example where your equal grew.
Lean penury within that pen doth dwell,
That to his subject lends not some small glory,
But he that writes of you, if he can tell,
That you are you, so dignifies his story.
Let him but copy what in you is writ,
Not making worse what nature made so clear,
And such a counterpart shall fame his wit,
Making his style admirèd every where.
  You to your beauteous blessings add a curse,
  Being fond on praise, which makes your praises worse.

85

My tongue-tied muse in manners holds her still,
While comments of your praise richly compiled,
Reserve their character with golden quill,
And precious phrase by all the Muses filed.
I think good thoughts, whilst other write good words,
And like unlettered clerk still cry Amen,
To every hymn that able spirit affords,
In polished form of well refinèd pen.
Hearing you praised, I say 'tis so, 'tis true,
And to the most of praise add something more,
But that is in my thought, whose love to you
(Though words come hindmost) holds his rank before,
Then others, for the breath of words respect,
Me for my dumb thoughts, speaking in effect.

86

Was it the proud full sail of his great verse,
Bound for the prize of (all too precious) you,
That did my ripe thoughts in my brain inhearse,
Making their tomb the womb wherein they grew?
Was it his spirit, by spirits taught to write,
Above a mortal pitch, that struck me dead?
No, neither he, nor his compeers by night
Giving him aid, my verse astonishèd.
He nor that affable familiar ghost
Which nightly gulls him with intelligence,
As victors of my silence cannot boast,
I was not sick of any fear from thence.
But when your countenance filled up his line,
Then lacked I matter, that enfeebled mine.

87

Farewell! thou art too dear for my possessing,
And like enough thou know'st thy estimate,
The charter of thy worth gives thee releasing:
My bonds in thee are all determinate.
For how do I hold thee but by thy granting,
And for that riches where is my deserving?
The cause of this fair gift in me is wanting,
And so my patent back again is swerving.
Thy self thou gav'st, thy own worth then not knowing,
Or me to whom thou gav'st it, else mistaking,
So thy great gift upon misprision growing,
Comes home again, on better judgment making.
  Thus have I had thee as a dream doth flatter,
  In sleep a king, but waking no such matter.

88

When thou shalt be disposed to set me light,
And place my merit in the eye of scorn,
Upon thy side, against my self I'll fight,
And prove thee virtuous, though thou art forsworn:
With mine own weakness being best acquainted,
Upon thy part I can set down a story
Of faults concealed, wherein I am attainted:
That thou in losing me, shalt win much glory:
And I by this will be a gainer too,
For bending all my loving thoughts on thee,
The injuries that to my self I do,
Doing thee vantage, double-vantage me.
  Such is my love, to thee I so belong,
  That for thy right, my self will bear all wrong.

89

Say that thou didst forsake me for some fault,
And I will comment upon that offence,
Speak of my lameness, and I straight will halt:
Against thy reasons making no defence.
Thou canst not (love) disgrace me half so ill,
To set a form upon desiréd change,
As I'll my self disgrace, knowing thy will,
I will acquaintance strangle and look strange:
Be absent from thy walks and in my tongue,
Thy sweet belovéd name no more shall dwell,
Lest I (too much profane) should do it wrong:
And haply of our old acquaintance tell.
  For thee, against my self I'll vow debate,
  For I must ne'er love him whom thou dost hate.

90

Then hate me when thou wilt, if ever, now,
Now while the world is bent my deeds to cross,
Join with the spite of fortune, make me bow,
And do not drop in for an after-loss:
Ah do not, when my heart hath 'scaped this sorrow,
Come in the rearward of a conquered woe,
Give not a windy night a rainy morrow,
To linger out a purposed overthrow.
If thou wilt leave me, do not leave me last,
When other petty griefs have done their spite,
But in the onset come, so shall I taste
At first the very worst of fortune's might.
  And other strains of woe, which now seem woe,
  Compared with loss of thee, will not seem so.

91

Some glory in their birth, some in their skill,
Some in their wealth, some in their body's force,
Some in their garments though new-fangled ill:
Some in their hawks and hounds, some in their horse.
And every humour hath his adjunct pleasure,
Wherein it finds a joy above the rest,
But these particulars are not my measure,
All these I better in one general best.
Thy love is better than high birth to me,
Richer than wealth, prouder than garments' costs,
Of more delight than hawks and horses be:
And having thee, of all men's pride I boast.
  Wretched in this alone, that thou mayst take,
  All this away, and me most wretched make.

92

But do thy worst to steal thy self away,
For term of life thou art assuréd mine,
And life no longer than thy love will stay,
For it depends upon that love of thine.
Then need I not to fear the worst of wrongs,
When in the least of them my life hath end,
I see, a better state to me belongs
Than that, which on thy humour doth depend.
Thou canst not vex me with inconstant mind,
Since that my life on thy revolt doth lie,
O what a happy title do I find,
Happy to have thy love, happy to die!
  But what's so blesséd-fair that fears no blot?
  Thou mayst be false, and yet I know it not.

93

So shall I live, supposing thou art true,
Like a deceivéd husband, so love's face,
May still seem love to me, though altered new:
Thy looks with me, thy heart in other place.
For there can live no hatred in thine eye,
Therefore in that I cannot know thy change,
In many's looks, the false heart's history
Is writ in moods and frowns and wrinkles strange.
But heaven in thy creation did decree,
That in thy face sweet love should ever dwell,
Whate'er thy thoughts, or thy heart's workings be,
Thy looks should nothing thence, but sweetness tell.
  How like Eve's apple doth thy beauty grow,
  If thy sweet virtue answer not thy show.

94

They that have power to hurt, and will do none,
That do not do the thing, they most do show,
Who moving others, are themselves as stone,
Unmovéd, cold, and to temptation slow:
They rightly do inherit heaven's graces,
And husband nature's riches from expense,
They are the lords and owners of their faces,
Others, but stewards of their excellence:
The summer's flower is to the summer sweet,
Though to it self, it only live and die,
But if that flower with base infection meet,
The basest weed outbraves his dignity:
  For sweetest things turn sourest by their deeds,
  Lilies that fester, smell far worse than weeds.

95

How sweet and lovely dost thou make the shame,
Which like a canker in the fragrant rose,
Doth spot the beauty of thy budding name!
O in what sweets dost thou thy sins enclose!
That tongue that tells the story of thy days,
(Making lascivious comments on thy sport)
Cannot dispraise, but in a kind of praise,
Naming thy name, blesses an ill report.
O what a mansion have those vices got,
Which for their habitation chose out thee,
Where beauty's veil doth cover every blot,
And all things turns to fair, that eyes can see!
Take heed (dear heart) of this large privilege,
The hardest knife ill-used doth lose his edge.

96

Some say thy fault is youth, some wantonness,
Some say thy grace is youth and gentle sport,
Both grace and faults are loved of more and less:
Thou mak'st faults graces, that to thee resort:
As on the finger of a thronéd queen,
The basest jewel will be well esteemed:
So are those errors that in thee are seen,
To truths translated, and for true things deemed.
How many lambs might the stern wolf betray,
If like a lamb he could his looks translate!
How many gazers mightst thou lead away,
If thou wouldst use the strength of all thy state!
But do not so, I love thee in such sort,
As thou being mine, mine is thy good report.

97

How like a winter hath my absence been
From thee, the pleasure of the fleeting year!
What freezings have I felt, what dark days seen!
What old December's bareness everywhere!
And yet this time removed was summer's time,
The teeming autumn big with rich increase,
Bearing the wanton burden of the prime,
Like widowed wombs after their lords' decease:
Yet this abundant issue seemed to me
But hope of orphans, and unfathered fruit,
For summer and his pleasures wait on thee,
And thou away, the very birds are mute.
  Or if they sing, 'tis with so dull a cheer,
  That leaves look pale, dreading the winter's near.

98

From you have I been absent in the spring,
When proud-pied April (dressed in all his trim)
Hath put a spirit of youth in every thing:
That heavy Saturn laughed and leaped with him.
Yet nor the lays of birds, nor the sweet smell
Of different flowers in odour and in hue,
Could make me any summer's story tell:
Or from their proud lap pluck them where they grew:
Nor did I wonder at the lily's white,
Nor praise the deep vermilion in the rose,
They were but sweet, but figures of delight:
Drawn after you, you pattern of all those.
  Yet seemed it winter still, and you away,
  As with your shadow I with these did play.

99

The forward violet thus did I chide,
Sweet thief, whence didst thou steal thy sweet that smells,
If not from my love's breath? The purple pride
Which on thy soft cheek for complexion dwells,
In my love's veins thou hast too grossly dyed.
The lily I condemnéd for thy hand,
And buds of marjoram had stol'n thy hair,
The roses fearfully on thorns did stand,
One blushing shame, another white despair:
A third nor red, nor white, had stol'n of both,
And to his robbery had annexed thy breath,
But for his theft in pride of all his growth
A vengeful canker eat him up to death.
More flowers I noted, yet I none could see,
But sweet, or colour it had stol'n from thee.

100

Where art thou Muse that thou forget'st so long,
To speak of that which gives thee all thy might?
Spend'st thou thy fury on some worthless song,
Darkening thy power to lend base subjects light?
Return forgetful Muse, and straight redeem,
In gentle numbers time so idly spent,
Sing to the ear that doth thy lays esteem,
And gives thy pen both skill and argument.
Rise resty Muse, my love's sweet face survey,
If time have any wrinkle graven there,
If any, be a satire to decay,
And make time's spoils despiséd everywhere.
Give my love fame faster than Time wastes life,
So thou prevent'st his scythe, and crookéd knife.

101

O truant Muse what shall be thy amends,
For thy neglect of truth in beauty dyed?
Both truth and beauty on my love depends:
So dost thou too, and therein dignified:
Make answer Muse, wilt thou not haply say,
'Truth needs no colour with his colour fixed,
Beauty no pencil, beauty's truth to lay:
But best is best, if never intermixed'?
Because he needs no praise, wilt thou be dumb?
Excuse not silence so, for't lies in thee,
To make him much outlive a gilded tomb:
And to be praised of ages yet to be.
  Then do thy office Muse, I teach thee how,
  To make him seem long hence, as he shows now.

102

My love is strengthened though more weak in seeming,
I love not less, though less the show appear,
That love is merchandized, whose rich esteeming,
The owner's tongue doth publish every where.
Our love was new, and then but in the spring,
When I was wont to greet it with my lays,
As Philomel in summer's front doth sing,
And stops her pipe in growth of riper days:
Not that the summer is less pleasant now
Than when her mournful hymns did hush the night,
But that wild music burthens every bough,
And sweets grown common lose their dear delight.
  Therefore like her, I sometime hold my tongue:
  Because I would not dull you with my song.

103

Alack what poverty my muse brings forth,
That having such a scope to show her pride,
The argument all bare is of more worth
Than when it hath my added praise beside.
O blame me not if I no more can write!
Look in your glass and there appears a face,
That over-goes my blunt invention quite,
Dulling my lines, and doing me disgrace.
Were it not sinful then striving to mend,
To mar the subject that before was well?
For to no other pass my verses tend,
Than of your graces and your gifts to tell.
  And more, much more than in my verse can sit,
  Your own glass shows you, when you look in it.

104

To me fair friend you never can be old,
For as you were when first your eye I eyed,
Such seems your beauty still: three winters cold,
Have from the forests shook three summers' pride,
Three beauteous springs to yellow autumn turned,
In process of the seasons have I seen,
Three April perfumes in three hot Junes burned,
Since first I saw you fresh which yet are green.
Ah yet doth beauty like a dial hand,
Steal from his figure, and no pace perceived,
So your sweet hue, which methinks still doth stand
Hath motion, and mine eye may be deceived.
  For fear of which, hear this thou age unbred,
  Ere you were born was beauty's summer dead.

105

Let not my love be called idolatry,
Nor my belovéd as an idol show,
Since all alike my songs and praises be
To one, of one, still such, and ever so.
Kind is my love to-day, to-morrow kind,
Still constant in a wondrous excellence,
Therefore my verse to constancy confined,
One thing expressing, leaves out difference.
Fair, kind, and true, is all my argument,
Fair, kind, and true, varying to other words,
And in this change is my invention spent,
Three themes in one, which wondrous scope affords.
  Fair, kind, and true, have often lived alone.
  Which three till now, never kept seat in one.

106

When in the chronicle of wasted time,
I see descriptions of the fairest wights,
And beauty making beautiful old rhyme,
In praise of ladies dead, and lovely knights,
Then in the blazon of sweet beauty's best,
Of hand, of foot, of lip, of eye, of brow,
I see their antique pen would have expressed,
Even such a beauty as you master now.
So all their praises are but prophecies
Of this our time, all you prefiguring,
And for they looked but with divining eyes,
They had not skill enough your worth to sing:
  For we which now behold these present days,
  Have eyes to wonder, but lack tongues to praise.

107

Not mine own fears, nor the prophetic soul,
Of the wide world, dreaming on things to come,
Can yet the lease of my true love control,
Supposed as forfeit to a confined doom.
The mortal moon hath her eclipse endured,
And the sad augurs mock their own presage,
Incertainties now crown themselves assured,
And peace proclaims olives of endless age.
Now with the drops of this most balmy time,
My love looks fresh, and death to me subscribes,
Since spite of him I'll live in this poor rhyme,
While he insults o'er dull and speechless tribes.
And thou in this shalt find thy monument,
When tyrants' crests and tombs of brass are spent.

108

What's in the brain that ink may character,
Which hath not figured to thee my true spirit,
What's new to speak, what now to register,
That may express my love, or thy dear merit?
Nothing sweet boy, but yet like prayers divine,
I must each day say o'er the very same,
Counting no old thing old, thou mine, I thine,
Even as when first I hallowed thy fair name.
So that eternal love in love's fresh case,
Weighs not the dust and injury of age,
Nor gives to necessary wrinkles place,
But makes antiquity for aye his page,
Finding the first conceit of love there bred,
Where time and outward form would show it dead.

109

O never say that I was false of heart,
Though absence seemed my flame to qualify,
As easy might I from my self depart,
As from my soul which in thy breast doth lie:
That is my home of love, if I have ranged,
Like him that travels I return again,
Just to the time, not with the time exchanged,
So that my self bring water for my stain,
Never believe though in my nature reigned,
All frailties that besiege all kinds of blood,
That it could so preposterously be stained,
To leave for nothing all thy sum of good:
For nothing this wide universe I call,
Save thou my rose, in it thou art my all.

110

Alas 'tis true, I have gone here and there,
And made my self a motley to the view,
Gored mine own thoughts, sold cheap what is most dear,
Made old offences of affections new.
Most true it is, that I have looked on truth
Askance and strangely: but by all above,
These blenches gave my heart another youth,
And worse essays proved thee my best of love.
Now all is done, have what shall have no end,
Mine appetite I never more will grind
On newer proof, to try an older friend,
A god in love, to whom I am confined.
Then give me welcome, next my heaven the best,
Even to thy pure and most most loving breast.

111

O for my sake do you with Fortune chide,
The guilty goddess of my harmful deeds,
That did not better for my life provide,
Than public means which public manners breeds.
Thence comes it that my name receives a brand,
And almost thence my nature is subdued
To what it works in, like the dyer's hand:
Pity me then, and wish I were renewed,
Whilst like a willing patient I will drink,
Potions of eisel 'gainst my strong infection,
No bitterness that I will bitter think,
Nor double penance to correct correction.
Pity me then dear friend, and I assure ye,
Even that your pity is enough to cure me.

112

Your love and pity doth th' impression fill,
Which vulgar scandal stamped upon my brow,
For what care I who calls me well or ill,
So you o'er-green my bad, my good allow?
You are my all the world, and I must strive,
To know my shames and praises from your tongue,
None else to me, nor I to none alive,
That my steeled sense or changes right or wrong.
In so profound abysm I throw all care
Of others' voices, that my adder's sense,
To critic and to flatterer stoppéd are:
Mark how with my neglect I do dispense.
You are so strongly in my purpose bred,
That all the world besides methinks are dead.

113

Since I left you, mine eye is in my mind,
And that which governs me to go about,
Doth part his function, and is partly blind,
Seems seeing, but effectually is out:
For it no form delivers to the heart
Of bird, of flower, or shape which it doth latch,
Of his quick objects hath the mind no part,
Nor his own vision holds what it doth catch:
For if it see the rud'st or gentlest sight,
The most sweet favour or deformed'st creature,
The mountain, or the sea, the day, or night:
The crow, or dove, it shapes them to your feature.
Incapable of more, replete with you,
My most true mind thus maketh mine untrue.

114

Or whether doth my mind being crowned with you
Drink up the monarch's plague this flattery?
Or whether shall I say mine eye saith true,
And that your love taught it this alchemy?
To make of monsters, and things indigest,
Such cherubins as your sweet self resemble,
Creating every bad a perfect best
As fast as objects to his beams assemble:
O 'tis the first, 'tis flattery in my seeing,
And my great mind most kingly drinks it up,
Mine eye well knows what with his gust is 'greeing,
And to his palate doth prepare the cup.
If it be poisoned, 'tis the lesser sin,
That mine eye loves it and doth first begin.

115

Those lines that I before have writ do lie,
Even those that said I could not love you dearer,
Yet then my judgment knew no reason why,
My most full flame should afterwards burn clearer,
But reckoning time, whose millioned accidents
Creep in 'twixt vows, and change decrees of kings,
Tan sacred beauty, blunt the sharp'st intents,
Divert strong minds to the course of alt'ring things:
Alas why fearing of time's tyranny,
Might I not then say 'Now I love you best,'
When I was certain o'er incertainty,
Crowning the present, doubting of the rest?
  Love is a babe, then might I not say so
  To give full growth to that which still doth grow.

116

Let me not to the marriage of true minds
Admit impediments, love is not love
Which alters when it alteration finds,
Or bends with the remover to remove.
O no, it is an ever-fixéd mark
That looks on tempests and is never shaken;
It is the star to every wand'ring bark,
Whose worth's unknown, although his height be taken.
Love's not Time's fool, though rosy lips and cheeks
Within his bending sickle's compass come,
Love alters not with his brief hours and weeks,
But bears it out even to the edge of doom:
  If this be error and upon me proved,
  I never writ, nor no man ever loved.

117

Accuse me thus, that I have scanted all,
Wherein I should your great deserts repay,
Forgot upon your dearest love to call,
Whereto all bonds do tie me day by day,
That I have frequent been with unknown minds,
And given to time your own dear-purchased right,
That I have hoisted sail to all the winds
Which should transport me farthest from your sight.
Book both my wilfulness and errors down,
And on just proof surmise, accumulate,
Bring me within the level of your frown,
But shoot not at me in your wakened hate:
Since my appeal says I did strive to prove
The constancy and virtue of your love.

118

Like as to make our appetite more keen
With eager compounds we our palate urge,
As to prevent our maladies unseen,
We sicken to shun sickness when we purge.
Even so being full of your ne'er-cloying sweetness,
To bitter sauces did I frame my feeding;
And sick of welfare found a kind of meetness,
To be diseased ere that there was true needing.
Thus policy in love t' anticipate
The ills that were not, grew to faults assured,
And brought to medicine a healthful state
Which rank of goodness would by ill be cured.
But thence I learn and find the lesson true,
Drugs poison him that so fell sick of you.

119

What potions have I drunk of Siren tears
Distilled from limbecks foul as hell within,
Applying fears to hopes, and hopes to fears,
Still losing when I saw my self to win!
What wretched errors hath my heart committed,
Whilst it hath thought it self so blesséd never!
How have mine eyes out of their spheres been fitted
In the distraction of this madding fever!
O benefit of ill, now I find true
That better is, by evil still made better.
And ruined love when it is built anew
Grows fairer than at first, more strong, far greater.
So I return rebuked to my content,
And gain by ills thrice more than I have spent.

120

That you were once unkind befriends me now,
And for that sorrow, which I then did feel,
Needs must I under my transgression bow,
Unless my nerves were brass or hammered steel.
For if you were by my unkindness shaken
As I by yours, y'have passed a hell of time,
And I a tyrant have no leisure taken
To weigh how once I suffered in your crime.
O that our night of woe might have remembered
My deepest sense, how hard true sorrow hits,
And soon to you, as you to me then tendered
The humble salve, which wounded bosoms fits!
But that your trespass now becomes a fee,
Mine ransoms yours, and yours must ransom me.

121

'Tis better to be vile than vile esteemed,
When not to be, receives reproach of being,
And the just pleasure lost, which is so deemed,
Not by our feeling, but by others' seeing.
For why should others' false adulterate eyes
Give salutation to my sportive blood?
Or on my frailties why are frailer spies,
Which in their wills count bad what I think good?
No, I am that I am, and they that level
At my abuses, reckon up their own,
I may be straight though they themselves be bevel;
By their rank thoughts, my deeds must not be shown
  Unless this general evil they maintain,
  All men are bad and in their badness reign.

122

Thy gift, thy tables, are within my brain
Full charactered with lasting memory,
Which shall above that idle rank remain
Beyond all date even to eternity.
Or at the least, so long as brain and heart
Have faculty by nature to subsist,
Till each to razed oblivion yield his part
Of thee, thy record never can be missed:
That poor retention could not so much hold,
Nor need I tallies thy dear love to score,
Therefore to give them from me was I bold,
To trust those tables that receive thee more:
  To keep an adjunct to remember thee
  Were to import forgetfulness in me.

123

No! Time, thou shalt not boast that I do change,
Thy pyramids built up with newer might
To me are nothing novel, nothing strange,
They are but dressings of a former sight:
Our dates are brief, and therefore we admire,
What thou dost foist upon us that is old,
And rather make them born to our desire,
Than think that we before have heard them told:
Thy registers and thee I both defy,
Not wond'ring at the present, nor the past,
For thy records, and what we see doth lie,
Made more or less by thy continual haste:
  This I do vow and this shall ever be,
  I will be true despite thy scythe and thee.

124

If my dear love were but the child of state,
It might for Fortune's bastard be unfathered,
As subject to time's love or to time's hate,
Weeds among weeds, or flowers with flowers gathered.
No it was builded far from accident,
It suffers not in smiling pomp, nor falls
Under the blow of thralléd discontent,
Whereto th' inviting time our fashion calls:
It fears not policy that heretic,
Which works on leases of short-numbered hours,
But all alone stands hugely politic,
That it nor grows with heat, nor drowns with showers.
  To this I witness call the fools of time,
  Which die for goodness, who have lived for crime.

125

Were't aught to me I bore the canopy,
With my extern the outward honouring,
Or laid great bases for eternity,
Which proves more short than waste or ruining?
Have I not seen dwellers on form and favour
Lose all, and more by paying too much rent
For compound sweet; forgoing simple savour,
Pitiful thrivers in their gazing spent?
No, let me be obsequious in thy heart,
And take thou my oblation, poor but free,
Which is not mixed with seconds, knows no art,
But mutual render, only me for thee.
  Hence, thou suborned informer, a true soul
  When most impeached, stands least in thy control.

126

O thou my lovely boy who in thy power,
Dost hold Time's fickle glass his fickle hour:
Who hast by waning grown, and therein show'st,
Thy lovers withering, as thy sweet self grow'st.
If Nature (sovereign mistress over wrack)
As thou goest onwards still will pluck thee back,
She keeps thee to this purpose, that her skill
May time disgrace, and wretched minutes kill.
Yet fear her O thou minion of her pleasure,
She may detain, but not still keep her treasure!
  Her audit (though delayed) answered must be,
  And her quietus is to render thee.

127

In the old age black was not counted fair,
Or if it were it bore not beauty's name:
But now is black beauty's successive heir,
And beauty slandered with a bastard shame,
For since each hand hath put on nature's power,
Fairing the foul with art's false borrowed face,
Sweet beauty hath no name no holy bower,
But is profaned, if not lives in disgrace.
Therefore my mistress' eyes are raven black,
Her eyes so suited, and they mourners seem,
At such who not born fair no beauty lack,
Slandering creation with a false esteem,
Yet so they mourn becoming of their woe,
That every tongue says beauty should look so.

128

How oft when thou, my music, music play'st,
Upon that blessèd wood whose motion sounds
With thy sweet fingers when thou gently sway'st
The wiry concord that mine ear confounds,
Do I envy those jacks that nimble leap,
To kiss the tender inward of thy hand,
Whilst my poor lips which should that harvest reap,
At the wood's boldness by thee blushing stand.
To be so tickled they would change their state
And situation with those dancing chips,
O'er whom thy fingers walk with gentle gait,
Making dead wood more blest than living lips,
Since saucy jacks so happy are in this,
Give them thy fingers, me thy lips to kiss.

129

Th' expense of spirit in a waste of shame
Is lust in action, and till action, lust
Is perjured, murd'rous, bloody full of blame,
Savage, extreme, rude, cruel, not to trust,
Enjoyed no sooner but despised straight,
Past reason hunted, and no sooner had
Past reason hated as a swallowed bait,
On purpose laid to make the taker mad.
Mad in pursuit and in possession so,
Had, having, and in quest, to have extreme,
A bliss in proof and proved, a very woe,
Before a joy proposed behind a dream.
  All this the world well knows yet none knows well,
  To shun the heaven that leads men to this hell.

130

My mistress' eyes are nothing like the sun,
Coral is far more red, than her lips red,
If snow be white, why then her breasts are dun:
If hairs be wires, black wires grow on her head:
I have seen roses damasked, red and white,
But no such roses see I in her cheeks,
And in some perfumes is there more delight,
Than in the breath that from my mistress reeks.
I love to hear her speak, yet well I know,
That music hath a far more pleasing sound:
I grant I never saw a goddess go,
My mistress when she walks treads on the ground.
  And yet by heaven I think my love as rare,
  As any she belied with false compare.

131

Thou art as tyrannous, so as thou art,
As those whose beauties proudly make them cruel;
For well thou know'st to my dear doting heart
Thou art the fairest and most precious jewel.
Yet in good faith some say that thee behold,
Thy face hath not the power to make love groan;
To say they err, I dare not be so bold,
Although I swear it to my self alone.
And to be sure that is not false I swear,
A thousand groans but thinking on thy face,
One on another's neck do witness bear
Thy black is fairest in my judgment's place.
  In nothing art thou black save in thy deeds,
  And thence this slander as I think proceeds.

132

Thine eyes I love, and they as pitying me,
Knowing thy heart torment me with disdain,
Have put on black, and loving mourners be,
Looking with pretty ruth upon my pain.
And truly not the morning sun of heaven
Better becomes the grey cheeks of the east,
Nor that full star that ushers in the even
Doth half that glory to the sober west
As those two mourning eyes become thy face:
O let it then as well beseem thy heart
To mourn for me since mourning doth thee grace,
And suit thy pity like in every part.
  Then will I swear beauty herself is black,
  And all they foul that thy complexion lack.

133

Beshrew that heart that makes my heart to groan
For that deep wound it gives my friend and me;
Is't not enough to torture me alone,
But slave to slavery my sweet'st friend must be?
Me from my self thy cruel eye hath taken,
And my next self thou harder hast engrossed,
Of him, my self, and thee I am forsaken,
A torment thrice three-fold thus to be crossed:
Prison my heart in thy steel bosom's ward,
But then my friend's heart let my poor heart bail,
Whoe'er keeps me, let my heart be his guard,
Thou canst not then use rigour in my gaol.
  And yet thou wilt, for I being pent in thee,
  Perforce am thine and all that is in me.

134

So now I have confessed that he is thine,
And I my self am mortgaged to thy will,
My self I'll forfeit, so that other mine,
Thou wilt restore to be my comfort still:
But thou wilt not, nor he will not be free,
For thou art covetous, and he is kind,
He learned but surety-like to write for me,
Under that bond that him as fast doth bind.
The statute of thy beauty thou wilt take,
Thou usurer that put'st forth all to use,
And sue a friend, came debtor for my sake,
So him I lose through my unkind abuse.
  Him have I lost, thou hast both him and me,
  He pays the whole, and yet am I not free.

135

Whoever hath her wish, thou hast thy will,
And 'Will' to boot, and 'Will' in over-plus,
More than enough am I that vex thee still,
To thy sweet will making addition thus.
Wilt thou whose will is large and spacious,
Not once vouchsafe to hide my will in thine?
Shall will in others seem right gracious,
And in my will no fair acceptance shine?
The sea all water, yet receives rain still,
And in abundance addeth to his store,
So thou being rich in will add to thy will
One will of mine to make thy large will more.
Let no unkind, no fair beseechers kill,
Think all but one, and me in that one 'Will.'

136

If thy soul check thee that I come so near,
Swear to thy blind soul that I was thy 'Will',
And will thy soul knows is admitted there,
Thus far for love, my love-suit sweet fulfil.
'Will', will fulfil the treasure of thy love,
Ay, fill it full with wills, and my will one,
In things of great receipt with ease we prove,
Among a number one is reckoned none.
Then in the number let me pass untold,
Though in thy store's account I one must be,
For nothing hold me, so it please thee hold,
That nothing me, a something sweet to thee.
Make but my name thy love, and love that still,
And then thou lov'st me for my name is Will.

137

Thou blind fool Love, what dost thou to mine eyes,
That they behold and see not what they see?
They know what beauty is, see where it lies,
Yet what the best is, take the worst to be.
If eyes corrupt by over-partial looks,
Be anchored in the bay where all men ride,
Why of eyes' falsehood hast thou forgéd hooks,
Whereto the judgment of my heart is tied?
Why should my heart think that a several plot,
Which my heart knows the wide world's common place?
Or mine eyes seeing this, say this is not
To put fair truth upon so foul a face?
  In things right true my heart and eyes have erred,
  And to this false plague are they now transferred.

138

When my love swears that she is made of truth,
I do believe her though I know she lies,
That she might think me some untutored youth,
Unlearnéd in the world's false subtleties.
Thus vainly thinking that she thinks me young,
Although she knows my days are past the best,
Simply I credit her false-speaking tongue,
On both sides thus is simple truth suppressed:
But wherefore says she not she is unjust?
And wherefore say not I that I am old?
O love's best habit is in seeming trust,
And age in love, loves not to have years told.
  Therefore I lie with her, and she with me,
  And in our faults by lies we flattered be.

139

O call not me to justify the wrong,
That thy unkindness lays upon my heart,
Wound me not with thine eye but with thy tongue,
Use power with power, and slay me not by art,
Tell me thou lov'st elsewhere; but in my sight,
Dear heart forbear to glance thine eye aside,
What need'st thou wound with cunning when
thy might
Is more than my o'erpressed defence can bide?
Let me excuse thee, ah my love well knows,
Her pretty looks have been mine enemies,
And therefore from my face she turns my foes,
That they elsewhere might dart their injuries:
Yet do not so, but since I am near slain,
Kill me outright with looks, and rid my pain.

140

Be wise as thou art cruel, do not press
My tongue-tied patience with too much disdain:
Lest sorrow lend me words and words express,
The manner of my pity-wanting pain.
If I might teach thee wit better it were,
Though not to love, yet love to tell me so,
As testy sick men when their deaths be near,
No news but health from their physicians know.
For if I should despair I should grow mad,
And in my madness might speak ill of thee,
Now this ill-wresting world is grown so bad,
Mad slanderers by mad ears believéd be.
That I may not be so, nor thou belied,
Bear thine eyes straight, though thy proud heart go wide.

141

In faith I do not love thee with mine eyes,
For they in thee a thousand errors note,
But 'tis my heart that loves what they despise,
Who in despite of view is pleased to dote.
Nor are mine ears with thy tongue's tune delighted,
Nor tender feeling to base touches prone,
Nor taste, nor smell, desire to be invited
To any sensual feast with thee alone:
But my five wits, nor my five senses can
Dissuade one foolish heart from serving thee,
Who leaves unswayed the likeness of a man,
Thy proud heart's slave and vassal wretch to be:
  Only my plague thus far I count my gain,
  That she that makes me sin, awards me pain.

142

Love is my sin, and thy dear virtue hate,
Hate of my sin, grounded on sinful loving,
O but with mine, compare thou thine own state,
And thou shalt find it merits not reproving,
Or if it do, not from those lips of thine,
That have profaned their scarlet ornaments,
And sealed false bonds of love as oft as mine,
Robbed others' beds' revenues of their rents.
Be it lawful I love thee as thou lov'st those,
Whom thine eyes woo as mine importune thee,
Root pity in thy heart that when it grows,
Thy pity may deserve to pitied be.
  If thou dost seek to have what thou dost hide,
  By self-example mayst thou be denied.

143

Lo as a careful huswife runs to catch,
One of her feathered creatures broke away,
Sets down her babe and makes all swift dispatch
In pursuit of the thing she would have stay:
Whilst her neglected child holds her in chase,
Cries to catch her whose busy care is bent,
To follow that which flies before her face:
Not prizing her poor infant's discontent;
So run'st thou after that which flies from thee,
Whilst I thy babe chase thee afar behind,
But if thou catch thy hope turn back to me:
And play the mother's part, kiss me, be kind.
So will I pray that thou mayst have thy Will,
If thou turn back and my loud crying still.

144

Two loves I have of comfort and despair,
Which like two spirits do suggest me still,
The better angel is a man right fair:
The worser spirit a woman coloured ill.
To win me soon to hell my female evil,
Tempteth my better angel from my side,
And would corrupt my saint to be a devil:
Wooing his purity with her foul pride.
And whether that my angel be turned fiend,
Suspect I may, yet not directly tell,
But being both from me both to each friend,
I guess one angel in another's hell.
Yet this shall I ne'er know but live in doubt,
Till my bad angel fire my good one out.

145

Those lips that Love's own hand did make,
Breathed forth the sound that said 'I hate',
To me that languished for her sake:
But when she saw my woeful state,
Straight in her heart did mercy come,
Chiding that tongue that ever sweet,
Was used in giving gentle doom:
And taught it thus anew to greet:
'I hate' she altered with an end,
That followed it as gentle day,
Doth follow night who like a fiend
From heaven to hell is flown away.
  'I hate', from hate away she threw,
  And saved my life saying 'not you'.

146

Poor soul the centre of my sinful earth,
My sinful earth these rebel powers array,
Why dost thou pine within and suffer dearth
Painting thy outward walls so costly gay?
Why so large cost having so short a lease,
Dost thou upon thy fading mansion spend?
Shall worms inheritors of this excess
Eat up thy charge? is this thy body's end?
Then soul live thou upon thy servant's loss,
And let that pine to aggravate thy store;
Buy terms divine in selling hours of dross;
Within be fed, without be rich no more,
  So shall thou feed on death, that feeds on men,
  And death once dead, there's no more dying then.

147

My love is as a fever longing still,
For that which longer nurseth the disease,
Feeding on that which doth preserve the ill,
Th' uncertain sickly appetite to please:
My reason the physician to my love,
Angry that his prescriptions are not kept
Hath left me, and I desperate now approve,
Desire is death, which physic did except.
Past cure I am, now reason is past care,
And frantic-mad with evermore unrest,
My thoughts and my discourse as mad men's are,
At random from the truth vainly expressed.
For I have sworn thee fair, and thought thee bright,
Who art as black as hell, as dark as night.

148

O me! what eyes hath love put in my head,
Which have no correspondence with true sight,
Or if they have, where is my judgment fled,
That censures falsely what they see aright?
If that be fair whereon my false eyes dote,
What means the world to say it is not so?
If it be not, then love doth well denote,
Love's eye is not so true as all men's: no,
How can it? O how can love's eye be true,
That is so vexed with watching and with tears?
No marvel then though I mistake my view,
The sun it self sees not, till heaven clears.
O cunning love, with tears thou keep'st me blind,
Lest eyes well-seeing thy foul faults should find.

149

Canst thou O cruel, say I love thee not,
When I against my self with thee partake?
Do I not think on thee when I forgot
Am of my self, all-tyrant, for thy sake?
Who hateth thee that I do call my friend,
On whom frown'st thou that I do fawn upon,
Nay if thou lour'st on me do I not spend
Revenge upon my self with present moan?
What merit do I in my self respect,
That is so proud thy service to despise,
When all my best doth worship thy defect,
Commanded by the motion of thine eyes?
  But love hate on for now I know thy mind,
  Those that can see thou lov'st, and I am blind.

150

O from what power hast thou this powerful might,
With insufficiency my heart to sway,
To make me give the lie to my true sight,
And swear that brightness doth not grace the day?
Whence hast thou this becoming of things ill,
That in the very refuse of thy deeds,
There is such strength and warrantise of skill,
That in my mind thy worst all best exceeds?
Who taught thee how to make me love thee more,
The more I hear and see just cause of hate?
O though I love what others do abhor,
With others thou shouldst not abhor my state.
  If thy unworthiness raised love in me,
  More worthy I to be beloved of thee.

151

Love is too young to know what conscience is,
Yet who knows not conscience is born of love?
Then gentle cheater urge not my amiss,
Lest guilty of my faults thy sweet self prove.
For thou betraying me, I do betray
My nobler part to my gross body's treason,
My soul doth tell my body that he may,
Triumph in love, flesh stays no farther reason,
But rising at thy name doth point out thee,
As his triumphant prize, proud of this pride,
He is contented thy poor drudge to be,
To stand in thy affairs, fall by thy side.
  No want of conscience hold it that I call,
  Her love, for whose dear love I rise and fall.

152

In loving thee thou know'st I am forsworn,
But thou art twice forsworn to me love swearing,
In act thy bed-vow broke and new faith torn,
In vowing new hate after new love bearing:
But why of two oaths' breach do I accuse thee,
When I break twenty? I am perjured most,
For all my vows are oaths but to misuse thee:
And all my honest faith in thee is lost.
For I have sworn deep oaths of thy deep kindness:
Oaths of thy love, thy truth, thy constancy,
And to enlighten thee gave eyes to blindness,
Or made them swear against the thing they see.
  For I have sworn thee fair: more perjured I,
  To swear against the truth so foul a lie.

153

Cupid laid by his brand and fell asleep,
A maid of Dian's this advantage found,
And his love-kindling fire did quickly steep
In a cold valley-fountain of that ground:
Which borrowed from this holy fire of Love,
A dateless lively heat still to endure,
And grew a seething bath which yet men prove,
Against strange maladies a sovereign cure:
But at my mistress' eye Love's brand new-fired,
The boy for trial needs would touch my breast,
I sick withal the help of bath desired,
And thither hied a sad distempered guest.
  But found no cure, the bath for my help lies,
  Where Cupid got new fire; my mistress' eyes.

154

The little Love-god lying once asleep,
Laid by his side his heart-inflaming brand,
Whilst many nymphs that vowed chaste life to keep,
Came tripping by, but in her maiden hand,
The fairest votary took up that fire,
Which many legions of true hearts had warmed,
And so the general of hot desire,
Was sleeping by a virgin hand disarmed.
This brand she quenchéd in a cool well by,
Which from Love's fire took heat perpetual,
Growing a bath and healthful remedy,
For men diseased, but I my mistress' thrall,
  Came there for cure and this by that I prove,
  Love's fire heats water, water cools not love.

NOTES

ABBREVIATIONS

(a) *Titles of Sh.'s plays, etc.*

Ado=*Much Ado about Nothing*; *All's*=*All's Well*; *Ant.*=*Antony and Cleopatra*; *A.Y.L.*=*As You Like It*; *Caes.*=*Julius Caesar*; *Cor.*=*Coriolanus*; *Cym.*=*Cymbeline*; *Err.*=*A Comedy of Errors*; *Gent.*=*Two Gentlemen of Verona*; *Ham.*=*Hamlet*; *1 H. IV*=*First Part of Henry IV*; *2 H. IV*=*Second Part of Henry IV*; *H. V*=*Henry V*; *1 H. VI*=*First Part of Henry VI*; *2 H. VI*=*Second Part of Henry VI*; *3 H. VI*=*Third Part of Henry VI*; *H. VIII*=*Henry VIII*; *K.J.*=*King John*; *L.C.*=*A Lover's Complaint*; *L.L.L.*=*Love's Labour's Lost*; *Lr.*=*King Lear*; *Lucr.*=*The Rape of Lucrece*; *Mac.*=*Macbeth*; *Meas.*=*Measure for Measure*; *M.N.D.*=*A Midsummer Night's Dream*; *M.V.*=*The Merchant of Venice*; *M.W.W.*=*The Merry Wives of Windsor*; *Oth.*=*Othello*; *Per.*=*Pericles*; *P.P.*=*The Passionate Pilgrim*; *R. II*=*Richard II*; *R. III*=*Richard III*; *Rom.*=*Romeo and Juliet*; *Shr.*=*The Taming of the Shrew*; *S.*=*The Sonnets*; *Tim.*=*Timon of Athens*; *Tit.*=*Titus Andronicus*; *Temp.*=*The Tempest*; *Troil.*=*Troilus and Cressida*; *Tw.Nt.*=*Twelfth Night*; *Ven.*=*Venus and Adonis*; *Wint.*=*The Winter's Tale*.

All references to the plays are to *New Cambridge Shakespeare*, its lineation, spellings and punctuation.

(b) *Technical terms*

adj.=adjective; adv.=adverb(ially); app.=apparently; ap.=apud; attrib.=attributive(ly); c., cent.=century; cf.=compare; comp.=compositor; conj.=conjecture; corr.=(1) corrupt(ion), (2) correction; e.g.=for example; edd.=editors, editions; Eliz.=Elizabethan; ellipt.=elliptical(ly); esp.=especially; exx.=examples; fig.=figuratively; ff.=following; Fr.=French; freq.= frequent(ly); i.e.=id est, that is; imp.=imperative; impers.=impersonal(ly); infin.=infinitive; interj.= interjection; int.=intransitive; It.=Italian; L=Latin; lit.=(1) literal(ly), (2) literature; mod.=modern; obj.=object; obs.=obsolete; orig.=origin(ally); p. pple=past participle; pass.=passive; perh.=perhaps; pl., plur.=plural; prep.=preposition; prob.=probably; Ps.=Psalms; Q=The 1609 quarto; Q (1640)= Benson's ed. (see Introd. p. xxii); q.v.=quod vide, which see; ref.=refer, reference, referring; Sh., Shn.= Shakespeare, Shakespearean; sb.=substantive; scil.= scilicet, that is to say; s.v.=sub voce, under the word; sing.=singular; sp.=spelling; trans.=(1) translation, (2) transitive; transf.=in a transferred sense; usu.= usually; vb., vbl.=verb, verbally; viz.=videlicet, namely. The sign † denotes emendation or suspected corruption in the text. Formulae like M†, Camb.†, in the Notes imply readings accepted by most editors since Malone, Camb., etc.

(*c*) *List of Principal Books and Articles consulted or referred to*

The following is a list, with abridged titles, of the books cited, consulted or alluded to in the Introduction and the Notes:

Abbott=*Sh. Grammar*, by E. A. Abbott, ed. 1870.

Acheson=*Sh. and the Rival Poet*, by A. Acheson, 1905.

Alden=*The Sonnets of Sh. from the Quarto of 1609*, ed. by R. M. Alden, 1916.

Anders=*Sh.'s Books*, by H.R.D. Anders, 1904.

Aubrey=*Brief Lives*, by John Aubrey, 1613, ed. by O. Lawson Dick, 1949.

B.=*The Sonnets of Sh.*, ed. by H. C. Beeching, 1904.
Barnes=*Parthenophil & Parthenophe*, by Barnabe Barnes, 1593.
Barnfield=*The Affectionate Shepherd*, by Richard Barnfield, 1574.
B.C.P.=The Book of Common Prayer.
Blunden=*The Mind's Eye*, by Edmund Blunden, 1934.
Boaden=*On the Sonnets of Sh. identifying the Person to whom they were addressed*, by James Boaden, 1837 [Pembrokeite].
Boswell='Boswell's Malone', i.e. *The Plays and Poems of William Sh.*, XXI vols., 1821 (vol. XX contains the Sonnets).
Bradley (1)=*Oxford Lectures on Poetry*, by A. C. Bradley, 1909.
Bradley (2)=*Shn Tragedy*, by A. C. Bradley, 1904.
Bray=*The Original Order of the Sonnets*, by Sir Denys Bray, 1925.
Brooke=*Sh.'s Sonnets*, ed. by Tucker Brooke, 1936.
Brown=*Sh.'s Autobiographical Poems being his sonnets clearly developed*, by C. Armitage Brown, 1838.
B.S.='The Order of Ss. 127–154', by Brents Stirling, in *Sh. 1564–1964*, ed. E. A. Bloom, 1964.
Bucknill=*The Medical Knowledge of Sh.*, by J. C. Bucknill, 1860.
Butler=*The Sonnets Reconsidered*, by Samuel Butler [in *Works*, vol. 14], 1899.
Buxton=*Elizabethan Taste*, by John Buxton, 1963.
Camb.=*The Cambridge Sh.*, ed. Aldis Wright (3rd ed. 1891–3). Refs. to Gildon and Sewell.
Cap.=Edward Capell's text of Sh., 1768.
Chambers (1)=*Shn Gleanings*, by E. K. Chambers, 1944—contains papers on: The order of the Sonnets; The youth of the Sonnets; The Mortal Moon.

Chambers (2) = *William Sh., a study of facts and problems*, by E. K. Chambers, 1930.
Chapman = *Poems*, by George Chapman, ed. by Phyllis Bartlett, 1941; *see also* Acheson.
Clar. = *The History of the Great Rebellion*, by the Earl of Clarendon, ed. by W. Dunn Macray, 1888.
Clemen = *Shakespeares Bilder*, by Wolfgang Clemen, 1936—cited from the revised English trans., *The Development of Sh.'s Imagery*: with a preface by J. Dover Wilson, 1951.
Coleridge = *Coleridge's Shn Criticism*, ed. by Raysor (q.v.), 1930.
Conrad = Hermann Conrad, as cited by Roll.
Constable = *Diana*, by Henry Constable, 1592.
Cruttwell = *The Shn Moment*, by P. Cruttwell, 1954.
D. = *The Sonnets of Sh.*, ed. by Edward Dowden, 1891.
Daniel = *Delia*, by Samuel Daniel, 1592.
Davies = *Microcosmos*, by John Davies of Hereford, 1600—as cited in Chambers, *Wm. Sh.* p. 213.
Davison = *Poetical Rhapsody*, by Francis Davison, 1602.
Drake = *Sh. and his Times*, by Nathan Drake, 1817. 2 vols. [Southamptonite].
Drayton = *Idea, the Shepherd's Garland*, by Michael Drayton, 1593, ed. in his *Works* by J. W. Hebel and Kathleen Tillotson, 1931–41.
E.D.D. = *English Dialect Dictionary.*
Ed. III = *The Reign of King Edward the Third*, 1596, cited from Tucker Brooke, *The Shn Apocrypha*, 1908.
Elton = *Modern Studies*, by Oliver Elton, 1907.
Empson = *Seven Types of Ambiguity*, by William Empson, 1931.
Fort = *The two dated Sonnets of Sh.*, by J. A. Fort, 1924.
F.Q. = *The Faerie Queene*, by Edmund Spenser.
Fripp = *Sh. Man and Artist*, by E. I. Fripp, 2 vols., 1938.

Gittings = *Sh.'s Rival*, by Robert Gittings, 1960.
Gold. = *The Metamorphoses of Ovid*, trans. by Arthur Golding, 1567, from the ed. by W. H. D. Rouse, 1904.
Granville-Barker = *A Companion to Sh. Studies*, by H. Granville-Barker and G. B. Harrison, 1934.
G.S., *see* Steev.
G.W., or W., *see* Wyndham.
Harbage = *Sir William Davenant*, by A. Harbage, 1935.
Harris = *The Man Sh. and his tragic Life Story*, by Frank Harris, 1909.
Harrison = *Sh. under Elizabeth*, by G. B. Harrison, 1933.
Herford = *Works of Sh.* (Eversley ed., vol. x), by C. H. Herford, 1899.
Hotson = *Sh.'s Sonnets Dated*, by Leslie Hotson, 1949.
Keller = trans. of the *Sonnets* in vol. xv of *Shakespeares Werke*, by Wolfgang Keller, 1916.
Ker = *Form and Style in Poetry*, by W. P. Ker, 1928.
Kinnear = *Cruces Shakespearianae*, by B. G. Kinnear, 1883 (cited from Roll.).
Kittredge = *An Address on Sh.*, by G. L. Kittredge, 1916.
Knights = *Sh.'s Sonnets*, by L. C. Knights, in *Scrutiny* 1934, III, pp. 133–60; reprinted in *Explorations*, 1946.
Krauss = Fritz Krauss (as cited by Roll.).
Landry = *Malone as Editor of Sh.'s Sonnets*, by Hilton Landry, in 'Bulletin of the New York Public Library', September 1963.
Lee = *Elizabethan Sonnets*, by Sidney Lee, 2 vols., 1904.
Elizabethan and other Essays, by Sidney Lee, ed. F. S. Boas, 1929.
Legouis = *Sh. et la Féodalité*, by Pierre Legouis, in *Filološki Pregled*, Belgrade, 1964.

Leish.=*Themes and Variations in Sh.'s Sonnets*, by J. Blair Leishman, 1961 [and private communications].

Lettsom, *see* W. S. Walker.

Lev.=*The Elizabethan Love-Sonnet*, by J. W. Lever, 1956.

Lodge=*Phillis*, by Thomas Lodge, 1593.

Lyly=*Works*, by John Lyly (ed. by R. W. Bond), 1902.

M.=Edmond Malone, text of Sh., 1790. (*See also* Landry and Boswell.)

Mackail=*The Approach to Sh.*, by J. W. Mackail, 1930.

McKerrow (1)=*A Dictionary of Printers and Booksellers in England, 1559–1640*, by R. B. McKerrow, 1910.

McKerrow (2)=*The Works of Thomas Nashe*, ed. by R. B. McKerrow, 1904.

Markham=Gervase Markham (see Introd. p. lxv).

Marlowe=*Poems of Christopher Marlowe*, ed. by L. C. Martin, 1931.

Mathew=*An Image of Sh.*, by Frank Mathew, 1922.

Mattingly='The Date of Sh.'s Sonnets', by Gerald Mattingly, in *P.M.L.A.* XLVIII (1933), 705–21.

Maxwell=J. C. Maxwell [private communications].

Minto=*Characteristics of English Poets*, by William Minto, 1874.

Muir=Article in Bloom, *Sh. 1564–1964* [also private communications].

Nashe, *see* McKerrow.

Naylor (1)=*Sh. and Music*, by E. W. Naylor, 1931.

Naylor (2)=*The Poets and Music*, by E. W. Naylor, 1928.

Nisbet=*The Onlie Begetter*, by Ulric Nisbet, 1936.

Noble (1)=*Sh.'s Biblical Knowledge*, by Richmond Noble, 1936.

Noble (2)=*Sh.'s Use of Song*, by Richmond Noble, 1923.

Noyes = 'The Origin of Sh.'s Sonnets', by Alfred Noyes, in *Bookman*, LXVII (1924), 159–62.

O.D.P. = *The Oxford Dictionary of Proverbs*, 1948 ed.

On. = *A Sh. Glossary*, by C. T. Onions, 1953 ed.

Ovid, *see* Rouse.

P.P. = *The Passionate Pilgrim.*

Prince (1) = 'The Sonnet from Wyatt to Sh.', by F. T. Prince, in *Elizabethan Poetry*, 1960.

Prince (2) = *Sh.: the Poems*, by F. T. Prince, 1963.

P. = *Sh.'s Sonnets*, ed. by C. K. Pooler (The Arden Sh.), 1918.

Raleigh = *Shakespeare*, by Sir Walter Raleigh, 1907.

Raysor = *Coleridge's Shn Criticism*, by T. M. Raysor, 2 vols., 1930.

Robertson = *The Problems of the Sh. Sonnets*, by J. M. Robertson, 1926.

Rolfe = *A Life of William Sh.* by W. J. Rolfe, 1904.

Roll. = *The Sonnets*, ed. by H. E. Rollins, 2 vols. A New Variorum Ed. of Sh., 1944.

Ronsard = *Œuvres Complètes*, by Pierre Ronsard, ed. H. Vaganay, 7 vols., 1923, 24.

Rouse = W.H.D. Rouse, *see* Golding.

Rylands = Introduction to Marlowe Society Record of the *Sonnets*, by G. H. W. Rylands, 1958.

Sch. = *Sh.-Lexicon*, by Alexander Schmidt, 1902.

Sh.'s Eng. = *Sh.'s England*, 2 vols., 1916.

Shaw = *The Dark Lady of the Sonnets*, by G. B. Shaw, 1914.

Sidney = *Complete Works*, of Sir Philip Sidney, ed. by A. Feuillerat, 4 vols., 1912–26, containing *Arcadia*, 1590, and *Astrophel and Stella.*

Simpson = *Shn Punctuation*, by Percy Simpson, 1911.

S.-Smith = *Sh.'s Sonnets*, by M. Seymour-Smith, 1963.

Spenser = *The Faerie Queene*, by Edmund Spenser, cited from 1909 ed.

Spurgeon = *Sh.'s Imagery*, by Caroline Spurgeon, 1935.
Staunton = *Sh.'s Plays*, vol. III, 1860.
Steev. = Notes by George Steevens to edd. of Sh. in 1773 and 1790 as found in the Variorum Malone of 1821.
Stirling = *Sonnets 127–154*, by Brents Stirling, in Bloom's *Sh. 1564–1964*.
Stopes = *Sh.'s Sonnets*, ed. by Charlotte C. Stopes, 1904.
Svensson = *William Sh., Sonnetter*, by K. A. Svensson, Lund, 1964.
Theob. = *The Works of Sh.*, ed. by Lewis Theobald, 1773.
Thomson = *Sh. and the Classics*, by J. A. K. Thomson, 1952.
Tilley = *A Dictionary of Proverbs in England in the sixteenth and seventeenth Centuries*, by M. P. Tilley, 1950.
Tuck. = *The Sonnets of Sh.*, ed. by T. G. Tucker, 1924.
Tottel = *Tottel's Micellany*, ed. H. Rollins, 2 vols., Harvard U.P., 1928.
T.T. = *Sh.'s Sonnets*, ed. by Thomas Tyler, 1890.
Ver. = *The Sonnets of Sh.*, ed. by A. W. Verity, in vol. 8 of the Henry Irving Sh., 1888–90.
Walker = *A Critical Examination of the Text of Sh.*, by W. S. Walker, ed. by W. N. Lettsom, 3 vols., 1860.
Watson = *The Hecatompathia, or Passionate Centurie of Love*, by Thomas Watson, 1582 (Arber's Reprints).
Wilde = *The Portrait of Mr W.H.*, by Oscar Wilde, 1889.
Wilson, F. P. = *Marlowe and the Early Sh.*, by F. P. Wilson, 1958.
W. = *The Poems of Sh.*, ed. by George Wyndham, 1898.
Yates = *A Study of L.L.L.*, by Frances A. Yates, 1936.

Section I: Sonnets 1–126

1–17: *The Marriage Sonnets*

General argument. The Poet implores a very handsome and evidently very distinguished young man to marry and beget heirs, that his beauty and grace be not lost to the world but carried on to succeeding generations. The Poet already knows, or knows of, the young man well enough to be sure that he was not only renowned for his beauty but took pride in the fact. Being therefore engaged (we cannot doubt by the family)* to prepare his mind for the idea of marriage and fatherhood, the Poet could confidently use this beauty as the basis of his argument. He is, he tells him, the handsomest youth of his time; he is 'the world's fresh ornament', which may suggest a recent arrival at court; the world will mourn him like a widow if he dies without passing on this beauty to a son. (One recalls the weeping crowds in February 1587 when Sir Philip Sidney was carried to his grave leaving no son to perpetuate his name.) He is the very image of his mother—who rejoices to see her young loveliness reproduced in him. Let him recapture her joy by seeing his beauty reproduced in turn. He is now in his golden time, at the pitch of his perfection, at the zenith of his glorious and lofty station in the eyes of an adoring world. But this cannot last, beauty must fade, old age cannot be avoided. The only way to defy decay, death, oblivion, is to live again in one's posterity. Not to do this is to act like the steward who buries the wealth lent for him to invest, and so has nothing to show when the audit comes. So you, the Poet tells him, by hoarding the gift Nature gave you, behave like an unthrifty miser, like an enemy to yourself.

Sources and parallels. The question of sources of the

* See Introd. p. xcix.

Sonnets as a whole has been dealt with in the final chapter of the Introduction. But this marriage section had a source peculiar to itself, as was originally pointed out by Massey,* namely a famous passage in the *Countess of Pembroke's Arcadia*, which Sir Philip Sidney wrote for his sister, the mother of William Herbert afterwards Lord Pembroke. In Book 3, Chapter 5 of *Arcadia*† the 'subtle Cecropia visits sad Philoclea' who had taken a solemn vow 'to lead a virgin's life' till the day of her death. Whereupon 'the shameless aunt' offers her modest niece a 'shrewd temptation to love and marriage', which consisted of a series of arguments virtually identical with those Shakespeare advances to the youth. Cf. 5. 9 note on 'Summer's distillation'.‡

In these opening sonnets, moreover, as often in his plays, Shakespeare did not hesitate to draw upon his own earlier writings. The same theme for example is treated in *Venus and Adonis*, ll. 163–74:

Torches were made to light, jewels to wear,
Dainties to taste, fresh beauty for the use,
Herbs for their smell, and sappy plants to bear;
Things growing to themselves are growth's abuse;
  Seeds spring from seeds and beauty breedeth beauty;
  Thou wast begot: to get it is thy duty.

Upon the earth's increase why should'st thou feed,
Unless the earth with thy increase be fed?
By law of nature, thou art bound to breed,
That thine may live when thou thyself art dead:
  And so, in spite of death, thou dost survive,
  In that thy likeness still is left alive.

* *Shakespeare's Sonnets never before interpreted*, by Gerald Massey, 1866.

† Pp. 379–81 of the 1590 text, ed. by Feuillerat (Cambridge English Classics).

‡ And see Erasmus's *De Conscribendis*, translated and made accessible in Wilson's *Arte of Rhetoricke*.

The thought, sometimes the very words, are the same. But how much more elaborate, more highly wrought, is the treatment in the *Sonnets*. It is arguable that the Poet has here taken up again and greatly developed subject-matter more simply and directly dealt with earlier, perhaps two or three years earlier. Closer I feel in style and diction to the *Sonnets* is the parallel from *Romeo and Juliet* (I. I. 216–19), also often quoted. See below p. 92.

The growth of intimacy in 1–17. Development is not only traceable from *Venus and Adonis* to the *Sonnets* but even within the first group itself. It is natural that sonnet 1 should be the most formal as it is artistically the most finished of the series, for it was important to arrest attention at the outset, and Shakespeare must have spent much time over it. Yet it does not mark the beginning of the friendship: Shakespeare is already addressing the lad as 'tender churl', and speaking of his 'sweet self', while in sonnet 3 he seems to know the family well enough to talk freely of the likeness between mother and son. But it is not until sonnet 10 that the friendship seems to begin ripening into love. He begs the youth even if he cannot love anyone else, to beget a son 'for love of me'. And if this is said casually, perhaps timidly, it is repeated in greater assurance in sonnet 13, where the young friend is addressed both as 'love' and as 'dear my love'.

A similar if hesitating advance is noticeable in the references to the Poet's verse. These do not begin until near the end of the series. In 12 he is still protesting that 'nothing 'gainst Time's scythe can make defence Save breed'. But in 15 he is himself making war on Time 'for love of' his friend, by engrafting anew in the verse that celebrates it, the beauty Time is robbing him of. In 16, however, 'breed' is still a mightier, more blessed means than the Poet's 'barren rhyme' for the friend to fortify himself with in his decay. And in 17 the two seem to claim an equal place; no one will believe my verse when you are dead, says the Poet, unless you leave a son behind to prove the verse is true.

And then comes sonnet 18; and there is no talk of marriage in it, or for ever afterwards; and how great is the contrast between the earlier 'sugréd sonnets', highly wrought, closely packed, deeply meditated, and this inspired, impassioned, simply phrased verse, which has all the inevitability of his best dramatic style. And the reason for the difference is obvious: while 1–17 are lovely exercises on a single theme, this sonnet is dramatic, lyrical-dramatic, a spontaneous cry from the heart. Compare a similar contrast between the expression of Romeo's artificial calf-love for Rosaline and that of his real passion for Juliet.

Benvolio. Then she hath sworn that she will still live chaste?
Romeo. She hath, and in that sparing makes huge waste:
For beauty, starved with her severity,
Cuts beauty off from all posterity. (1. 1. 216–19)

Romeo. But soft! What light through yonder window breaks?
It is the east, and Juliet is the sun.
Arise, fair sun, and kill the envious moon,
Who is already sick and pale with grief
That thou, her maid, art far more fair than she.
Be not her maid, since she is envious.
Her vestal livery is but sick and green,
And none but fools do scorn it: cast it off.
It is my lady, O it is my love;
O that she knew she were! (2. 2. 1–10)

* * * * *

I

The young man's duty to Nature and Society at large: gardeners cultivate to produce the finest flowers and fruits, cattle-breeders to develop the finest stocks; if you, loveliest of men, neglect to do likewise, you will rob the world of its due by wasting your own rich substance.

1. *creatures* products of the creation, viz. all forms of life. *increase* crops, fruit, progeny—the usual sense in Shakespeare. Cf. 97. 6 'the teeming autumn, big with rich increase', and Ps. 67. 6 'Then shall the earth yield her increase'.

2. *That...die* That beauty may continue to blossom for ever. *beauty's rose* Q 'beauties *Rose*'. Cf. *O.E.D.* 'rose' 5 (*transf.*), 'A peerless or matchless person; a paragon; esp. a woman of great beauty, excellence, or virtue', and *Ham.* 3. 1. 155 'Th'expectancy and rose of the fair state'.

3. *as the...decease* as the ripening 'creature' must perish in course of time. Cf. *Mac.* 5. 5. 17 'she should have died hereafter'.

4. *His*=its. *tender* Cf. *R. III*, 5. 3. 95 'thy brother, tender George' and the mod. idiom 'at the tender age of'. *bear* carry on. *memory* memorial, Cf. B.C.P. 'in perpetual memory of that his precious death'.

5. *contracted* betrothed, wedded. Cf. S. 56. 10. 'A reference to the fable of Narcissus who fell in love with his own reflection' (B.). Alden suggests 'limited', i.e. not able to see beyond the limit of your eyesight.

6. *Feed'st...fuel* 'You feed your sight on the sight of yourself' (W.) The same image is elaborated in 73. 9–12. Here 'the life of one who dies unmarried is likened to a fire that is allowed to burn itself out' (Fort *ap.* Roll.).

thy light's flame the 'bright eyes' are imaged as consuming, like a fire, what they have in view. *self-substantial* i.e. supplied by your own personal interests and desires. The hyphen is Malone's.

9. *the world's*='society's' or 'the time's'. *ornament* Surely an apt compliment for a budding young courtier.

10. *only...spring* 'the first bright flower of a new spring' (B.) i.e. leader of those who salute the dawn of a new age. *herald*=harbinger, proclaimer. Cf. *Rom.* 3. 5. 6 'the lark, the herald of the morn'. Does this imply a consciousness on Shakespeare's part that a new age was dawning in the nineties? Cf. the reference to 'this growing age' at 32. 10. But in B.'s view 'The idea seems to be that W.H. might if he pleased enrich the world with a more beautiful race of mortals'. *gaudy*= gay, festive. Not pejorative.

11. *content* satisfaction with thy bachelor existence. To 'bury one's content in oneself' is to have 'no desires outside' (B.).

12. *tender churl* dear young miser (cf. 'tender' l. 4). *mak'st...niggarding* An oxymoron i.e. you waste your capital by hoarding it. Cf. *Rom.* 1. 1. 217 cited above p. 92.

13–14. *Pity...thee* 'The rhyme in this couplet occurs in Ss. 3 and 4.' (Ver.).

14. *by the grave and thee* 'i.e. not only by allowing the *grave* ultimately to devour it, but also by thus devouring it yourself' (T.).

2

What will happen when you grow old and have no child to perpetuate your grace and beauty?

1. *forty* 'Used indefinitely to express a large number' (On.). Shakespeare himself was about thirty when he wrote this.

1–2. *besiege...field* Metaphor from siege warfare. *trenches* Cf. *Tit.* 5. 2. 23 'those trenches made by grief and care' and 19. 9.

3. *proud* magnificent, gorgeous. *youth's...livery* Cf. *Ham.* 4. 7. 78, 'the light and careless livery that it [youth] wears'.

4. *tattered weed* ragged garment; 'tott'red' (Q) is the form always found in Sh. Cf. Q. 26. 11.

6. *lusty* 'full of animal life and spirit' (Sch.). Cf. 5. 7 'lusty leaves'=leaves full of sap.

8. *were...praise.* 'Such gluttony would be a shame, and self-praise could not profit' (B.). *thriftless praise* Cf. 'thriftless sighs' *Tw. Nt.* 2. 2. 39 (Ver.).

9. *thy beauty's use* i.e. if you had put your beauty out to interest, by investing it in a son.

10–11. M.'s quotation-marks.

11. *Shall sum...excuse* Commercial language. The beauty of this child of mine will stand for the whole treasure of the beauty once committed to me, and serve as an excuse for the loss of beauty in old age. Cf. *2 H. IV*, 1. 1. 166–7.

3

Just as your mother when looking at you can see herself as she was in the fresh beauty of her girlhood, so you, when womanlike you look in the glass to see how to keep your face in repair, will realize that the only way to do so is to hand on that face to your child, as your mother handed her lovely one to you—and what woman would refuse to become the mother of such a child or indeed what other man would so defeat his own interest as to deny posterity to himself? Die single, your loveliness dies with you and you choose to be forgotten.

1. *glass* 'There are two kinds of mirrors—first that

of glass; secondly, a *child* who reflects his parent's beauty' (D.).

3. *fresh repair* the 'fresh bloom' of his complexion.

4. *unbless some mother* deprive some woman of her joy of motherhood.

5–6. *uneared...tillage...husbandry* 'uneared'=un-tilled. 'husbandry' has its double sense. Cf. *Ant.* 2. 2. 228 'He ploughed her and she cropped'; Ded. to *Ven.* 'Never after ear so barren a land'.

7. *fond* foolish.

7–8. *the tomb...posterity* Cf. 1. 13–14. Ver. cites *Ven.* 757–60.

8. *self-love* M.'s hyphen.

9–10. *Thou...her prime* W.H.'s mother was evidently beautiful, and he was very like her. S. 20 stresses his feminine type of beauty, while 'Calls...the lovely April of her prime' implies boyhood in the son. Cf. 'tender churl' 1. 12. *thy mother's glass...her prime* Ver. cites *Lucr.* 1758–64:

> Poor broken glass, I often did behold
> In thy sweet semblance my old age newborn, etc.

11–12. *So thou...golden time* M. cites *Lover's Complaint*, ll. 12–14:

> Time had not scythéd all that youth began
> Nor youth all quit; but spite of heaven's fell rage
> Some beauty peeped through lattice of seared age.

12. *golden time* Also prob. implies boyhood; cf. *Cym.* 4. 2. 262 'Golden lads and girls'.

14. *image* Q 'Image'.

4

'In S. 3 Shakespeare had viewed his friend as an inheritor of beauty from his mother; this legacy of beauty is now regarded as the bequest of nature. The idea of "unthriftiness" (l. 1), and "niggardness" (l. 12) is another form of the "sum my count" of 2. 11. The new idea introduced in this sonnet is that of usury, which reappears in 6. 5–6' (D.).

Steev. notes that Milton imitates this sonnet in *Comus* 679–84; and, closer, cf. ll. 739–42:

> Beauty is Nature's coin; must not be hoarded,
> But must be current; and the good thereof
> Consists in mutual and partaken bliss,
> Unsavoury in the enjoyment of itself.

3. *Nature's bequest gives nothing but doth lend* Ver. cites Lucretius, 'Vitaque mancipio nulli datur' and *Meas.* 1. 1. 29–31:

> Thyself and thy belongings
> Are not thine own so proper as to waste, etc.

and D. cites the rest of the passage

> spirits are not finely touched
> But to fine issues: nor Nature never lends
> The smallest scruple of her excellence,
> But, like a thrifty goddess, she determines
> Herself the glory of a creditor,
> Both thanks and use.

4. *free* frank, liberal.
8. *live* = make a living.
9. *For having...alone* 'A usurer who lent money only to himself could not live on the proceeds of his trade' (B.).
10. *deceive* defraud, cheat.
12. *audit* Q 'Audit'. A statement of account rendered by a steward or factor to the owner of the property. Had Shakespeare in mind the parable of the Unjust Steward, who buried the talent in a napkin? Matt. xxv. 14. Cf. l. 13 'Thy unused beauty... tombed'.

14. *which...lives* i.e. as your child. *executor* In the testamentary sense of one who carries out the terms of a will or bequest by assigning the property to the heirs of a deceased.

5 and 6

In this pair of sonnets youth and age are compared with the seasons of the year, and the argument runs: In time your beauty must fade as that of summer must be destroyed by the oncoming of winter. Yet as the scents of summer can be enjoyed in winter when its flowers have been distilled and preserved in a phial, so your beauty can be distilled and preserved in the children you beget. The reference to 'use' (interest) in ll. 4–6 S. 6 links it with 4, while the imagery of summer and winter naturally leads on to the imagery of morning and evening in 7.

5

1. *hours* Q 'howers'—so pronounced. *gentle work* delicate workmanship. Cf. *Ham.* 2. 2. 307 'What a piece of work is a man'. *frame* Q 'frame,'.

2. *gaze* (Sb.) 'that which is gazed or stared at' (*O.E.D.*). Cf. *Mac.* 5. 8. 24 'the show and gaze o'th' time', and above 2. 3.

4. *that unfair* make that unfair; for 'unfair' (vb.) cf. 'unbless' in 3. 4. *fairly* 'in beauty' (On.).

5–8. *For never-resting time...everywhere* Leish. (p. 34) finds here a possible echo of Horace *Ode* IV. 7, 'Diffugere nives'.

never-resting M.'s hyphen.

6. *confounds* destroys.

7. *lusty* full of sap. Cf. 2. 6 'lusty days'. *gone,* (M.) Q 'gon'.

8. *bareness everywhere* Cf. 73. 4 'Bare ruined

choirs', and 97. 4 'December's bareness everywhere'. *everywhere* (M.) Q 'every where,'.

9. *summer's distillation* e.g. rose water. Cf. S. 54 as a whole. B. notes 'This is a thought with which Sh. seems to have been much pleased'; and M. cites *M.N.D.* 1. 1. 76 'the rose distilled'. B. suggests that Sh. took the image from *Arcadia* (1590), III, 5 (Feuillerat ed., 1. 380) though Sidney applies it differently. 'Have you ever seen a pure Rose-water kept in a chrystall glass; how fine it looks, how sweet it smells, while that beautiful glasse imprisons it?' Sh.'s 'liquid prisoner' suggests an echo of Sidney's 'imprison' though the latter is speaking of the 'restraint of crystalline marriage'. For Sh.'s keen sense of smell see Spurgeon's *Sh.'s Imagery*, pp. 78 ff. He seems to have been particularly sensitive to personal smells, often bad smells (e.g. 'stinking breath', *Caes.* 1. 2. 247) but sometimes delicious ones (e.g. *Oth.* 4. 2. 68–70);

O, thou weed,
Who art so lovely fair and smell'st so sweet
That the sense aches at thee.

Is 'buds of marjoram' (99. 7) a reference to the scent of the blossom? Cf. *Lr.* 4. 6. 93 'sweet marjoram'.

11. *Beauty's...bereft* Both beauty and the product or fruit of beauty would be destroyed. Cf. On. 'bereave 2. to rob of its strength or beauty'.

12. *Nor it...was* 'Neither it nor any resemblance of what it was remaining' (Ver.).

14. *Leese* lose. *show...substance* A common antithesis with Sh. and other sixteenth-century writers.

6

The argument was not completed in 5, so 6 begins with 'Then'.

1. *ragged* (Gild. & edd.) Q 'wragged'; Cap. MS 'rugged'. Cf. *R. III*, 4. 1. 102 (of the Tower of London) 'Rude, ragged nurse'. Sh. seems to use 'ragged' and 'rugged' indifferently with the same meaning. *O.E.D.* notes under 'rugged' that 'the precise relationship to "ragged" is not quite clear, but the stem is no doubt ultimately the same'.

3–4. *treasure...treasure* The duplication suggests corruption, the comp. catching the word from the next line. P. cites *Cor.* 3. 3. 115 'treasure of my loins' (of a son) which supports 'beauty's treasure'. For 'treasure' as trans. vb. *O.E.D.* cites only this and another (doubtful) instance. A trochee meaning 'enrich' or 'endow' is needed. Lowell suggested 'pleasure'.

4. *self-killed* M.'s hyphen.

5. *use* 'interest paid for borrowed money' (Sch.). *forbidden usury* Usury, condemned in scripture and forbidden by the Church, was reluctantly legalized by the Act of 1571 which allowed interest up to 10% (see *Sh.'s Eng.* 1, 332). A second Act, 1597, admitted usury to be necessary and profitable. But the contemptuous attitude of Antonio towards 'interest' in *M.V.* (1. 3. 72 ff.) suggests what the gentry thought about it.

7. *to breed* 'Breed' (sb.) was often used in the sense of 'interest'. Cf. *M.V.* 1. 3. 131. So Middleton's *Black Book*: 'Coming to repay both the money and the breed of it' (Ver.).

8. *be it ten for one* Prob. alludes to 'ten per cent' interest allowed.

10. *thee* (M.) Q 'thee,'.

7

The transience of youth's beauty is now compared with the daily passage through the heavens of the sun. The sonnet develops the popular adage (Tilley, S 979) 'The rising not the setting sun is worshipped by most men'. From Erasmus *Adagia* 'Plures adorant solem orientem, quam occidentem'. See Introd. to S. 59.

1. *light* (M.) Q 'light,'.

2–4. *each under eye...Serving* Cf. *Wint.* 4. 2. 35 'I have eyes under my service' (D.).

3. *his...sight* i.e. at the appearance of dawn. *new-appearing* M.'s hyphen.

4. *Serving with looks...majesty* Perh. alluding to the practice of courtiers to keep facing a monarch while in his presence or of the similar practice of priests before the altar.

5. *the steep-up...hill* Cf. *P.P.* ix. 5 'upon a steep-up hill' [M.], and *Oth.* 5. 2. 283 'steep-down gulfs'. M.'s hyphen.

6. *Resembling strong youth* M. cites Ps. xix. 5, but that speaks of a bridegroom not a youth. But cf. *3 H. VI*, 2. 1. 21 ff. which develops the image:

> See now the morning opes her golden gates
> And takes her farewell of the glorious sun!
> How well resembles it the prime of youth,
> Trimmed like a younker prancing to his love!

clearly l. 23 here and 7. 6 are closely connected.

9. *pitch* Falconry term; cf. *2 H. VI*, 2. 1. 5 f. *weary car* Cf. *Err.* 1.2.7 'ere the weary sun set in the west', and *Ven.* 529.

10. *reeleth from the day* D. cites *Rom.* 2. 3. 3–4:

> And darkness fleckéd like a drunkard reels
> From forth day's pathway, made by Titan's wheels.

11. *fore* Old form of 'before' and needs no apostrophe.

13. *thy self out-going...noon* 'passing beyond thy meridian beauty, and so declining' (B.).

14. *get a son* Quibble on 'sun'. Cf. *L.L.L.* 4. 3. 366; *Tit.* 5. 3. 18.

8

If interpreted literally the first four lines of this sonnet give us interesting news about W.H.: (1) that he was not only beautiful to look at but endowed with a lovely voice; (2) that he loved music but, like Jessica (*Mer.* 5. 1. 70), was 'never merry when he heard sweet music'.

1. *Music to hear* Vocative. Ver. cites S. 128:

> How oft when thou, my music, music play'st.

sadly? (M.) Q 'sadly,'.

3–4. B. paraphrases: 'If you listen to music sadly, it must mean that you receive not gladly what you love, or that you tolerate what annoys you.'

5–6. *the true...married* It must be recollected that Sh. speaks of polyphonic music. *unions* combinations (*O.E.D.* 7). George Herbert employs the same image in his 'Easter':

> Consort both heart and lute and twist a song
> Pleasant and long:
> Or, since all music is but three parts vied
> And multiplied,
> O let thy blessed spirit bear a part
> And make up our defects with thy sweet art.

well-tuned M.'s hyphen.

7. *confounds* Shn. 2nd pers. sing.

10. *Strikes each in each* 'in' = on.

14. *Thou single wilt prove none.* 'One is no number' was a prov. saying. Cf. Marlowe, *Hero & Leander*, l. 255,

> One is no number; maids are nothing then,
> Without the sweet society of men.

see also S. 136. 8 and Tilley O 54.

thee, '*Thou...none*' (M.) Q 'thee thou...none'.

9

If you excuse your remaining single, because you wish to spare a widow her tears, remember that at your death you will make the whole world a widow, one for ever lamenting that you left no child behind (see above, p. 89), when any individual widow has her husband's likeness alive in the children he gave her. When too an ordinary man wastes his wealth it goes into another man's pocket; but if you waste yourself the world's loss is absolute.

3. *Ah*, Q 'Ah;'.

4. *makeless* without a mate.

5. *still* for ever.

8. *By children's eyes* in the very eyes of her children.

10. *Shifts but his place* i.e. from one man's pocket to another's. *it*; (M.) Q 'it'.

11–12. *But beauty's waste...destroys it.* Ver. cites Marlowe, *Hero & Leander*, l. 328: 'Beauty alone is lost, too warily kept.'

14. *murd'rous shame* = shameful murder.

10

In this sonnet the Poet speaks for the first time in his own person, begging W.H. to beget a child 'for love of me'. It also gives us another glimpse of W.H. himself in the petition:

> Be as thy presence is gracious and kind.

Furthermore the whole sonnet is an acknowledgement of the fact that W.H. is determined not to marry,

> But that thou none lov'st is most evident,

and even that he hated women, although it is also evident that many women love him. D. best brings out the general sense: 'The "murderous shame" of 9. 14 reappears in the "For shame" and "murderous hate" of 10.'

1–2. *For,..unprovident* i.e. in being so reckless of yourself you prove that you have no love for anyone in the world. *unprovident.* (M.) Q 'vnprouident'.

5. *murd'rous hate* scil. against yourself.

7–8. *Seeking...desire* D. argues that 'ruinate' implies that the father of the Friend is dead. But 'The "beauteous roof" called in 13. 9 "so fair a house" is the person of his friend' (B.). To the Elizabethans the 'body' was the dwelling-place of the spirit.

8. *repair* i.e. keep in repair. Cf. 3. 3.

9. *thought* i.e. his 'resolution not to marry' (Ver.). *my mind* 'my opinion of thy character' (Lee).

11. *thy presence...gracious and kind* Reveals the Friend's attitude towards Sh., the attitude surely of one higher in rank.

12. *kind-hearted* M.'s hyphen.

13. *for love of me* If you will not do so for the love

of any woman or for love of yourself, beget a son for my sake. Sh. can now confidently appeal to the boy's love for him. The marriage theme is weakening.

II

D. notes: The first five lines 'enlarge on the thought (10. 14) of beauty living "in thine"; showing how the beauty of a child may be called "thine"'.

2. *that...departest* 'a slip of thee' (B.). *departest* 'separatest off'. 'Used actively as in the old form of the marriage vow, "till death us depart"' (B.). Cf. On. 3 '"depart with", part with, give up, *L.L.L.* 2. 1. 144; *K.J.* 2. 1. 563'. Refers, not to 'the period of youth you leave behind' (G.W.), but to the 'fresh blood' the Friend must gradually surrender as age and 'cold decay' advance but bestows upon the child he begets 'youngly', i.e. in the prime of life; cf. *Cor.* 2. 3. 235.

4. *convertest* changest. But cf. 14. 12.

7–8. *If all...away* Cf. *Ven.* ll. 11–12.

7. *so*=like the latter. *the times* Cf. *Ham.* 3. 1. 70 'the whips and scorns of time'. Thus in plur. 'the times'='the generations of men' (D.).

8. *year* often plur. in Sh. *make...away* destroy. Cf. *2 H. VI*, 3. 1. 167; *Ven.* 763 (On.).

9. *those...made for store* i.e. those 'fairest creatures' from which 'we desire increase' (see 1. 1). To 'keep for store'=to reserve young animals for breeding (see *O.E.D.* 'store' 8, 13*c*.).

10. *perish:* (M., etc.) Q has comma.

11. *Look whom*=whomsoever. See *O.E.D.* 'look' 4*b*. Cf. 37. 13. *thee more* (M., etc.) Q 'the more'. Camb.+D. follow Q but do not understand the idiomatic 'look whom' which makes 'thee' certain. The

whole line='To whomsoever Nature gave her best she gave thee more'.

12. *in bounty* 'By being bountiful, i.e. prolific' (P.). *cherish:* (M.) Q has comma.

13. *seal* i.e. that which authenticates a document or article as genuine or unique when it leaves its stamp upon it. Cf. The Great Seal.

14. *not* (Q) Misprinted 'nor' in the eighteenth century and often still. *copy*=original from which an impression should be taken. *that copy* must=the *original* seal, otherwise 'die' would be pointless, and the ref. to *Tw. Nt.* 1. 5. 247 (where it=transcript), often made, is therefore irrelevant.

12

'This sonnet seems to be a gathering into one of 5, 6 and 7' (D.). Time brings all loveliness and strength to an end: the light of day, the tender beauty of the flower, the majestic beauty of the tree, the splendour of summer. How can your beauty escape? By breed and breed alone.

With this colour group (violet, sable, silver, white, green) cf. those in Ss. 73 and 99, and see Spurgeon pp. 68–9.

The theme of devouring time and the transience of beauty is here introduced for the first time. But see S. 19 and Introd. p. cix.

1. *count the clock...the time* i.e. mark the passage of the hours.

2. *brave day* radiant day. *hideous* Cf. 'hideous winter' 5. 6.

3. *the violet past prime* D. cites *Ham.* 1. 3. 7 'A violet in the youth of primy nature'. But 'past prime' here, as the context shows, ='faded', not 'after springtime'.

4. *all silvered o'er* (M.) Q 'or siluer'd ore'. Ver. conj. 'o'er-silvered all'. For *sable curls...silvered* cf. *Ham.* 1. 2. 242 'His beard was...a sable silvered'.

5–8. *When lofty trees...bristly beard* Lines quoted by Keats, in a letter to Reynolds of 22 November, 1817. And C. L. Finney cites from the *Grecian Urn*:

> Fair youth, beneath the trees, thou canst not leave
> Thy song, nor ever can those trees be bare

as prob. echoing Sh.'s lines. (Roll.).

7–8. *summer's green...beard* Cf. *M.N.D.* 2. 1. 94 f. 'the green corn | Hath rotted ere his youth attained a beard' [Cap. cited M. 1821]. 'Harvest-home is transmuted into a funeral and the waggon laden with ripened corn becomes a bier bearing the aged dead' (T.T.). Rollins cites a description of a harvest home procession in the streets of Windsor described by Paul Hentzner in 1598 (see W. B. Rye, *England as seen by foreigners*, 1865, p. 111, *ap.* Roll.).

7. *girded up* Rollins cites 'tied firmly or confined' from *O.E.D.* 'gird' vb. 8. But the meaning is more personal, viz. = 'with a girdle about his waist', since the image is that of an old man being carried to his grave.

8. *bristly beard* suggests barley.

9. *do I question make* 'the phrase now survives only in the negative' (B.).

10. *the wastes of time* Cf. S. 30. 4 'my dear time's waste'. On. glosses 'things devastated by Time'.

11. *themselves forsake* 'depart from what they were' (T.) or 'change for the worse' (P.).

14. *brave* defy.

13

This seems to mark a distinct increase in intimacy, it being the first time W.H. is addressed as 'love' (l. 1), later emphasized as 'dear my love' (l. 13). It is also the first time he is addressed as 'you' and not 'thou', perhaps because it was then felt to be less formal. But such deductions are dangerous in view of the apparently haphazard use of these pronouns elsewhere in the sonnets. Dowden notes: 'In the first fifty sonnets, *you* is of extremely rare occurrence; in the second fifty *you* and *thou* alternate in little groups of sonnets, *thou* having still a preponderance, but now only a slight preponderance; in the remaining twenty-six [of the first Section] *you* becomes the ordinary mode of address and *thou* the exception. In the sonnets to a mistress, *thou* is invariably employed.' (P. xlvi.)

1. *O that you were yourself* This deliberately arresting opening is expanded and so explained in ll. 6–8.

5–6. *lease...determination* Ver. notes: '*Lease* implies a short time' and cites Ld. Campbell: *Sh.'s Legal Acquirements*, p. 101, 'the word "*determination*" is always used by lawyers instead of "end"'.

7. *your self's* (edd.) Q 'you selfe'.

9. *so fair a house* Repeats 10. 7–8 (see note *ad loc.*).

10. *husbandry* (*a*) good management of the estate; (*b*) marriage.

14. *You had a father* Meaning disputed by adherents of the rival candidates for identity of W.H. D. (*pro* Southampton) cites *All's Well* 1. 1. 18 '[She] had a father—O, that "had", how sad a passage 'tis', and deduces 'The father of Sh's friend was probably dead'; and P. agrees. T.T., G.W., T., B. (*pro* Herbert) citing *M.W.W.* 3. 4. 36, 'thou hadst a father,' interpret 'Your father begot you; go and do likewise'. Rollins, supporting neither candidate himself, can find no reason why l. 14 should mean literally that the boy's father was dead. See 10. 7–8.

14

The only astrological knowledge or prognostication the Poet can command is that which he derives from those fixed stars, his Friend's eyes. And from them he learns that Truth and Beauty live with him and must perish from the world if he leaves no child to carry them on.

2. *astronomy* No distinction between this and astrology in Sh.'s day, the latter being dependent on the Ptolemaic system, still the accepted theory of the universe. But Sh.'s line has been misinterpreted. It need not mean that he believes in astrology. On the contrary, he goes on to disclaim such a belief by giving a list of all the stock matters on which the astrologers prognosticate and he does not. Yet he *has* astrology and can prognosticate by gazing at those fixed stars, the young man's eyes. Cf. Berowne's astrology 'first learned in a lady's eye' (*L.L.L.* 4. 3. 324.). It is doubtful whether Sh. believed in astrology at all (cf. *Caes.* 1. 2. 140 and note). D. and others find Sh.'s source here in Sidney's sonnet 26 (*Astrophel and Stella*, 1598):

> Though dusty wits do scorn astrology
> . . . .
> proof makes me sure,
> Who oft fore-judge my after following case
> By only those two stars in Stella's face

Sh's 'oft predict' seems to echo Sidney's 'oft fore-judge'. But Sidney's argument seems to run the other way to Sh.'s.

6. *Pointing* appointing. *to each* to each minute.

8. *oft predict*=constant or frequent prognostication. Every crowned head in Europe entertained a busy astrologer at this date.

9. *But from thine eyes* see *L.L.L.* quoted in note 2.

10–11. *read such art As* gather the following knowledge. *art*=knowledge or science; generally= 'knowledge' acquired by magic or astrology.

12. *If...convert* If by begetting a son you perpetuate your stock of fresh blood—lit. exchange your individual self for precious stock; cf. 11. 4. *convert*=turn. 'In Daniel, *Delia*, son. 11, "convert" rhymes with "heart"' (D.).

14. *Thy end...doom* Cf. *Ven.* 1019:

> For he being dead, with him is beauty slain.

15, 16 and 17

These three sonnets form a trio on the subject of Time and Beauty, number 16 beginning 'But' following directly upon 15 in which the subject of the Poet's verses is introduced for the first time. 17 is intended as the conclusion of the series. For the number 17 see Introd. p. c.

15

2. *Holds in perfection*=Retains its full perfection.

3–4. *this huge stage...comment* Cf. 'All the world's a stage' (*A.Y.L.* 2. 7. 139) and 'This great stage of fools' (*Lr.* 4. 6. 182)—a constant thought with Sh.; upon which, as he says in *Meas.* 2. 2. 122–3, we men like a pack of quarrelsome apes

> Play such fantastic tricks before high heaven
> As make the angels weep.

To grasp the full meaning of this vision of the world, the earth must be thought of as the centre of the Ptolemaic universe, the events and doings upon which are at once subject to the influence, for good or ill, of the stars above it, and to the comments of the angelic beings who inhabit these stars. Cf. *M.V.* 5. 1. 61:

> There's not the smallest orb that thou behold'st
> But in his motion like an angel sings,
> Still choiring to the young-eyed cherubins.

And for the 'comments' of the cherubs, so 'young-eyed' (=keen-sighted) that they see into the bottom of men's souls, cf. Hamlet's retort to Claudius at 4. 3. 47: 'I see a cherub that sees them.'

3. *stage* (Q) M.+ read 'state'. 'But the word "present" like "show" is theatrical and confirms the text of the Q' (D.). *presenteth* represents. *shows* (*a*) i.e. theatrical displays; (*b*) shadows, illusions.

For later stage imagery or possible allusions to the stage see 23, 25, 29, 36, 37, 39, 110, 111, 112.

4. *influence* 'The supposed flowing or streaming from the stars or heavens of an ethereal fluid acting upon the character and destinies of men, and affecting sublunary things generally' (*O.E.D.*).

6. *Cheered and checked* encouraged and disapproved of.

7. *Vaunt* exult. *youthful sap* the vigour of youth. 'sap' has a wide reference in Sh.; almost=the mod. 'spunk'. *at height decrease* Cf. *Caes.* 4. 3. 215 'We, at the height, are ready to decline'.

8. *wear...state* The image is that of clothes, as is shown by 'wear' (=wear out) and 'brave' which On. glosses 'finely arrayed'. *out of memory* i.e. until their tattered bravery has passed from memory.

9. *the conceit* the thought, the recognition. *inconstant stay* Lit.=unstable duration (of things in general). This is an Ovidian sonnet; see introd. to sonnet 59.

10. *Sets...sight* Brings you in your glorious youth vividly before my mind.

11. *Where*=in circumstances in which (On.). *debateth* Not as usual and as On. ('combat') but 'discuss', 'consider', almost 'plot together'. See Sch. 'debate' (3).

12. *sullied night* Cf. 27. 11.

13–14. *And all in war with Time* etc. Because I love you I declare war upon time and replant you as you decay. This is the first time Sh. refers to his desire to immortalize W.H. in verse—and only timidly as it were, since verse is not mentioned.

16

But my rhyme is barren and cannot give you children. Why do not you yourself, now at the most radiant moment of youth, make war upon this tyrant Time in a more effective fashion, by renewing yourself in the children that many a virtuous maiden would be only too willing to give you—a likeness of yourself much more life-like than that portrait you have just had painted, for they are living portraits drawn by your own art?

2. *Time?* Q 'time?' Cf. 15. 13.

3. *fortify yourself* repair yourself.

4. *barren rhyme* The 'barren' is not primarily intended, I think, as self-depreciative, but rather as unproductive.

5. *stand...hours* Wordsworth echoes this in the even more famous lines of *The Prelude*:

> France standing on the top of golden hours
> And human nature seeming born again.

7. *bear you* (M.+) Q 'bear your'—which D. supports, noting '"your living flowers" stands over against "your painted counterfeit"'; B. objects—'to repeat "your" forces the antithesis too much'. The

sentence at full length is: 'Many maiden gardens would bear you living flowers which would be much liker you than your painted counterfeit is.'

9. *the lines of life that life repair* 'Playfully applicable both to lineage and the lines drawn by artist and poet' (Alden). But D. thinks it refers also to the 'eternal lines' which form the climax of 18. This seems most likely and if correct would link 18 with 15, 16 and 17.

10. *Which this (Time's pencil) or my pupil pen* Q, 'Which this (Times pensel or my pupill pen)'. In Q the comp. has carelessly carried on the second arm of the bracket to the end of the line. M. and most edd., including Camb. and D., read commas instead of brackets. 'This time's pencil' = a contemporary artist and 'my pupil pen' = these unpolished sonnets neither able to withstand the ravages of Time. The grammatical order of words is 'that life, which neither this time's pencil nor my pupil pen can make you live yourself'.

11. *fair* = beauty, as in 18. 7, 68. 3, 83. 2.

12. *men.* (M + inc. S-S.) Q. 'men,'

13. *To give away yourself...still* 'To produce likenesses of yourself (that is, children) will be the means of preserving your memory' (M.).

17

Develops what 16 says of the Poet's 'pupil pen' (ll. 10–14).

3–4. *a tomb...life* Ver. cites S. 83. 12.

4. *shows not...parts* Alluding to the customary description of a deceased, engraved on the outside of his tomb.

6. *fresh* '"lively and beautiful" to match the Friend's "graces"'. See 1. 9; 104. 8; 107. 10 (B.). *numbers* verse. *number* enumerate.

8. *touches* lit. 'strokes of the brush' (On.); but here, Ver. thinks, vaguer, 'equivalent perhaps to *traits*'. Cf. *A.Y.L.* 5. 4. 27, 'some lively touches of my daughter's favour'. *touched* painted (Sch. 3).

11. *true rights* 'due praise' (P.). *poet's rage* 'Applied in contempt to poetic inspiration' (Sch.). Rather, I think, in hyperbole, than 'in contempt'. Cf. the Lat. 'furor', used for the inspired prophetic and poetic frenzy; or 'rabies', the word Virgil uses to describe the inspiration of the Sibyl (*Aen.* VI. 49). In S. 100. 3 it becomes the Muse's 'fury' while in *M.N.D.* 5. 1. 12 Sh. speaks of the 'poet's eye, in a fine frenzy rolling' which is persiflage, certainly not contempt. One feels that he found the classical use of 'furor', *μαντεία*, etc., for poets rather amusing. It had not yet become conventional, a stock poetic counter, as it did in eighteenth century diction, e.g. in Gray's famous lines:

> Chill Penury repressed their noble rage
> And froze the genial current of the soul.

12. *stretchèd metre...song*=strained, affected verse of some quaint old poet. Keats adopts this line as a motto for his *Endymion*, 1818. Does this betray a feeling on Sh.'s part that all these marriage sonnets are rather artificial in diction and content? Anyhow, ll. 13–14 are the last we hear of marrying or begetting, and there is nothing strained or artificial about S. 18.

18

The Coming of Love (cf. above p. 92).

In this sonnet we step straight from a series of lovely poetical exercises, probably composed to order, into an eager and impassioned love-poem, one of the finest in the language, addressed by one lover to another; for Sh. could never have offered love in these terms had he not been sure that the love was reciprocated. Nor, I think, would a humble player have dared so confidently to promise immortality to a young lord had he not been conscious, and known that the fair youth was conscious, that all the great lyrical poets from the classics downwards had made similar promises of immortality to their patrons. Something had happened between Ss. 17 and 18; all barriers were down. The Poet had found a Friend; the 'lovely boy' had convinced him that it was not a bride forced upon him by parents eager for an heir, who was to be honoured by his love, but he, the Poet, who could offer in exchange something far better than an heir according to the flesh, the heritage of eternal fame.

'The beginning of this friendship', wrote A. C. Bradley, 'seems to have been something like a falling in love'. True, but to bring out the full meaning of the situation we must add the words *on both sides*, bearing in mind however that the intensity and depth of love depends on the depth of the spirit that offers it, and that what the *Sonnets* express is only one side.

3. *darling* something very dear, to be much cherished. *May* D. notes that according to the pre-Gregorian calendar, May ran up into nearly midsummer.

4. *date* duration ('the prevailing meaning in Sh.' On.).

5. *the eye of heaven* see also *R. II*, 3. 2. 37 and *Lucr.* 356 (M.).

7. *some time* Q 'some-time'; M. 'sometime'.

8. *By chance...untrimmed* Stripped of its ornaments by accident or in the course of the changing seasons.

9–14. *But thy...to thee* Cf. Leishman, ch. 1.

10. *that fair...ow'st* that beauty thou possessest.

12. *grow'st*=becomest a part of.

19

It was not possible to remain long upon the heights of rapture attained in 18. So the Poet returns to the theme of the tyranny of Time, already touched on in Ss. 15 and 16. But whereas 'breed' is there presented as the sovereign remedy against the ravages of Time, the Poet now claims this virtue for his verse and boldly forbids the tyrant to lay a finger on his beloved's brow.

In Ss. 15 and 16 Time is a 'bloody tyrant'; but in this sonnet, however, there is an unmistakable echo of Ovid's 'Tempus edax rerum' (*Met.* xv. 234). See Leish. p. 134; Lee, pp. 123–4. Alden cites *L.L.L.* 1. 1. 4 'spite of cormorant devouring Time'. Cf. also *Lucr.* 995ff, in which Time is reproached by Lucrece for affording Tarquin the opportunity to betray her. But for Ovidian influence in later Sonnets see head-notes 55 and 59.

1. *Time* Q 'time'.

2. *brood* Cf. 'breed' in 12. 14 (Roll.).

3. *jaws* (M.) Q 'yawes'.

4. *long-lived* M.'s hyphen.

5. '*fleet'st*'. Shn. 2nd pers. sing., rhyming with 'sweets'.

10. *antique pen* 'May mean not merely "old" (cf. 106. 7) but also "a pen that plays pranks, that draws

grotesque lines"' (E. B. Reed, *ap*. Roll.) An 'antic' = at once a buffoon and a death's head or skull, poss. in reference to the grotesque masks that buffoons wore. Cf. *R. II*, 3. 2. 162.

11. *course* i.e. cursus vitae. *untainted* untouched (by decay, corruption).

13. *Time: despite* (M.) Q 'Time dispight'.

14. *My love...young* The Time theme, begun in 15, is now dropped until resumed in 59.

20

On this much-debated because much misunderstood sonnet M. spoke in 1780 the final (if almost the earliest) word: 'Such addresses to men, however indelicate [i.e. unrefined] were customary in our author's time, and neither imported criminality nor were esteemed indecorous [i.e. indecent].' The quibbles on 'thing' and 'prick' both referring to the penis, imply a frankness about the human body general with the Elizabethans but outmoded by the prudery of the Victorians. The sonnet might have been occasioned by a bathe in the Thames and in any case in lines 11 and 14 the Poet expressly dissociates his affectionate admiration for the beauty of his Friend's physique from any question of sexual desire, though we cannot consider it impossible that the frank disclaimer may have been needed with a youth of this character.

1. *with nature's own hand* i.e. not by Art (P.). Cf. 21.

2. *master mistress* Hyphenated by Cap. and most edd. Does not perhaps mean *man*-mistress but *sovereign* mistress (M.). *passion* Almost certainly = love-poetry. Thomas Watson called all the sonnets in his *Hecatompathia* (1582) 'passions'.

7. *A man in hue* Q. 'hew'. *O.E.D.* glosses 'hue' as appearance, colour or complexion; but whichever meaning Sh. intended, 'a man in hue' would ill accord with the rest of the sonnet, the whole point of which is to emphasize the boy's feminine appearance. B. therefore proposes to read 'maiden' for 'man in'—an easy misreading in Sh.'s hand—and notes 'A manly hue (appearance or "complexion") would neither steal men's eyes nor surprise women's souls'. Again, 'In the previous two lines his "eye" has been compared with a woman's and we should expect a similar comparison as to his "hue" to preserve the balance of the double comparison in the first quatrain'. The reasons are enough to stamp 'A man in' as certainly corrupt and to lend strong support to 'A maiden hue'. For 'steal' he cites *Per.* 4. 1. 42ff 'That excellent complexion (=appearance, form) which did steal| The eyes of old and young'.

all hues in his controlling Here 'his' =its, as often in Sh.; while since 'control' <orig. contre-roll =a copy of a roll of accounts, etc., kept for purposes of checking [see *O.E.D.* 'control' (v.) and countra-roll (sb.).], the line means that the boy's 'hue' sets the standard against which all other human 'hues' must be judged.

10, 12. *doting...nothing.* Rhymes. Cf. *Ado*, 2. 3. 54, 56.

11. *defeated* defrauded. Cf. *M.N.D.* 4. 1. 156.

12. *thing* 13. *pricked* 14. *use* All equivocal.

13. *pricked thee out* to prick out =to select specially, lit. to mark or indicate a particular person or object by a 'prick' or tick; cf. *Caes.* 4. 1. 1, *2 H. IV*, 3. 2. 114. But often with a quibble.

14. *their love's use* Cf. 40. 6, etc. 'to use' =to have sexual intercourse with.

21

Having extolled in the simplest verse the face 'with Nature's own hand painted', Sh. contrasts this with the highly artificial style of a poet inspired by a 'painted beauty', alias a whore. To Wyndham this sonnet represents Sh.'s 'first attack on the false art of a Rival Poet'. But B. insists that if so he cannot be the same rival poet who later (Ss. 78–86) is mentioned as praising the Friend, because *ex hypothesi* that young man was not a 'painted beauty'. In any case, if the Rival Poet in Ss. 78 *et seq.* be Chapman, as I believe he was, Sh. is certainly making fun of him in this sonnet, as Acheson first observed in 1903.* For if 'painted' apart from its cosmetic sense be taken to mean fictitious, pretended or false, as it often does in Sh., the 'painted beauty' whose qualities or aspects this poet compares with sun and moon and stars, 'with April's flowers', and 'all things rare' must stand for the 'mistress Philosophy' in honour of whom Chapman had in 1595 fashioned a '*Coronet*' of sonnets and a whole '*Amorous Zodiac*'† of comparisons with the delights of philosophy, i.e. contemplation. And that this all points to Chapman seems confirmed by the play upon his name, chap-man, in the proverbial conclusion to the sonnet.

This gentle raillery seems to be Sh.'s reply to the arrogant attack upon him in the *Coronet* which begins:

> Muses that sing Love's sensual empery,
>   And lovers kindling your enraged fires
> At Cupid's bonfires burning in the eye,
>   Blown with the empty breath of vain desires—

* Pp. 63 ff. *Sh. and the Rival Poet* (1903), by Arthur Acheson.

† A translation from the French by Giles Durrant, according to C. S. Lewis, *op. cit.* p. 513.

lines obviously aimed at the author of *Venus and Adonis*, to say nothing of the first draft of *Love's Labour's Lost* with its burlesque of a little academy of 'philosophers',

Still and contemplative in living art

which is presently betrayed by Berowne the champion of Love and Ladies' eyes.

Sonnet 21 is an episode in the war between Poetry and Pedantry, and Chapman is a figure of fun; he is not yet, I think, a rival to be feared. That comes later in Ss. 78–85.

1. *muse*, (M.) Q 'Muse,'.

1. *couplement* combination, union.

7. *first-born* M.'s hyphen.

8. *That...this huge rondure hems*=that is contained within the mighty circle of the firmament. A reference to the Ptolemaic universe, at the centre of which lay the firmament, a kind of hollow ball or inverted cup that held within it all the heavenly bodies, sun, moon, stars, together with the earth and 'all that therein is' at the centre, around which the heavenly bodies moved in their various orbits. Cf. *Ham*. 2. 2. 302: 'This goodly frame the earth...this most excellent canopy the air... this brave o'erhanging firmament, this majestical roof fretted with golden fire.' *hems*. (M.) Q 'hems,'.

12. *candles* stars. Cf. *Rom*. 3. 5. 9; *Mac*. 2. 1. 5; *M.V*. 5. 1. 221.

13. *like of*=like. *hearsay* i.e. tittle-tattle.

14. *I will not praise...sell*. Proverbial. Cf. *Troil*. 4. 1. 80 'We'll but commend what we desire to sell'; *L.L.L*. 4. 3. 237 'To things of sale a seller's praise belongs'.

22

The praise of the Friend's beauty suggests by contrast Sh.'s own face marred by time. He comforts himself by 'claiming the Friend's beauty as his own' (D.)—a theme developed again in 62. But the main purport of the sonnet is that Poet and Friend have exchanged hearts.

1. *old* References to the poet's advanced age were traditional with sonneteers. Lee (*Life* 1898, pp. 85 ff.) derives it from Petrarch and notes its occurrence in Daniel (aged 29), Barnfield (aged 20), Drayton (aged 31).

3. *furrows* (M.+) Q 'forrwes'.

4. *expiate* M. explains the line: 'then do I expect that death *should fill up the measure* of my days', and cites *R. III*, 3. 3. 23, 'the hour of death is expiate'. The word is unusual in this sense, and W. notes 'Expiate = to atone for a crime and thus to close the last chapter of his history. Here the sense of completing is kept and the sense of atoning dropt'.

5–7. *For...as thine in me* Cf. Sidney's 'My true love hath my heart, and I have his' (*Arcadia*, 1593, bk. III, *Works*, II, p. 17).

11–14. *Bearing thy heart...again.* D. finds here 'the first hint of possible wrong committed by the youth against friendship'. But surely this is to read too much into an expression of deep affection.

12. *ill.* (M.+) Q 'ill,'.

13. *Presume not on* 'Do not expect to receive back'.

23

Drawing upon his knowledge of nervous actors on the stage the Poet protests that his self-distrust and the depth of his feeling prevents him saying all that is in his heart. He begs his friend therefore to 'hear with eyes', to perceive the force of the Poet's love from his face.

1. *unperfect* not yet perfect (in his 'part').

2. *beside* (M.) Q 'besides', out of.

3. *some...rage* 'a wild beast overwhelmed with rage' (Adams, *ap.* Roll.).

5. *for fear of trust* mistrusting myself, or fearing to be overconfident, 'not knowing what reception I shall get' (B.)—like an actor as he appears before the audience.

6. *rite* (M.) Q 'right'. Q's is the usual Shn. sp. The sense of ritual is needed by the context.

9. *looks* (Cap. *ap.* M.) Q 'books'. Some edd. defend Q, e.g. D. who refers to l. 13 'O learn to read what silent love hath writ' and supposes Sh. refers to the manuscript books in which he wrote his sonnets. But B. asks 'How could a book be a "presage of speech"?', and 'Why should anyone have to learn to read his sonnets? The "books" is not to the point'. And Tuck. finds 'looks' 'entirely necessary'.

10. *dumb presagers* i.e. like the dumb-shows which commonly enacted silently the burden of the dialogue that followed in the play. Cf. the Dumb-show in *Hamlet* (discussed in my *What Happens in Hamlet*, pp. 144 ff.). 'The image of the imperfect actor is still maintained; though he has lost command of his tongue, he can still plead by his looks' (B.).

12. *More...expressed* i.e. to a greater degree 'than that tongue (the tongue of another) which hath more fully expressed more ardours of love, or more of your perfections' (D.). Is this a reference to a rival poet?

14. *with eyes* Q 'wit eies'. *wit* Q 'wiht'.

24

This looks like a continuation of S. 22 and perhaps both orig. belonged to a group of four Ss., 43 and 45 being the other two. B. comments: this S. has the air of being a half-humorous, half-serious parody of a common type of sonnet, such as the following of Constable's *Diana*:

> Thine eye, the glass where I behold my heart,
> Mine eye, the window through the which thine eye
> May see my heart, and there thyself espy
> In bloody colours how thou painted art.

The S. as a whole is a complicated conceit, and Tuck. speaks of 'the far-fetched conceits of this trifling composition'.

1. *stelled*, (Dyce <Cap.; B. and most mod. edd.) Q 'steeld,'.. 'stelled' (a term of painting) = fixed, placed (cf. 'installed') Cf. *Lucr.* 1444:

> To this well-painted piece is Lucrece come,
> To find a face where all distress is stelled

where the word also clearly means 'fixed', as here

2. *table* The regular name for the board on which a picture was often painted at this period. Cf. *All's*, 1. 1. 97; *K.J.* 2. 1. 503.

3. *'tis* (M.+edd.) Q 'ti's'.

4. *perspective* 'Used ambiguously' (P.) = (*a*) the art of giving an appearance of solidity, due proportion and distance to objects painted on a flat surface. *O.E.D.* 3 cites 1601 Holland *Pliny*, 'so excellent he was in this perspective, that a man would say, his even, plaine and flat picture were embossed and raised work'; (*b*) an optical instrument for looking through (*O.E.D.* 2). Cf. Ben Jonson, *E.M.O.*, (1599) iv, 4 'To view 'hem (as you'ld do a piece of Perspective) in at a key-hole'. Here the Poet's 'eye' is the perspective through which

to look into his heart in which the true image of the beloved is pictured.

5, 6. *you your* Contrast 'thy', 'thee', 'thine' in ll. 2, 8, 10, 12. May not 'you', 'your' be used indefinitely? Cf. *All's*, 1. 3. 61. 'Your marriage comes by destiny | Your cuckoo sings by kind.'

7. *my bosom's shop* The imagery changes; a shop, either a store-house or a workshop.

9. *good turns* Q 'good-turns'.

12. *thee*; (M.+edd.) Q 'thee'.

13. *art*, (M.) Q 'art'.

13–14. *Yet...heart* P. sees this conflict as the serious part of the S. and compares 92. 14. 'Thou mayst be false, and yet I know it not'. I feel no such intimation. The sonnet is playful throughout and such playfulness denotes intimacy.

25

D. summarizes: 'In this sonnet Sh. makes his first complaint against fortune, against his low condition. He is about to undertake a journey on some needful business of his own [26, 27], and rejoices to think that at least in one place he has a fixed abode, in his friend's heart.' B. ignores this penetrating note, and writes: 'The general impression given by this sonnet is that Sh.'s friend was not himself a "great prince's favourite"; for in that case, the poet's fortune, being involved in his friend's, would have lacked this perfect security (ll. 13, 14)'. But that is an editorial inference, and even if valid, is misleading since it is certainly not the point Sh. wished particularly to make, which was, as D. says, that he loved and was beloved. But what about going on a journey, which D. found in the sonnet and B. could not? This is an editorial inference also but I think implied by the concluding couplet, which not only emphasizes the unshakable constancy of the love on both sides but also its continued existence whether they are together or apart. But the key to all this is to be found in 36, which we shall see has been misplaced by Thorpe, and should be read after 25.

1. *in favour with their stars* Astrologically, rank, profession, health, etc., were supposed to be determined by the position and condition of the stars at the hour of a man's birth. Cassius in *Caes.* 1. 2. 139 questions this:

> Men at some time are masters of their fates:
> The fault, dear Brutus, is not in our stars,
> But in ourselves, that we are underlings.

And in this sonnet, secure in the love of his friend, Sh. can say with Romeo 'I defy you, stars!'.

3. *whom fortune...bars* Probably refers to his social standing as a common player. See Introd. p. xlviii.

4. *Unlooked for* *O.E.D.* glosses 'disregarded, unheeded'. But here the meaning is surely 'unexpected, unhoped for', cf. *K.J.* 2. 1. 560, *3 H. VI.*, 3. 2. 131.

5–6. *Great princes. favourites...sun's eye* 'No two lines could have been penned more apposite to the fall and disgrace of Essex after his military failure in Ireland' (W.) B. agrees. But the S. was assuredly written before 1599. And why need the fallen favourite be a contemporary? The Poet was a dramatist with half-a-dozen histories to his credit, and there are two or three 'marigolds' in *Richard III* alone, and he had only to look at his Plutarch to find warriors 'famoused for fight' dishonoured by defeat at the end.

9. *painful* toiling (On.). *fight* (M.) Q 'worth'.

11. *quite*. Theobald conj. 'forth'.

13–14. See headnotes 25 and 26, and Steev.

26

'A love-letter, in the language of a vassal doing homage to his liege lord' (Lord Campbell). But why this sudden formal 'written embassage' (l. 3)? Most critics explain it as some sort of dedicatory epistle and the resemblance of expression in it to those in the prose dedication of *Lucrece* has persuaded many to assume that it was a sonnet Sh. wrote to accompany the MS when presenting *Lucrece* to Southampton in 1594. And after Drake (following Cap.) had drawn general attention to these parallels in 1817, it became 'the starting-point of the Southampton theory', addicts to which have 'greatly overstressed it' (Roll.). For Rollins observes with B. and P. that the resemblance ceases to be significant when we discover that dedications of books to patrons at this time were much alike in their language and dealt with much the same topics.

No one, however, seems to have perceived that all such speculations are beside the point if we take 'this written embassage' as 'this letter' or 'this sonnet'. Yet surely that is the natural and obvious way of taking it? And when we do so and assume with D. that Ss. 25, 26, 27, 28 form a series written just before or during a journey, the present letter is seen to be a half-playful and at the same time—in view of the Friend's exalted rank—half-serious despatch by Shakespeare to the 'Lord of his Love', in which he pretends the journey to be one of diplomatic importance and the writer to be a royal ambassador paying his respects the day after his departure, assuring him of his devotion—as it might be a diplomatic emissary of the Queen paying his respects on the eve of taking ship for the continent. What was the purpose of Sh.'s journey we do not know. If it was undertaken on behalf of the Friend or his family, the language would have given additional point to the sonnet. But see the note on 36.

2. *thy merit* etc. i.e. you deserve all the service I can render you. *hath...knit* D. cites *Mac.* 3. 1. 15:

> Let your highness
> Command upon me, to the which my duties
> Are with a most indissoluble tie
> For ever knit—

a close parallel but the sonnet is more concise than Banquo's rigmarole and may therefore be earlier.

3. *embassage* (M.) Q 'ambassage'. *written* Because an 'embassage' was generally delivered by word of mouth.

4. *wit*=skill.

7. *good conceit*=favourable opinion.

7–8. *I hope...bestow it* I hope you will think well enough of it to take it to your heart, poor verse though it is.

9–10. *Till...aspect* Until the enterprise I am now engaged upon begins to promise success. *moving*=(*a*) journey; (*b*) existence, on the analogy of 'moving'=motion of the stars. *Points on* 'sends rays upon' (Sch.). *aspect* (*a*) appearance; (*b*) astrol.; the position of a heavenly body in relation to an observer on earth.

11–12. *And puts...respect*=(*a*) makes me fit for company; (*b*) gives me a chance of writing something worthy.

11. *tattered* (M.+edd.) Q 'tottered'. Cf. 2. 4.

12. *thy* (M.) Q 'their'. see p. xxvi.

13–14. *Then...prove me.* Then I can return to claim your friendship, till when you will not see me.

27 and 28

One of the linked pairs of sonnets discovered by Chambers (*Gleanings*, pp. 113–14). See Introd. above, p. xxix. Note that 28. 1 harks back to 26. 11.

27

The first of a pair of sonnets describing in simple and vivid language the reality of the journey so hopefully introduced in 26. The pessimistic tone together with the allusions to his 'outcast state' suggest that the Poet may have been forced to go on tour in the country owing to the closing of the theatre because of the plague, the hostility of a puritan mayor and corporation, or as I argue in notes 36 the disapprobation of the government. Brooke found the expression 'tattered loving' (26. 11) a reflexion of the 'out-at-elbows' condition of actors on tour, a condition to which many actors were reduced during the disastrous plague years 1592–3. It may be so; yet it is generally supposed that Sh. was then occupied in writing *Venus and Adonis* and *The Rape of Lucrece*, while there is no evidence that he ever went on tour himself though his company did at times. Moreover the impression that 27 and 28 seem to convey is one of solitude and post-haste speed, neither suggestive of a company of players trudging along the muddy roads of Elizabethan England. All the sonnets tell us is that he had fallen into some kind of trouble which compelled him to leave London, or at any rate the neighbourhood of his Friend, and that he hoped to return eventually 'in happy plight'. But see comment on S. 36.

1. *toil* the fatigue of travel (as in 28. 7) (B.).
2. *travel* (M.+edd.) Q 'travaill'.

4. *to work my mind*=to keep my mind active. Cf. 93. 11 'thy heart's workings'; working=mental operation of any sort. See my note on *Ham*. 2. 2. 137.

6. *Intend* set out upon. *a pilgrimage* For lovers as pilgrims and their beloveds as saints see *Rom*. 1. 5. 93 ff.

7. *eyelids* Q 'eye-lids'.

9. *imaginary* acting by the imagination alone.

10. *thy* (Cap.) Q 'their'. Cf. Introd. p. xxvi. *shadow* 'image produced by the imagination' (Sch.).

11. *like a jewel...night* 'Refers to the idea that some stones could be seen in the dark' (Ver.). Cf. *Tit*. 2. 3. 226–30. Cf. *Rom*. 1. 5. 45–6:

> It seems she hangs upon the cheek of night
> As a rich jewel in an Ethiop's ear

'the comparative vagueness of the expression in the sonnet would suggest that it was a reminiscence of the earlier passage in the play. It is only the word "face" that shows us the image intended' (B.).

14. *For...self* 'By day my limbs find no quiet on account of my journey, by night my mind finds no quiet on account of your image' (Rolfe).

28

1. *return in happy plight* scil. with the 'apparel' he had hoped to 'put on' his 'tattered' condition (26. 11) at his departure. The link shows (*a*) that 26 is rightly placed in Q; and (*b*) that a sonnet can carry a double meaning: a tribute to the Friend's beauty and grace and beneath that a plea for sympathy and perhaps help for the Poet; 'tattered loving' being as it were the key word.

3. *oppression* distress.

5. *enemies to either's* (M.) Q 'enimes to ethers'. *either's* each other's (as usual in Sh.).

6. *shake hands* to ratify agreement.

7. *to complain* An ellipse—by causing me to complain.

8. *I toil* Cf. 27. 1 n. Here the vb.=to travel. *still* ever.

9–12. *I tell the day...the even* 'There must be correspondence here; "I please the day by telling it... I flatter the night by telling it"' (Leishman, pencilled note). All the four lines 9–12 must be taken together and the lovely hyperbole intended is that however dark the day, or pitch-black the night, the Friend is still bright enough to bring comfort to the world.

11. *flatter* gratify. *swart-complexioned* M.'s hyphen.

12. *twire* peep, twinkle. M., to whom the word was unknown, read 'twirl', but Boswell discovered it in Ben Jonson *The Sad Shepherd*, 2. 3. 17, 'Which maids will twire at, 'tween their fingers, thus' (ed. Herford and Simpson, vol. VII).

12. *gild'st the even* (M.+edd.) Q 'guil'st th' eauen'.

13, 14 *longer,...length seem stronger* (Q and M.). Mod. edd. follow Dyce (<Cap. MS and Collier conj.) in reading 'strength'. Dyce cites *2 H. IV*, 2. 3. 54.5:

> Then join you with them, like a rib of steel,
> To make strength stronger.

29

'These are the night-thoughts referred to in the last line of 28; hence the special appropriateness in the image of the lark rising at break of day' (D.). Roll. ignores this brilliant comment on a wonderful sonnet.

2. *outcast state* A reference surely to his state as a common player. Cf. Introd. p. xlviii.

4. *fate*, (M.+ inc. S.-S.) Q. '*fate*,'.

7, 8. *Desiring...scope, With what I most enjoy contented least* On l. 8 D. writes 'the preceding line makes it not improbable that Sh. is here speaking of his own poems'.

11–12. (*Like...earth*) (M.) Q. closes brackets at end of l. 11.

12. *sings hymns* etc. Cf *Cym.* 2. 3. 19.

30

'Sonnet 29 was occupied with thoughts of present wants and troubles; 30 tells of thoughts of past griefs and losses' (D.). The train of thoughts is natural but l. 1 shows that they are no longer night thoughts.

1–2. *to the sessions...I summon up* Cf. *Oth.* 3. 3. 143. S.-Smith thinks the legal metaphor 'adds the notion of guilt and punishment to that of nostalgia. "And I mourn again the precious time I have wasted in seeking for what I did not find".'

5. *an eye* (*unused to flow*) Cf. *Oth.* 5. 2. 351:

> whose subdued eyes,
> Albeit unusèd to the melting mood,
> Drop tears

6. *dateless* endless. Freq. in Sh. Cf. *R. II*, 1, 3, 152 and 'date' S. 14. 14.

8. *th' expense...sight* Refers to the notion that sighing involved a loss of blood. *vanished*=escaped.

sight sigh. See *O.E.D*. 'sight[2]'. But the ordinary word 'sight', favoured by a number of edd., also gives quite good sense, and goes more naturally with 'vanished'.

9. *foregone* gone by.

10. *heavily* sadly. *tell* count.

13. *dear friend* 'The first use of this term' (Brooke).

31

A development and explanation of the last line in 30. D. notes the close parallel in *A Lover's Complaint* where 'the beautiful youth pleads to his love that all earlier hearts which had paid homage to him now yield themselves through him to her service'. And under l. 10 he quotes *L.C.* l. 218:

> Lo, all these trophies of affections hot

1. *endeared* 'enhanced in value' (On.).

3. *there reigns love...parts* Cf. *Tw. Nt.* I. I. 36 ff.

5. *obsequious* Sh. can use this in either of two senses (cf. *O.E.D.* obsequious, obsequy), both prob. felt here: (1) dutiful, obedient (perh. even) fawning, e.g. cf. in love *M.W.W.* 4. 2. 2; cf. fondness *Meas.* 2. 4. 29; (2) dutiful in performing funeral rites, cf. *Tit.* 5. 3. 152, 'To shed obsequious tears'.

8. *But things removed*=only things absent. *thee* (M.+edd.) Q 'there' Cf. Introd. p. xxvi. W. follows Q as referring back to 'thy bosom'. But 'hidden in there' is awkward, and had Sh. meant that, he would have written 'therein'. It is also harsh after 'appear' (l. 7).

9. *Thou art the grave...live* A similar image occurs in *2 H. IV*, 5. 2. 123:

> My father is gone wild into his grave!
> For in his tomb lie my affections.

Cf. Introd. p. lxxv ff.

10. *trophies*=memorials Cf. On. 2 'emblem or memorial placed over a grave'; and the scroll hung about Hero's grave, in *Ado*, 5. 3.

32–3

There is clearly some kind of break here, there being no sort of connexion between 32 and 33. On the other hand, 32 might well be connected with what looks a small self-contained group (Ss. 71–4) all concerned with the Poet's death. What we know actually follows 32 is a group of liaison sonnets, though not I believe the earliest of that group; and it was the practice of the interpolator, as I have shown in the Introd. pp. xxix ff., to select sonnets from the main series to lend plausibility to the operation. Thus, though the ingenuity of D. was not able to trace any link between 32 and 33, Thorpe might have supposed the Poet's death and the Friend's sunset to be sufficiently akin for his purpose.

32

D. comments 'From the thought of dead friends of whom he is the survivor Sh. passes to the thought of his own death, and his Friend as the survivor'. He continues more doubtfully: 'This sonnet reads like an Envoy', though he is surely right in observing that 'a new group seems to begin' with 33.

1. *my well-contented day* 'The day whose arrival will well content me' (B.). The tone is still melancholy. M.'s hyphen.

2. *that churl death* 'Death is represented as a grave-digger' (B.).

3. *re-survey* Q 're-suruay'.

4. *lover*=intimate friend. Cf. *Cor.* 5. 2. 14.

5–6. *Compare...every pen* 'May we infer from these lines (and 10) that Sh. had a sense of the wonderful progress of poetry in the time of Elizabeth?' (D.).

7. *Reserve*=preserve.

10–14. M. first supplied quot. marks.

12. *equipage* equipment, generally mil. equipment. 'To march (or walk) in equal (or better) equipage' was a cliché of the period; Cf. Nashe, 'Pref. to *Menaphon*,' 1589 (ed. McKerrow, III, 320) who speaks of certain writers of Latin verse who 'march in equipage of honour with any of our ancient poets'.

33, 34, 35

B. heads this group: 'The friend's wrong-doing, confession and forgiveness', and he adds in a note 'the sensual fault' (35. 9) 'seems to be that which is more plainly indicated in the series 40, 41, 42'. Developing this in the Introd., pp. lvii ff., I argue that one can trace the story of the Friend's wrong-doing by reading Ss. 48, 57, 58, 61; 40, 41, 42; 33, 34, 35; and perhaps also 92, 93, 94—taken in that order.

But apart from the liaison affair, the group has features of relevance to the *Sonnets* as a whole. In an article in *Sh. Survey* 15, 1962, M. M. Mahood goes some way towards establishing the date of the *Sonnets* by demonstrating their close connexion with the plays of the middle period, a conclusion the more persuasive that the writer appears unaware that Beeching had been before her. Both critics also find the most striking of the connecting links in *1* and *2 Henry IV* and surprisingly close in the parallelism between Ss. 33, 34 and Prince Hal's speech at *1 H. IV*, 1. 2. 189–195—an important matter on which I must refer the reader to my Introd. (pp. lxxvii ff.).

33

2. *Flatter* A monarch's eye is said 'to flatter whatever it rests upon' (B.).

5. *basest* darkest. Cf. *Tit.* 4. 2. 71.

6. *Ugly* (Gild.) Q 'ougly'. *rack* 'mass of clouds driven before the wind in the upper air' (On.). Cf. *Temp.* 4. I. 156 'Leave not a rack behind'.

8. *this disgrace* i.e. the concealing clouds (see Mahood cited above). Cf. 'when heaven's sun staineth' (l. 14), which also implies that the sun was guilty. Miss Mahood would have found the sonnet less difficult had she seen its allusion to the liaison.

10. *all triumphant* (Q+M.) Dyce first suggested the hyphen which appears in most modern edd.

12. *The region cloud*=another term for 'the rack'.

14. *stain...staineth* Used as a vb. neuter (M.) and carries a double meaning, (*a*) become corrupt (cf. *O.E.D.* 5); (*b*) grow dim, be obscured (Sch.) Q 'stainteh'.

34

P. notes 'As lines 1 & 2 have been taken literally [e.g. by Samuel Butler] it is necessary to explain that the sun is Sh.'s friend; the beauteous day, fidelity in friendship; and the cloak, caution against treachery'. That this is what Sh. meant to convey and that the sonnet followed upon a painful scene, the details of which are hinted at in ll. 5–14, can hardly be denied. The metaphor, ambiguous in 33 though carried on, wears thin beneath the agitation of the Poet.

3–4. *base clouds...rotten smoke?* This might well stand for the gathering suspicions referred to in Ss. 57, 58, etc. if my reconstruction of the story be correct. *base*=(*a*) evil; (*b*) dark-coloured. *rotten smoke* unwholesome fog. Fogs and fen-mists were commonly thought to carry plague. Cf. Caliban's curse in *Temp.* 1. 2. 322. *brav'ry* splendour (Sch.). *smoke?* Q 'smoke.'

5. *that...break* i.e. when he seeks out the Poet to say how sorry he is. Cf. 'salve' (l. 7).

6. *my storm-beaten face* What a picture that calls up!

7. *well...can speak* can say much in favour. *salve.* 'The salve is the friend's repentance already pictured as the sun breaking through the clouds' (P.).

8. *That heals the wound...disgrace* Echoes the prov. 'Though the wound be healed yet the scar remains.' Cf. *Lucr.* 732 and Tilley, W 929. Does 'disgrace' allude to the cuckold's?

12. *cross* (M.) Q 'losse'. Cf. 42. 10, 12 and *A.Y.L.* 2. 4. 12 'I should bear no cross if I did bear you'. *the strong offence's* Together with 'my grief' (l. 9) this suggests that the mistress' treachery was almost as painful to Sh. as the Friend's.

13–14. *Ah...ill deeds* It is characteristic that after the scarcely concealed condemnation of the boy's conduct he finds the spectacle of love 'in tears' irresistible. And once so moved, he goes on in 35 to forgive, to find excuses and even to blame himself as an 'accessary'.

13. *sheds,* Q. 'sheeds,'.

35

'The "tears" of 34 suggest the opening. Moved to pity, Sh. will find guilt in himself rather than in his friend' (D.), and ll. 5, 6 D. paraphrases 'and even I am faulty in this, that I find precedents for your misdeed by comparisons with roses, fountains, sun, and moon'. See Introd. p. xxxi, and note how by using the word 'guilt' D. begins to forge his ingenious but misleading link with 36.

3. *stain.* Cf. 33.

4. *canker* worm that preys upon blossoms (Sch.).

6. *Authorizing* justifying.

7. *corrupting salving* Cap. conj. 'Corrupt in salving'.

8. *thy...thy* (M.) Q 'their...their'. Cf. Introd. p. xxvi. *Excusing...are* 'More sinful in excusing them than they themselves are sinful' (Leishman, pencilled note).

9. *sense* reason.

11. *commence:* (M.) Q 'commence,'.

14. *that sweet...from me.* Lee cites Barnfield, first sonnet addressed to *Cynthia* (1595):

> There came a thief, and stole away my heart,
> (And therefore robbed me of my chiefest part)

me. Q 'me,'.

36–9

See Chambers (1) (pp. 113–18) on linked sonnets.* These four constitute an elaborately planned group, not noted by Chambers, in which the sonnets are linked by the repetition of words and rhymes, tied up as it were by the rhymed couplet 'twain—remain', at the end of 39 repeating the rhymes at the beginning of 36. Thus:

36	1 twain	3 remain	37	1 delight	3 spite
	2 one	4 alone		10 give	12 live
	6 spite	8 delight		13 thee	14 me
	9 thee	11 me			
38	5 thee	7 me	39	2 me	4 thee
	6 sight	8 delight		5 live	7 give
				6 one	8 alone
				13 twain	14 remain.

and note how the rhyme 'thee—me' runs like a refrain throughout.

* And my Introd. pp. xxix ff.

36

D. writes, 'according to the announcement made in 35 Sh. proceeds to make himself out the guilty party'. To this B. objects, rightly, 'But the poet has made no such announcement; he has called himself an accessory more to blame than the principal because he defends his action by arguments of reason; but that is a long way from making himself out the guilty party. The sonnets from 36–39 must refer to a different topic.* 36 refers to some "blots" upon the Poet and 37 to the Friend's "truth" [loyalty] as atoning for the spite of fortune. The subject of the Friend's wrong to the Poet is resumed in 40.' Further, in support of B. note that if 'blots' refers to the liaison, the arguments of 36 and 37 lose all point. Sonnets 36–9 have therefore, as B. suggests,† been misplaced; and P. who agrees, proposes that they should rightly be a continuation of 29, while he too suggests that the 'blots' in 36 refers to his 'disgrace with Fortune and men's eyes' (29. 1). This is my view also, except that I should carry the prelude to 36 further back, to 25, in which as D. observes we first hear Sh. complaining 'against Fate and his low condition'.

It follows from all this that what is called in 36 'blots' or a 'separable spite', and seems to refer in 29 to the Poet's 'outcast state' can only mean the 'disgrace in men's eyes' that was at that period the lot of one who had to earn his bread as a 'common player'. As there is no hint of this in the first twenty-four sonnets, it may be that at their first meeting the young Friend accepted Sh. as his Poet, as the famous author of *Venus and Adonis*, and was either ignorant of or preferred to overlook the separable spite of their respective ranks.

* See my Introd. p. xxx. † See his Introd. pp. lxv–lxvi.

But what about 'bewailéd guilt'? One is not guilty of the accident of one's birth, or of the Fate that determines one's rank in society—irrevocably at that period. Shakespeare must have committed some act or become involved in some situation which laid him open to the disapproval of the Friend's relations and acquaintances or to the condemnation of the legal authority; and he was so keenly aware of this that, fearing his beloved boy might himself incur shame or dishonour by associating with the guilty party, he writes to tell him they must part:

> Let me confess that we two must be twain.

What had happened? Or what had Sh. done? Clearly a crisis of some kind had occurred and it is natural to suppose it concerned him as an actor, probably as a member of an acting company. Indeed, as I read the sonnet, the 'blots' and the 'guilt' though not the same thing were closely associated. In other words, his 'guilt' had revealed to the world the fact that the Poet whom the Friend had taken to his heart was nothing but a common player.

I believe too, as many others have believed, that the guilt was not so much a personal one but shared by Shakespeare with his company. And one may learn how it affected them by glancing over the score or more sonnets that follow S. 25. For it is certain that about fifteen or more were written in absence, while here and there interspersed among them are to be found sonnets written at the end of exhausting days' travel and travel on horseback. The inference is surely obvious; Sh. and his company had been forced to leave London and to go on tour in the country; forced, because the theatres had been closed by the authorities. Moreover, if we may judge the length of the tour by the number of the sonnets written in absence, it must have extended over several weeks. Further, I assume that it probably took place in 1597, since, as stated in the Introduction, I accept Beeching's argument for the year as that in which Poet and Friend first met.

Now it so happens that the only extended tour of the acting profession between the disastrous Plague Years of 1592–3 and the death of Elizabeth took place in August and September 1597 when the Privy Council, enraged by the production at the Swan Theatre of a so-called 'seditious' play entitled *The Isle of Dogs*, issued an injunction on 28 July ordering the arrest of all those implicated, to be followed by the closing and dismantling of all the theatres. Their orders seem to be phrased for all time, but early in October plays were being performed once again and two of the players who had been imprisoned together with Ben Jonson, who had a hand in writing the 'book', were at large. Nashe, another part author and probably the principal, managed to escape to Yarmouth. All this would account for the fifteen sonnets in absence, together with the riding on horseback. But the 'bewailéd guilt' is still unexplained. I can hazard but one guess: the play, as the evidence shows, was of composite authorship (like *Sir Thomas More*). If Sh. was discovered to have had a hand in it would not that complete the story of what lies behind S. 36? He was not of course 'guilty' in the eyes of the Friend: the words 'our undivided loves' shows that. But, if my guess be sound, he was guilty of sedition in the eyes of the Privy Council, and was not that something to 'bewail'?

Having said this, however, let me admit that there is not a tittle of evidence associating Sh. in any way with this ill-fated play. Not that much more than a tittle of information has survived about the play itself, since nothing is known of its contents.

One fact alone seems to emerge from the sonnet: that Sh. went a journey of some kind on horseback and was absent from his Friend for several weeks. Moreover, inasmuch as the sonnets during this time make no allusion to the liaison, though suspicion seems to creep into them towards the end, I infer that the Friend's treachery took place during the absence of the Poet who did not discover it until his return. But that even at his happiest moments he was haunted by fears that he might be robbed of his greatest treasure, as Miss Mahood urges, I think most likely.

1. *twain* parted, separated. Cf. *Troil.* 3. 1. 101 'she'll none of him; they two are twain'.

3. *blots* See headnote.

5. *one respect* mutual regard.

6. *a separable spite* 'a cruel fate that spitefully separates us from each other' (M.), i.e. the difference in social status.

7. *sole effect* emotions that no other experience can give.

8. *delight.* (M.+edd.) Q 'delight,'.

9. *not evermore* no longer, ever again (*O.E.D.* citing this). *acknowledge thee* show that I know you when we meet. Cf. *Err.* 5. 1. 323.

10. *bewailed guilt* See headnote.

11–14. *Nor thou...* From this 'it is reasonable to infer that the friend is a man of high rank' (Brooke). See Introd. p. xlviii.

11. *public kindness* i.e. a public recognition by a nobleman.

12. *Unless...name* Unless you are ready to run the risk of dishonouring yourself by so doing.

37

'Continues the thought of 36, 13–14' (D.). Cut off from his brilliant young friend by his social disability and his bewailed guilt, Sh. professes to find comfort in watching the activities of this splendid youth from afar.

1–2. *father...child* The father-son relationship here glanced at is significant.

3. *made lame* Cap. and Butler take this literally and picture Sh. hobbling on to the stage at the Globe! An interesting close parallel occurs in the 1608 Quarto of *Lear* (4. 6. 219), two years later than the Sonnets. cf. also 89. 3. *by Fortune's dearest spite* Cf. 36. 6. *dearest* Two senses for 'dear' in Eliz. English, of different origins, (i) precious, beloved, etc.; (ii) as here but now obs. except as 'dire' = grievous, hard, bitter.

4. *worth* 'Must be construed in terms of what follows' (B.). Implies high rank.

5. *beauty, birth, or wealth, or wit* 'As the Friend's beauty is sufficiently certified by the rest of the sonnets the presumption is that his birth and wealth and wit are equally matters of fact' (B. p. xxx) and equally denied by fortune to Sh. who had no 'worth'!

7. *Entitled...sit* 'Perhaps—sit as rightful kings among your other good qualities. Cf. "part" 74. 6' (P.). B. cites *L.L.L.* 5. 2. 807–8:

> If this thou do deny, let our hands part,
> Neither entitled in the other's heart.

thy (M.) Q 'their'. Cf. Introd. p. xxvi.

8. *engrafted* 'Grafted upon all this riches (this 'store') and so drawing life and strength from it, as a graft does from the stock' (Tuck). *store* = lit. storehouse or rich stock.

10. *shadow...substance* The contrast between shadow and substance was an Eliz. cliché, freq. in Sh. But here this 'shadow'='the metaphorical union of Sh.'s love with his friend's other possessions, and the substance is the real support [his "comfort"] derived from the imaginary union' (P.).

12. *by a part...live* It suffices that he lives by his love which is itself but a part of the friend's glorious being.

38

In 37. 14 the poet is 'ten times happy' in the contemplation of the young friend's glory and this reminds him of the Muses; and the thought in 39 follows directly upon 38.

1. *to invent*=to write poetry about. Invention (the power of) imaginative or poetic creation. Cf. *Ven.* Ded. 'the first heir of my invention'.

2. *pour'st* (Gild.) Q 'poor'st'.

3. *argument* subject, theme. Cf. 76. 10.

3–4. *too excellent...rehearse?* too great for any common versifier (like myself) to celebrate. *paper* a rather contemptuous term for 'poem'. *rehearse* relate, give an account of.

3. *too:* Q 'to'.

4. *rehearse?* Q 'rehearse:'.

6. *stand...sight* strike your notice.

13. *curious* critical.

39

Not very easy to follow, the point at ll. 5–8 being obscure. 'In 38', D. explains, 'Sh. declares that he will sing his friend's praises, but in 37 he had spoken of his friend as the better part of himself. He now asks how he can with modesty sing the worth of his own better part. Therefore he returns to the thought of 36, 'We two must be twain".' So much for ll. 1–4 and the links that bind the group 36–9 together; but it does not help with the rest of the sonnet, which a note of P.'s explains satisfactorily. 'In 36, their lives were divided though their loves were one lest the friend's character might be blemished, here a fanciful reason is put forward for a more complete separation, that Shakespeare's praise coming as from a stranger may seem in better taste.'

4. *thee?* Q 'thee,'.

7–8. Q's double colon here is not, as might be thought, inadvertent duplication by the comp. but by its pauses isolates and emphasizes the passionate l. 8 and gives ll. 7–8 the effect of a concluding couplet, the sestet being virtually a separate stanza.

9–14. *O absence...remain* Here Sh. explains his device for complete separation. N.B. the relatives 'thou', 'thy' refer to 'absence' throughout.

10. *sour leisure* bitter opportunity, i.e. for thought as he journeys away. This 'somewhat archaic sense of leisure is freq. in Sh.' (On.).

12. *doth* (M.) Q 'dost'.

13–14. Steev. cites *Ant.* I. 3. 102 (Ant. to Cleop.):

> Our separation so abides and flies,
> That thou residing here, goes yet with me,
> And I hence feeling, here remain with thee.

'Absence teaches how to make of the absent beloved two portions, one, absent in reality, the other present to imagination' (D.).

40

According to the theory worked out in the Introd. pp. xxxi ff. and lvii ff., this has no connexion with the extreme self-effacement of 39, being in fact the fourth of a collection of twelve sonnets concerned with the youth's treachery. That this is its subject is clear from ll. 9–14 and from the two following sonnets, while for its proper understanding 48, 57, 58, 61 should be read first. This thesis is a development of B.'s view and he comments on 40, 'With the three ensuing sonnets should be read Ss. 133–6, 143, 144 [sect. II], which deal with the same subject, an intrigue of the poet's friend with some lady unknown'. D., on the other hand, attempts to link 40 with 39 thus: 'In 39 Sh. desires that his love and his friend's may be separated in order that he may give the friend what otherwise he must give also to himself. Now, separated, he gives his beloved all his love.' As far as ll. 1–4 go, the link might seem obvious. And I suspect that Thorpe thought it would seem so since it offers an apparently satisfying explanation of why he inserted this liaison sonnet at this particular point.

1–4. As often in the plays, and elsewhere in the sonnets, Sh. resorts to quibbling or word-play at moments of emotional intensity.

3. *that thou...call* The love offered him by the mistress was certainly no 'true love', cf. 152. 2 'twice forsworn'.

4. *mine* i.e. my true love.

5. *my love...my love* In two senses—If for love of me you give my mistress welcome. For *receivest* cf. *O.E.D.* 'receive II 8' 'to admit (a person) into some relation with oneself'. May not this give us a hint of how the mistress may have gained access to the Friend during Sh.'s absence?

6. *useth* are familiar with, here in sense of sexual intercourse. Cf. *Oth.* 5. 2. 73.

7. *thy self* (Gild.) M. 'thyself'; Q 'this selfe'. *deceiveth* Cf 4. 10 'deceive' = betray, be false to, cheat (yourself).

8. *By...refuseth* 'by taking in wilfulness my mistress whom yet you do not love '(B. conj.) I agree, but suggest 'wantonness' for 'wilfulness'.

9. *robbery* Cf. 35. 14.

10. *all my poverty* my ewe lamb (P.).

12. *love's wrong* P. cites *Gent.* 5. 4. 71.

41

In the first eight lines Sh. refers lightly to the various adventures with women the youth indulges in when his Poet is not there to look after him; in the rest he speaks of 'love's wrong' but less bitterly than in 40. Perhaps there had been some conversation between the two meanwhile.

1. *pretty wrongs* i.e. the sins that 'well show' because committed so gracefully. Cf. *M.V.* 2. 6. 37:

> But love is blind, and lovers cannot see
> The pretty follies that themselves commit.

liberty (*a*) licence; (*b*) privilege of dispensing with ordinary conventions.

3. *thy years* Implies that he has not reached the years of discretion.

5. *Gentle...won* i.e. a noble and therefore a prize worth winning. cf. 1 *H. VI*, 5. 3. 79.

5–8. *Gentle...prevailed* This, though general in relevance, was, I think, intended to hint particularly at the conduct of the mistress, and is directly supported by S. 143 which shows the mistress in hot pursuit.

8. *sourly* rudely; cf. 35. 14. *he* M. reads 'she' saying 'the lady and not the man' is 'supposed the wooer'. Yet Sh. knew the man. See Landry, p. 437. Nearly all edd. agree with M., but male readers,

except those who know less about sex than Sh., will agree, I think, with Q.

prevailed? (Gild.) Q 'prevailed.'.

9. *my seat* Cf. *Oth.* 2. 1. 289–90 'I do suspect the lusty Moor | Hath leaped into my seat'.

10. *straying* Cf. *O.E.D.* (fig.) citing *Shorter Cat.* 'filthy and straying lust'.

11. *riot* dissolute conduct esp. of young men sowing their wild oats. Often applied to Prince Hal in *1 H. IV*.

12. *truth* loyalty, pledge of loyalty.

42

Sh. affects to find excuses for the treachery of mistress and friend by pretending that they must have fallen in love with each other because each knew the other was in love with their Poet. It was a pretty fancy intended no doubt to persuade a rather shallow young man that after all his Poet could make light of the whole thing. But the bitterness (sourness) is ill-concealed; he loved the woman 'dearly' and yet deeply resented her robbery of the most precious thing in his life, the loyal affection of his beloved Friend. He puts it all more frankly in 133 and 134, and 135 and 144.

3. *wailing* to wail = to grieve bitterly (not necessarily with loud cries). Cf. *O.E.D.* 'wail' 4.

7. *abuse* grossly deceive. 'Precise meaning often doubtful' (On.). Often in Sh. for deceive in love or wedlock, Cf. frequency in *Oth.*

8. *approve* (*a*) look favourably upon; (*b*) taste (cf. 40. 8). *her.* Q 'her,'.

14. *flattery* 'gratifying deception' (On.).

43–5

A linked group (*Gleanings*, pp. 114–15).

43

Even D. can discover no connexions here and asks 'Does this begin a new group of sonnets?' I comment: Having done his best with the liaison topic for a while, Thorpe now returns to his main text which continues the absence theme and in particular to the Poet's wearisome journey on horseback and thoughts of the Friend during sleepless nights at the end of tiring days, first spoken of in Ss. 27, 28, 29. He is still riding in 51, and there seems no reason to suppose any disturbance of the chronological order in the meantime.

N.B. We get liaison sonnets again in 57, 58, 61; and as 53 and 54 lay special emphasis upon the youth's constancy and truth (loyalty) it looks as if 57, 58, 61 are more liaison interpolations. See also note on 48. Now 61 is, like 43, a nightpiece, but as unhappy as 43 is happy. I conjecture that the interpolator carelessly transposed them and as 43–5 and 57–8 are both linked groups the confusion was perhaps the easier.

1. *wink* shut the eyes. Here=sleep.

2. *unrespected* unnoticed, i.e. that do not attract my attention.

4. *darkly bright* secretly cheerful. Cf. *Mac.* 3. 2. 28 'Be bright and jovial'. *darkly* freq. 'secretly' in Sh. *are bright in dark directed* can see clearly what they are looking at in the dark.

5. *whose shadow...bright* 'whose image makes bright the shades of night' (D.). For 'shadow'= 'image, portrait, likeness' see On.

6. *thy shadow's form* 'the form which casts your shadow' (On.).

8. *so!* Q. 'so?'

10. *day,* (M.) Q. 'day?'

11. *thy fair* (Cap., M.) Q 'their faire'. Introd. xxvi.

imperfect 'because it is only the shadow of what is perfect—the friend' (P.).

12. *stay!* Q. 'stay?'

14. *me.* Q. 'me,'.

44

In 43 he is carried into the bright presence of his Friend in dream; now he wishes that he could be transported thither by the mere process of thought. This leads on to a consideration, half fanciful, of the four elements that make up the composition of man (according to the Galenic physiology of Sh.'s day). Note the possible indications that Sh. had now reached a distant country, in his journey (? Scotland).

1. *dull substance* Cf. *M.V.* 5. 1. 65 'This muddy vesture of decay'—composed of the two heavier elements, earth and water. *thought* Here=imagination, cf. *H. V*, 1 Prol. 28, but in l. 9 it=melancholy.

2. *stop my way* i.e. to get to you.

4. *limits* regions (On.). *where* i.e. to where.

9. *thought kills* Cf. *Caes.* 2. 1. 187.

11. *so much...wrought* i.e. being so largely composed of these two ponderous elements Cf. *Ant.* 5. 2. 288 'I am air and fire; my other elements|I give to baser life' (Steev.).

12. *attend, time's leisure...moan* wait sorrowfully till time has leisure to reunite us (P.).

13. *nought* (Sewell) Q 'naughts'.

45

'Sonnet 44 tells us of the duller elements of earth and water; this sonnet of the elements of air and fire' (D.). It also speaks of letters passing to and fro between Poet and Friend (ll. 10–12).

1. *slight air...fire* Cf. Cleopatra in *Ant.* 5. 2. 288, cited at 44, 11. *purging fire.* Cf. the cleansing fire of Purgatory, and *M.N.D.* 3. 1. 151.

4. *present-absent* Because 'sliding' to and fro between them. Hyphened by M.

6. *embassy of love* Cf. 26. 3 'written embassage'.

8. *melancholy* Sh. gen. gives this our mod. accent; here both rhyme and rhythm seem to require 'melanchóly'.

9. *life's composition* i.e. of the four humours. *recured* restored. Cf. *Tw. Nt.* 2. 3. 10 'Does not our life consist of the four elements?'

9. *life's* (Sewell) Q 'liues'.

10–12. *those swift...health* letters or messengers return to say you are well.

12. *thy* (M+) Q 'their'. Introd. xxvi.

46 and 47

Conceits of eye and heart are in the convention of Eliz. sonneteers. Cf. Watson's *Tears of Fancy*, 1593 (19 and 20); Constable's *Diana* 1594 (III. 9; VI. 7); Drayton's *Idea*, 1619 (33) (W.). B. speaks of 'the feeling of boredom induced in modern readers by these occasional lapses into the conventional strain'. We have already had an example of it in 24. But 46 and 47 are different, being written in absence (47. 10), to return thanks for a portrait just received from the Friend (47. 6), and intentionally so obscurely expressed that only one critic has, I think, understood it (see ll. 1–2). But so interpreted, 46 and 47 are seen to be the conventional type amusingly made use of to turn a riddling compliment.

46

1–2. *Mine eye...thy sight* This states the theme of 46—a debate in legal terms between the Poet's eye and heart: which is the true portrait, the 'painted banquet' (47. 6) before his eye or the one he treasures in his heart? No critic except Brooke seems to have understood that a real picture is involved. P. sees 46, 47 as a development of 24, and D. thinks they are a pair of opposites (like 44, 45), the eye meaning the senses and the heart love.

2. *the conquest*=(*a*) the spoils of war; (*b*) property or goods awarded in a legal action.

3, 8. *thy* (M.+) Q 'their'. Introd. xxvi.

3–6. *Mine eye...eyes* The eye would lodge an objection in court to the heart's title to the picture: the heart would deny the eye's right to see the picture that lies within it as a jewel lies in a casket.

9. *side* 'to assign to a side or party' (On., who cites this Sonnet.).

12. *moiety* and *part* have much the same meaning.

13, 14. *thy...thy* (M 1780+many) M. 1790+ Camb., etc. 'thine...thine', Q 'their...their'.

47

The 'mortal war' of 46 is followed by a league.

2. *good turns* Cf. 24. 9 'Now see what good turns eyes for eyes have done'.

3. *famished for a look* Cf. 75. 10 'clean starved for a look' (D.).

7–8. *Another time...a part* i.e. the eye can reproduce his picture from the heart's thoughts (by imagination *or* in memory).

8. *his* i.e. the heart's.

10. *art* (Cap.+) Q 'are'.

11. *not* (1640+edd.) Q 'nor'.

48

I agree with P. who writes, 'An anticipation of estrangement, and therefore out of place' and with D. that it alludes to Sh.'s suspicions of a liaison with the mistress, in fact I believe it to be the earliest of the sonnets on that matter, written just about the time of his arrival back in London, a time which seems implied by the words 'when first I took my way', i.e. set out on my journey. And if I am right, the Friend whose constancy had been the Poet's theme for some two months had been amusing himself with the Dark Woman meanwhile.

We have seen above (Introd. p. xxxi) how Thorpe found places in the text for sonnets he had to insert, and how he often misled D. in so doing. He does both here; for the treasure locked in a chest (48) could well be linked with the reference to the closet in the first of the pair 46–47. Shakespeare makes use elsewhere of the 'closet' metaphor (e.g. in 52 and 75), but I do not think that this necessarily implies any connection with the circumstances of the liaison.

1. *when I took my way* i.e. began my travels.

4. *trust!* Q 'trust?'

6. *most worthy* most precious. *comfort*=both 'solace' and 'delight'. Cf. 144. *now...grief* 'because absent' suggests P. Surely because he has fears he may be 'stolen'.

12. *come and part* come and go.

14. *For truth...so dear*. Prov., see Tilley, P. 570, 'The prey entices the thief', and *Ven.* 724 'Rich preys make true men thievish'.

49

P. heads 88 'Perhaps a continuation of 49', and I am persuaded he is right, the more so that, as Miss Mahood points out, it gives one a remarkably detailed reflexion of the rejection of Falstaff at the entrance to the Abbey; see Introd. pp. lxxvii ff. This would make 49 the second of the Farewell sonnets; see headnote to 87–94.

If P. be right the sonnet is misplaced, and no doubt Thorpe is responsible. But I can offer no reason for his action.

3. *When as* when. *cast...sum* 'A metaphor from closing accounts or a dissolution of a partnership' (after P.). How bitter is this base commercialism!

4. *called...respects* i.e. set down in the statement a deliberate consideration of our respective indebtedness.

5. *strangely* like a stranger.

8. *reasons...settled gravity* 'reasons for changing to a grave and reserved deportment' (B.). *gravity;* (M.) Q 'gravitie.'.

9. *ensconce me* take refuge. A term of siege warfare.

11. *my hand...uprear* 'as a witness in court of law' (B.).

50

D. writes 'This sonnet and the next one a pair, as 44 and 45 are, and 46 and 47'.

3. *that ease and that repose* i.e. refreshment and bed

at the end of the day's journey (after Tuck). Cf. *1 H. IV*, 3. 3. 81 'Shall I not take mine ease in mine inn?'

4. *'Thus far...friend.'* Cf. 28. 8 (P.). Marked as a quotation by M.

6. *dully* (M.) Q 'duly'. Supported by the context and by 51. 2, 11. See Landry, p. 438. *that weight in me* i.e. the heaviness of my grief.

8. *being...from thee* Refers to 'speed', i.e. the faster he trots the further he carries me from you.

14. *my joy behind* i.e. he is still travelling *away* from the Friend.

51

In 50 we had the dull plodding *away* from the Friend; this sonnet continues it, while imagining how different might be a return journey.

1. *slow offence*=offence of slowness (Schm.).

3. *thence?* (Gild.) Q 'thence,'.

4. *posting*=riding at full speed.

6. *swift extremity*=extreme swiftness. For similar construction see 'separable spite' (36. 6). *slow?* (Gild.) Q 'slow,'.

7. *mounted...wind* M. compares *2 H. IV*. Induct. l. 4: 'making the wind my post-horse'.

8. *In winged speed...know*='though I were flying, my impatience would make me think I was standing still' (P.).

10. *perfect'st* Q 'perfects'.

11. *Shall neigh (no dull flesh) in his fiery race* The subject of the sentence is 'desire'. For desire, being made of perfect love, will neigh in its excitement and exultation, in its fiery race—not like this dull old horse I am riding upon. I adopt M.'s brackets.

12–14. *But love...to go.* 'For the love shown by my horse in going slowly away from you, I shall in my love of you forgive him for returning slowly; but I shall hasten on before him' (P.).

13. *wilful-slow* Hyphened by M.

14. *go*=walk, not run.

52

This and 75 are both sonnets on a casket for jewels; this beginning 'so am I' and that 'so are you', and B. therefore thought these a pair. I believe the resemblance to be accidental; see note on sonnet 75.

6. *seldom* M. cites close parallels at *1 H. IV*, 1. 2. 198; and 3. 2. 57–9. See my Introd. p. lxxvi. Ver. (1890) compares Florio's *Montaigne* (1603), 1, 42 (Tud. trans. 1892, 1. 305): 'Feasts, banquets, revels, rejoice them that seldom see them, and that have much desire to see them: the taste of which becometh cloysome and unpleasing to those that daily see.'

8. *captain*=of superior worth (M.). *carcanet*=an ornament worn round the neck (M.).

9–11. *So is the time...special-blest* Steev. cites *1 H. IV*, 3. 2. 55 ff.

> Thus did I keep my person fresh and new,
> My presence like a robe pontifical,
> Ne'er seen but wond'red at.

M.'s hyphen.

12. *his imprisoned pride* magnificence (On.)

53

Thoughts in absence; the Friend's beauty and truth. 'Compare the finer sonnet, 56' (P.). But a finer sonnet and a much closer parallel is 106 which I read as an obvious prelude to this. See comment on 106.

2. *strange* 'not properly your own' (B.).

5–7. *Adonis...Helen* At once the most beautiful and the most effeminate of myth. figures. He has no doubt well-known pictures in mind.

54

Continues l. 14 of 53. Here Sh. declares that the constant heart makes beauty more beautiful, must outlive all loveliness and will be the theme of his verse after beauty has faded.

2. *truth* fidelity. *give!* (M.+edd.) Q 'give,'.

5, 6. *canker* or 'canker-rose' = the dog rose or wild rose (M.). *tincture* colour.

7. *wantonly* playfully.

8. *their masked...discloses* M. cites *Ham.* I. 3. 36–40:

> The chariest maid is prodigal enough
> If she unmask her beauty to the moon.
> Virtue itself 'scapes not calumnious strokes.
> The canker galls the infants of the spring
> Too oft before their buttons be disclosed.

B. notes that 'unmask' and 'canker' (though in a different sense) occur in both passages and it is not impossible that the two passages were written at much the same time.

11. *Die to themselves* = die without profit to others (P.).

13. *Beauteous and lovely* 'lovely' = lovable; Lat. *amabilis* (Tuck). Cf. 5. 2, 18. 2, 79. 5

14. *vade* (Q+Camb.) M. reads 'fade'. Cf. *O.E.D.* 'vade' a variant of 'fade' very commonly found 1530–1630 applied to colours and flowers. *by verse* (Q+Camb.) M. reads 'my verse'. Acc. to Landry, p. 437 n. 9, one of M.'s 'poor or unnecessary emendations'.

55

A remarkable sonnet in more ways than one.

Ovid's *Met.* in Golding's translation had been Sh.'s standby since the beginning; and the well-known vaunt at the end of *Met.* xv (871–9 Gold. 984–95) was a commonplace with most Renaissance poets, especially those who claimed that their own verse would ensure immortality for their patrons. Thus traces of this influence have already been visible in the sonnets, especially in 19, which invokes 'Devouring Time', and is an echo of *Met.* xv, 234–6 *Tempus edax rerum* etc.; while for later influence see headnote 59. Sonnet 55 however, is peculiar in that lines 7–14 make a clear echo, almost a translation, of Ovid's famous conclusion:

> Iamque opus exegi, quod nec Iovis ira nec ignis
> nec poterit ferrum nec edax abolere vetustas.
> cum volet, illa dies, quae nil nisi corporis huius
> ius habet, incerti spatium mihi finiat aevi:
> parte tamen meliore mei super alta perennis
> astra ferar, nomenque erit indelebile nostrum,
> quaque patet domitis Romana potentia terris,
> ore legar populi, perque omnia saecula fama,
> siquid habent veri vatum praesagia, vivam.

—in the Loeb translation:

And now my work is done, which neither the wrath of Jove, nor fire, nor sword, nor the gnawing tooth of time shall ever be able to undo. When it will, let that day come which has no power save over this mortal frame, and end the span of my uncertain years. Still in my better part I shall be borne immortal far above the lofty stars and I shall have an undying name. Wherever Rome's power extends over the conquered world, I shall have mention on men's lips, and, if the prophecies of bards have any truth, through all the ages shall I live in fame.

For Sidney Lee on Ovid and the Sonnets, see my note to S. 59. In his *Problems of Shakespeare's Sonnets* (1928), J. M. Robertson suggested that S. 55 is a commendatory poem intended for inclusion in a volume of love-poetry. Following this up, Mona Wilson (*Sir Philip Sidney*, 1931) pointed out that it fits *Astrophel and Stella* better than any other production of the early nineties. In 1965 my friend Kenneth Muir argued strongly that the reference to Sidney is a mare's nest; and indeed there is no reason why the sonnet should not be one of the most splendid tributes offered to the Friend.

1. *monuments* (M.) Q 'monument,'. The rhyme and the plur. 'princes' confirm M. For 'gilded monuments' cf. 66.5 a 'gilded honour'.

4. *unswept stone* The stone of course bore an inscription to the dead man, the letters of which had become obscured, 'sluttish' (= dirty) in course of time.

7. *Nor...sword* The verb 'destroy' is understood. *burn:* (Q) Emphasizing next line. All edd. except S.-Smith omit colon.

9. *all-oblivious enmity* oblivion that wars against the memory of all men. M.'s hyphen. Q. 'Emnity'.

10. *pace forth* go forward.

12. *wear...out* outlast.

56

This sonnet puzzles all the critics. But, as D. suggests, 'the "love". Sh. addresses is the love in his own breast'. The grand passion of 55 is naturally followed by a reaction, while the 'interim' (l. 9) I feel sure refers to the Poet's absence from the Friend. In a word, he is still on his journey. Note that ll. 13–14 suggest the coming of winter (for which see 97).

6. *wink* shut in sleep (B.).

8. *dulness* insensibility.

9. *sad interim* period of apathy (B.). Period of estrangement or possibly absence (P.).

10. *contracted new* lately betrothed, see 1. 5 (P.).

11. *see*: (Q+S.-Smith) most edd. omit colon, which makes 'return of love' emphatic.

13. *Or* (M.) Q 'As'. *it* i.e. the 'sad interim'.

57–8

A linked pair (see *Gleanings*, pp. 115–16).

57

A sonnet after the discovery expressed in the form of extreme irony. See Introd. p. lvii for my suggestion that 48 introduces the 'liaison group'. The fear openly stated in 48 that 'Truth proves thievish for a prize so dear' was, I conjecture, followed by a request for an interview, and what happens then is related in 57, 58, 61.

Internal stylistic links: 57. slave, hours and times, time, hour, absence, slave, stay, ill; 58. slave, times, hours, stay, absence, time, ill.

5. *the world-without-end hour*=the hour as if it would never end (M.). Sh. prob. echoes the Gloria in B.C.P., but the exp. goes back to the *Ancren Riwle* (thirteenth century) at least. See *O.E.D.* Cf. *L.L.L.* 5. 2. 785, 'a world-without-end bargain' (M.). M.'s hyphens.

9. *jealous* Q 'iealious'—a freq. sixteenth–seventeenth c. sp.; suspicious, apprehensive of evil.

12. *Save...those*=save that how happy you make those where you are.

13. *So true a fool is love* So easy it is to deceive a true (loyal) lover. *in your will*=when you wish. Q puts 'Will' but no name-pun is, I think, intended, though a glance at 'will'=sexual desire may well be. Cf. 135. 2.

58

A continuation of 57.

1. *That god* (Dyce) Q 'That God'.

6. *Th'imprisoned...liberty* 'A typical instance of violent compression. The writer is imprisoned (i.e. cut off from the society of his friend) by the friend's absence, which is due to the friend's liberty of action' (Ridley *ap.* Roll.). Note the violence of the compression conveys the sense of insufferable restraint which the situation puts upon the Poet.

7. *tame to* (M+) Q 'tame, to'. *tame to sufferance* The image is that of a high-spirited horse or wild animal. The word 'check' = (*a*) rebuke (? here = hindrance); (*b*) curb, rein.

8. *injury* injustice (Sch.), insult.

9–10. *charter...privilege* sb. and vb. have much the same meaning and both imply the unquestionable privilege of rank.

11. *To* (Q) M+ 'Do'. B. 'the rhythm and sense of the quatrain are against Q. "Do what you will" answers rhetorically to "Be where you list".' Landry (p. 437) rightly claims M. 'violates the idiom and punctuation of Q'.

12. *self-doing* committed by yourself. The line makes it clear that the writer takes no responsibility for the crime. The tone becomes different in the later written 34, 35.

59

The text now leaves the liaison affair, at any rate for some time, and there follows (except for 61) a series of over a dozen sonnets, all, like 55, reflecting Ovid's *Metamorphoses* xv. They are as follows: 59, 60, 62, 63, 64, 65, 66, 67, 68, 71, 72, 73, 74 and its sequel 81 (see note). Though 69 and 70 have no connexion with Ovid, the whole series is clearly in the order in which Shakespeare wrote them.*

I believe too that all were written in absence while Shakespeare was travelling on the two months' journey referred to in my notes on 36.

The sonnet 55 is also Ovidian; this and the others of the same kind reflect the cosmology that Ovid made popular—though it was derived chiefly from Pythagoras and the Stoics—a cosmology the central doctrine of which was the indestructibility of life, its transmigration through a variety of forms, and the eternal recurrence of all things and persons.

For such periods of recurrence Sh. uses the term 'revolution', a term he did not, I think, find in either Ovid or Golding. Orig. it was an astrological term denoting the rotatory movement of the Ptolemaic universe round about the earth at its centre every twenty-four hours, but came to be used for any such cosmic rotatory movement. And what Ovid had in mind was clearly a 'revolution' much longer in duration, during which such changes are complete. (Cf. *O.E.D.* 2*b*, 'A cycle or recurrent period of time', citing Hooker, *Eccl. Pol.*, 1597, 'The day...changed in regard of a new revolution begun by Our Saviour Christ'.)

* See Introd. pp cxiv ff.

We owe our recognition of Ovid's widespread influence on the sonnets to a posthumous essay by Sidney Lee (in *Elizabethan and other Essays*, 1929); see my Introd. p. cxv. It is nevertheless necessary to insist that what Lee calls the Ovidian sonnets are poetry, not scientific statements, inasmuch as Lee writes as if Sh. were some sort of second-rate sixteenth-century scientist or 'philosopher'. Speaking for instance about the sestet of the present sonnet, he writes: 'Sh. though tempted to assent, stays hesitating at the threshold. In Sonnet 13 he takes a bolder position, though again his intellectual courage evaporates when in face of the inevitable conclusion' (Lee, p. 132). It seems incredible that a scholar who had been reading Sh. all his life should have so completely misunderstood the processes of his mind.

As pointed out in my Introd. p. lxxvii, here as in 33 there is a close parallel with *Henry IV* at this time, e.g. here with *2 H. IV*, 3. 1. 45 ff.—so close once again that the two must surely have been written at much the same time, though I fancy the sonnet comes first.

1–2. *If there...beguiled* Note how personal the old adage, 'nothing new under the sun', has become. Suppose this praise has all been offered before to another person like you 500 years ago [see 5–8 below]! Tuck cites Eccles. i. 9.

5–8. *O that record...done* i.e. 'Would that I could read a description of you in the earliest manuscript that appeared after the first use of letters' (M.). As the Herberts claimed descent from 'Herbertus Camerarius, a companion in arms of William the Conqueror, *five hundred years* before the time at which Sh. wrote', Mary Suddard (*ap*. Roll.) thinks this may be a reference to the Pembroke family.

10. *To...frame* To this marvellously fashioned body of yours.

11. *are mended* have improved, (or) are made better. Cf. On. '"make better, improve" in various contexts, is the most freq. sense'. *or whether* Q has 'where'—a freq. contracted form. Cf. *Ven.* 304. M. 'whe'r'.

12. *whether revolution* 'Whether time in its course produces the same things, same qualities, same kinds of men' (Ver.).

13. *the wits* men of intelligence and discernment.

60

Based on an earlier passage in *Met.* xv, viz. ll. 176–84.

1–4. *Like as the waves...* Cf. Gold. pp. 298–9, ll. 197–205 (I have modernized the sp.):

In all the world there is not that that standeth at a stay.
Things ebb and flow, and every shape is made to pass away.
The time itself continually is fleeting like a brook.
For neither brook nor lightsome time can tarry still. But look
As every wave drives other forth, and that that comes behind
Both thrusteth and is thrust itself: even so the times by kind
Do fly and follow both at once, and evermore renew.
For that that was before is left, and straight there doth ensue
Another that was never erst.

5. *light,* (Gild.) Q 'light.'.

5–6. *Nativity...Crawls to maturity* Nativity (abstract for concrete) = newborn child. *the main of light* = the ocean of light. A summary of several lines in Golding describing the daylight that greets the newborn's eyes. *Crawls to maturity* is a compressed borrowing from Golding, ll. 243–6:

The child newborn lies void of strength. Within a season though
He waxing fourfooted learns like savage beasts to go.
Then somewhat faltering, and as yet not firm of foot, he stands
By getting somewhat for to help his sinews in his hands.

Roll. notes that the borrowing from Ovid was seen long ago by Walker (*Critical Examinations*, 1860, I, pp. 152).

7. *crooked eclipses* malignant influence of the stars—that have governed him from birth.

8. *Time* Q 'time'.

9. *Time doth transfix the flourish* Time with its dart splits the plume on the crest of youth.

61

Another liaison sonnet, as the final couplet shows, see Introd. p. lvii, making the third of a trio following upon 57 and 58. D. alone seems to have perceived that 'the jealous feeling of 57 reappears in this sonnet'. Most critics have missed the humble irony of the whole, the accusations implied in the octet, and the passionate outburst of the sestet. They compare 43; but what a contrast! Deliberate, I suspect.

4. *mock*=deceive by imitation.

7. *shames and idle hours* 'A hendiadys, the meaning being "to see how badly I spend my spare time"' (P.).

8. *the scope and tenure*='the essential content or meaning' (Alden *ap*. Roll.). 'tenure' is the Q reading. Landry, p. 437 n. 9, calls M.'s emendation to 'tenour', which is generally followed, unnecessary.

11. *mine own true love* the inference is surely clear enough. *defeat*=destroy.

13. *watch and wake* A pointed antithesis; a watch-

man=one on guard; the implication here (and elsewhere) is that in Sh.'s eyes the intrigue is not only robbery. P. cites 144. 11. 'But being both from me both to each friend.'

62–8

These seven sonnets, clearly connected with each other, make a series not at first easy to place, nor have they been found by the critics easy to interpret. P.'s comments on individual sonnets display his usual percipience, but D. goes far astray in an attempt to connect 62 with jealousy and the liaison affair. My solution is a simple one: the group is a continuation of the Ovidian series begun in 59, though there are several earlier ones influenced by Ovid as well as 55. The failure to realize this is, I think, due to the fact that 62 seems at first sight to be an isolated sonnet. It is, however, indisputably a prelude to 63, while as Lee (p. 135) observes, 63. 5

> Hath travelled on to age's steepy night

is a reflexion of Golding (ed. 1904, foot of p. 299):

> Through drooping age's steepy path he runneth out his race.

But to see the relation to Ovid at this point, 62 and 63 which form a pair should be taken together and read with the relevant lines from Golding before one. Ovid is describing the effects of old age (xv. 227–236; Golding, 249–260): and after the line about 'drooping age's steepy path' we have five lines describing how Milo wept when he saw the effects of old age upon his body. Whereupon follows

> And Helen when she saw her aged wrinkles in
> A glass, wept also: musing in herself what men had seen,

That by two noble princes' sons she twice had ravished been.
Thou Time, the eater up of things, and age of spiteful teen,
Destroyest all things.

In 62 we have the once lovely face gazing into the looking-glass and in 63 we have the lines and wrinkles in which Time's injurious hand had drained the blood and

youthful morn
Hath travelled on to age's steepy night.

And so Ovid's wrinkled Helen has become through the Poet's transmigration the middle-aged Shakespeare seeing his face

Beated and chopt with tanned antiquity

as he gazes into the glass. And note too that the Helen passage leads straight on to one of the most famous of Ovid's declamations:

Tempus edax rerum, tuque, invidiosa vetustas,
Omnia destruitis.

And so we get ll. 1–4, 'wrinkles' and all.

The truth is, as already stated, that behind these seven sonnets and a good many others elsewhere there lies a very careful reading or at least a vivid memory of Ovid's account of the philosophy of Pythagoras, which occupies a considerable portion of Book xv of the *Metamorphoses*, and probably at many places the actual words of Golding's translation.

62

'A compliment in the form of a confession of vanity' (P.). Note the similarity of 61 and 62. Both affect an identity or interchange of personality and both make it clear in the concluding lines: in 61 'It is my love', etc. in 62 ''Tis thee (my self)', etc. Thus though the second deals with a totally different situation from the first it is not difficult to see why Thorpe placed the liaison sonnet (61) at this point.

2. *all and my every part* Sch. cites *K.J.* 4. 2. 38.

4. *grounded...heart* From B.C.P. 'grafted inwardly in our hearts' (P.). Communion Collect *ad fin.*

5. *gracious* attractive, lovely (On.).

6. *true...truth* Not intended, I think, to be ironical. Points therefore to a date before the Friend's treachery. Lee cites *Lr.* 1. 2. 8 'my shape as true'.

7. *for my self* 'for my own satisfaction' (D.). Poss. 'privately'.

8. *As*=as though (B.). *other* i.e. others.

10. *Beated and chopt* For 'beated' see *O.E.D.* 'beat' 17 crush, batter (B.) and 'chopt'=marked with cracks, seamed, cf. *Lucr.* 1452, 'Her cheeks with chops and wrinkles were disguised' (B.). 63. 2 'crushed and o'erworn' give the same meaning. N.B. Sh. is here describing his own face; have we any other self-portrait?

On. adopts Herford's conj. for 'beated'=flayed. Properly an agricultural term (still used in Devonshire) for paring away the sods from moorland. Surely somewhat far-fetched.

11. *read:* (S.-Smith) Q. 'read'. The hyphens in this and the next line are not in Q but are warranted by 'self-love' in l. 1 which is.

13. *'Tis thee...praise* 'Tis thee, myself (i.e. who art myself) that for myself (i.e. as if myself) I praise' (Ver.).

14. *Painting...days.* 'By identifying myself with you, I fancy myself beautiful' (Harrison *ap.* Roll.). Q 'daies,'.

63, 64, 65

A linked triplet of sonnets (see Chambers (1), p. 116).

The stylistic links are: 63. love, Time's, hand, age's, night, beauties, sight, away, time, age's, love's beauty, lover's, beauty, black. 64. Time's, hand, age, brass, mortal, decay, Time, love away. 65. brass, mortality, beauty, days, Time decays, Time's, hand, beauty, might, black, love, bright.

63

A direct continuation of 62.

2. *Time's* Q has no cap. *crushed and o'erworn* See 62. 10 'beated and chopt'. Tuck. suggests a metaphor from old clothes: 'As of a garment which has lost its nap. So "crushed" implies crumpled.'

3. *filled* (edd.) Q 'fild'.

8. *spring:* (M.) Q 'Spring.'.

10. *confounding...knife* i.e. the scythe of Time as in 100. 14 (Sch.).

64

1–4. *Time's fell hand...brass eternal* This echoes at once Ovid's *tempus edax rerum* (see 63. 3, 10) and Horace's *aere perennius* (Odes, III, 30). See also 55. *Time's* Q has no cap.

2. *rich-proud* M.'s hyphen.

cost=anything that costs expense; here of buildings.

3. *down-rased* M.'s hyphen.

4. *mortal rage* deadly fury.

5–9. *When I have seen...state* Lee (p. 130) points out that here Sh. follows Golding almost verbally, even to identifying himself with Ovid, though he might well have observed such things on the east coast of England. See Gold. p. 300, ll. 287–9:

Even so have places oftentimes exchanged their estate.
For I have seen it sea which was substantial ground alate,
Again where sea was, I have seen the same become dry land.

8. *store* plenty, abundance (Sch.).

9–10. *state...state* Used in different senses: state (9) from Golding=condition; state (10) =greatness—as in 96. 122 (B.). Cf. Introd. p. xlviii. P. suggests that the second 'prob.=the "rich proud cost" of l. 2'. But 'interchange' hardly agrees with this. B. has the lines from *2 H. IV* in mind (3. 1. 45–51):

> O God! that one might read the book of fate,
> And see the revolution of the times
> Make mountains level, and the continent,
> Weary of solid firmament, melt itself
> Into the sea! and, other times, to see
> The beachy girdle of the ocean
> Too wide for Neptune's hips.

See Introd. pp. lxxvii. The punctuation of the Q is rhetorically most effective in this sonnet.

65

Though this looks like a poss. alternative to 63, the fact that the two are members of the same triplet forbids it (see *Gleanings*).

1–2. *Since brass...power* A summary of the arguments in 64. 1–10.

3. *this rage* (Q.) M. conj. 'his' cf. 64. 4 'mortal rage'.

3–4. *hold a plea...action* Legal terminology (D.). B. objects that 'action'=vigour (cf. *Caes.* 1. 3. 77). But Sh. quibbles as usual.

5. *summer's honey breath* The scent now stands for the flowers themselves, and the metaphor, legal in

ll. 3, 4, is now that of siege warfare, with winter as 'one of the forces of time' (B.).

6. *wrackful* (Q) M.+Camb. 'wreckful'.

10. *Time's best jewel...hid* Elliptical: i.e. 'Where shall what is Time's best jewel be hidden so as to escape being seized and locked up in his chest?' (B.)—citing *Troil.* 3. 3. 145 where Time has a wallet into which he puts good deeds as food for devouring Oblivion. Q has no caps. here.

12. *of* (M.) Q 'or'.

14. *in black ink* cf. 63. 13 'in these black lines', and see headnote, p. 169.

66

'Compare Hamlet's celebrated soliloquy [3. 1. 56–88] with this sonnet' (Cap.). 'From the thought of his friend's death Sh. turns to think of his own, and of the ills of life from which death would deliver him'. (D.).

1. *these* i.e. the following evils.

3. *needy nothing* 'needy' used as predicate = in need of; *O.E.D.* 1*c* (rare); not in On. 'Opposed to "desert", what lacks all merit' (B.). *trimmed in jollity* Cf. *3 H.VI*, 2. 1. 24 'Trimmed like a younker prancing to his love'. *jollity* = finery.

4. *unhappily* = miserably. *forsworn* abandoned, lit. renounced on oath.

5. *gilded honour* With Sh. 'gilt' seems to imply something specious or spurious.

8. *strength...disabled* It is tempting to suspect a glance at the control of the State (including vigorous military men like Raleigh and Essex) by the limping Robert Cecil.

9. *art...authority* 'Can this refer to the censorship of the stage?' (D.). If it does 'the troubles of 1596 and

1597...are more likely to be in point than those of 1600' (Chambers (2), 1, 562).

10. *doctor-like* pedant-like. Holofernes in *L.L.L.* is Sh.'s portrait of him in action.

11. *simplicity* stupidity. Q hyphens *simple truth*.

12. *captive good* i.e. 'good helpless in the hands of evil' (P.). Q hyphens.

14. *alone*. Alden remarks on the unlikelihood of Sh. 'leaving alone' after his death such a personage as an earl. The best reply to this is the impossibility of such thoughts occurring to Sh. in such a sonnet. The meaning here is clearly 'unprotected by me'; and 67 gives something of a reply.

67

'This sonnet and the next are, like the last, in dispraise of the present evil times; but they are concerned with a more superficial fault, namely, the use of cosmetics and false hair, which, as we may judge from certain passages in the plays, seems to have been especially repugnant to Sh. See *Tw. Nt.* 1. 5. 240; *Ham.* 3. 1. 145; *M.V.* 3. 2. 92; *Tim.* 4. 3. 146' (B.).

1, 2. *infection...impiety* i.e. this sinful world (B.). *with infection*='in an age of corruption' (P.).

4. *lace* embellish, as in *Mac.* 2. 3. 112 (D.).

6. *dead seeming* (Cap. and Farmer conj.) Q+M.+Camb.+B. 'dead seeing'. But Cap. gives a sense more obviously in keeping with the context. Tuck. pronounces the emendation 'highly probable'.

7. *poor*=so destitute as to be dependent upon the gifts or alms of others for subsistence. See *O.E.D.* 'poor' B. 1. 1 legal sense. *indirectly* at second hand.

10. *Beggared...veins* And therefore dependent upon cosmetics to supply the lack of blood to blush with. *lively*=living hue.

11–14. *no exchequer...days long since* 'Nature is represented as proud of her many beautiful forms "in days long since"; he is the only one actually in existence and her reputation depends on him' (P.).

12. *gains* earnings—what his imperishable beauty continues to accumulate or add to Nature's exchequer or store.

68

Continues and develops 67: the friend the last representative of the age of simplicity.

1. *map* 'a detailed representation in epitome, also embodiment, very picture or image (*of* something).' On.

4. *inhabit* dwell.

13–14. *And him...doth Nature store* etc. Cf. couplet of 67. *Art* Q: antithesis with 'Nature'.

69–70

A pair of sonnets apparently referring to rumours reaching Sh. which seem to have brought the Friend into disrepute with the world; sonnets that seem quite independent of those that precede or follow, though it is arguable that the theme of 67–8, the Friend as the sole surviving representative, in an evil world, of the age of antiquity.

When beauty lived and died as flowers do now, naturally led Sh. to consider what happens to his beloved when he lives with infection and graces impiety with his presence.

He seems but recently come to Court or at least to London and his conduct is being narrowly watched. None can but praise his beauty and charm, but judging his character by his deeds they privately comment unfavourably upon it. Sh. does not more than hint at his own unfavourable opinion (e.g. 'so thou be good'

70. 5). What he counsels the youth is that since great beauty always arouses envy and provokes suspicion, his wisest course is to give people few opportunities of criticism by ceasing to court popularity.

69

2. *Want...mend* i.e. the world can see nothing but perfection in thy *outward* parts.

3. *that due* (Cap., M.) Q 'that end'. The letters *d* and *e* being formed alike in the secretary hand, the misreading was natural and apparently justified by the rhymes in ll. 2 and 4.

4. *bare* Emphatic (Ver.). *even...commend* 'i.e. without exaggeration' (P.). Q prints 'Commend' with a capital C, which may be a link with the author, who commonly wrote initial *c* as a capital; see *Sh.'s Hand in Sir T. More*, pp. 115–16.

5. *Thy outward* (M. 1780) Q 'Their outward'. *outward*=(sb.) appearance, exterior; (adj.) superficial, without an intimate knowledge of; cf. *All's*, 3. 1. 11.

8. *By seeing* The subj. is 'those who speak' understood from 'tongues' (<Tuck.).

10. *thy deeds* Anon. conj. (Camb.) gives 'their deeds', which some read, but B. asks Why should people be called 'churls' for judging a man by his own deeds?

12. *weeds:* (M.+edd.) Q 'weeds,'.

14. *soil* (Camb.<Cap. and Delius conj.). Q 'solye', a misp. of 'soyle'. Cf. Camb. note 1 (Sonnets): 'As the vb. "to soil" is not uncommon in Old English [late M.E.], meaning "to solve", as for example: "This question could not one of them all soil" (Udal's *Erasmus, Luke*, fol. 154*b*), so the substantive "soil" may be used in the sense of "solution".' There is of

course a play upon "soil"=blemish, fault. *common* not vulgar in the mod. sense, so much as hail-fellow-well-met. B. glosses 'too little choice in your company' and cites *Cor.* 2. 3. 100, while P. more appositely cites *1 H. IV*, 3. 2. 40–1. See Introd. p. lxxvi above.

70

Develops the same theme as 69. But the nature of the unsavoury deeds is now more clearly hinted at and learning of his lasciviousness from other sonnets, we can guess what it was. From ll. 8–10 I infer that the sonnet was written (1) soon after the Friend's first arrival in London and (2) before the discovery of the liaison.

1. *art* (edd.) Q 'are'.

2–3. *slander's mark...suspect* Refers to the prov. Tilley B 163: 'Beauty and chastity (honesty) seldom meet.' Cf. Hamlet's use of this in the Nunnery scene (*Ham.* 3. 1. 111 ff.). *mark* for a missile (Tuck.).

3. *The ornament* etc. M. cites Pettie, *Civil Conversation*, 1581 (ed. 1925, II, 10 ff.) 'it is a matter almost impossible, and seldom seen, that beauty and honesty agree together...it falleth out seldom but that exquisite beauty is held in suspicion'.

4. *A crow* the c. was a black and filthy bird. Cf. *Lucr.* 1009 (Tuck.).

5–8. *So thou be good* etc. 'The argument is that as temptation to vice is greatest in the case of youths whose attractiveness renders them popular, so the fact of being slandered is a testimony to popularity, and does not matter provided there is no ground for the slander' (B.). *approve* prove.

6. *Thy* (M.) Q 'Their'. *wooed of time*='courted by the world' (B., who quotes 'the whips and scorns of time' *Ham.* 3. 1. 70, and *Son.* 117. 6).

7. *the sweetest buds* Cap. *ap* M. compares *Gent.* 1. 1. 42 ff. 'in the sweetest bud|The eating canker dwells'.

9–10. *Thou...charged* I paraphrase 'You have so far escaped the temptation of youth, either not tempted or if tempted emerging victorious'. *Either* See Abbott for other examples of the softening of the 'th' in either.

11–12. *Yet this...enlarged* 'You must not expect your former good reputation to safeguard you against criticism of your present conduct' (Brooke).

12. *evermore enlarged* perpetually released, always rampant.

71

After the pessimistic 66, Sh. concentrates almost entirely on that aspect of the Ovid 'revolution' that concerns decay and death. In 66 he passes from the tyranny of Time as seen in the realm of nature including the human body to a consideration of Death, his own and the Friend's, and this topic now forms the main theme of 67, 71, 72, 73, 74 and perhaps 81. But, as the headnote to 62–8 points out, the influence of Ovid *Met.* xv is never very far from Sh.'s mind.

D. comments on 71: 'Sh. goes back to the thought of his own death from which he was led away in 66. 14 ("to die, I leave my love alone"). The world in this sonnet is the "vile world" described in 66.'

1–3. Cf. 2 *H. IV*, 1. 1. 102:

as a sullen bell,
Remembered tolling a departing friend.

2. *Than* (M.) Q 'Then'—a common form of 'than'.

10. *compounded...clay* M. cites *2 H. IV*, 4. 5. 115 'Only compound me with forgotten dust'—K. Henry

to Prince Hal. 'compound' = blend. Cf. *Ham.* 4. 2. 6 ff. 'What have you done, my Lord, with the dead body?—Compounded it with dust whereto 'tis kin', and *2 H. IV*, 1. 2. 7: 'this foolish-compounded clay-man'.

13. *the wise world* Sh. implies that 'the world will judge his shortcomings only too well' (Tuck.)—as expounded in 72.

72

1. *recite* relate.

4. *prove* find out by experience or examination.

13. *that which I bring forth* Does this refer to the sonnets or to the plays? Critics are divided. B. interprets l. 14 as 'the first notice that Sh.'s friend takes any interest in his poems'.

73

'Still, as in 71–2, thoughts of approaching death' (D).

1–4. Cf. Ovid, *Met.* xv, 199–213, likening the body's changes from birth to death with the changes in nature from spring to winter, and note esp. Gold. xv, 231 ff. (p. 299):

> Then followeth Harvest when the heat of youth grows somewhat cold,
> ...And somewhat sprent with grayish hairs. Then ugly winter last
> Like age steals on with trembling steps, all bald, or overcast
> With shirle [i.e. rough] thin hair as white as snow.

The description may have been apt to a prematurely bald man as the Stratford bust suggests Sh. to have been.

4. *Bare...sang* The monasteries, most of which had been dissolved about 1535, a generation before Sh.'s birth, will have fallen into 'cureless ruin' by 1590. The sweet birds, I take it, stand for the 'sweet singing in the choir' celebrated in the old carol of the Holly and the Ivy. *ruined* (edd.) Q 'rn'wd'.

5–8 *In me...rest* May well have been suggested by *Met.* xv. 186–98 (the change from Day to Night).

8. *Death's second self* Cf. *Mac.* 2. 2. 38 '[sleep] the death of each day's life'.

9–12. *In me...nourished by.* 'Wasting away on the dead ashes which once nourished it with living flame, (D.). Derived like the image at 1. 6 'Feed'st thy life's flame with self-substantial fuel' from the practice of raking up a fire in ashes to keep it alight. If not so covered up it dies, smothered by the ashes about it. Cf. Gray's *Elegy*, 92 'E'en in our ashes live their wonted fires'.

74

'An immediate continuation of 73' (D.).

1. *But...arrest* 'There is perhaps nothing, even in the Sonnets, equal in dignity and beauty to this calm opening' (B.). Cap. first noted the close parallel in *Ham.* 5. 2. 334 ff. 'this fell sergeant, Death, | Is strict in his arrest'. Which was written first? *But be contented when* (Q) M. and most edd. read 'But be contented: when'.

2. *bail* In its mod. meaning.

3. *this line* this verse. *some interest* 'some revenue of fame falling in, year by year, after my death' (W.).

6. *consecrate* the older form of 'consecrated'.

7. *The earth...due* Cf. Eccles. xii. 7 'Then shall the dust return to the earth as it was: and the spirit shall return unto God who gave it' (Carter *ap.* Roll.). M. notes the resemblance to the words of the Burial Service.

8. *the better part of me* Leishman (pp. 60–2) notes the echo here of Ovid, *Met.* xv, 875–6:

> Parte tamen meliore mei super alta perennis
> Astra ferar

and that Sh. may have been reminded of the Ovid by lines in Ronsard's *Élégie à Marie* which was certainly, he thinks, inspired by the Ovid *locus.*

11. *The coward...knife* The words so precisely recount the details and circumstances of Marlowe's death that it seems impossible that they should not be intended to allude to them and to suggest that Sh., another dramatic poet, might perhaps come to a like base end. And this meaning would have been clear had the line begun with *Or* instead of *The* which Thorpe reads. Line 10 begins with *The* and no type of misprint is more common than one due to a compositor's eye catching the initial word of the line above.

13. *that* the body.

14. *this* the spirit of the poet.

75

'So' = it follows that 'the better part of me' is that which keeps me alive. A supreme example of this 'better part' was S. 55, and the present sonnet shows how the Poet's mind swings between exaltation and depression, as it evidently does in the passage from 55 to 56.

2. *sweet-seasoned* M.'s hyphen. 'of the sweet season, i.e. April' (P.).

3. *the peace of you* the peace I enjoy when with you. 'antithesis to strife' (D.).

6–8. *Doubting...my pleasure* The lines imply that the Friend is now well known in London.

6. *Doubting* fearing.

8. *bettered* P. glosses 'made happier or prouder'. Cap. conj. 'better', which follows on 'best' more neatly.

13. *pine* starve.

14. *gluttoning* With these passionate terms compare the language of 56. *away* Q 'away,'.

76, 78, 79, 80, 82–6

The 'Rival Poet' series. Printed in the right order, which is however interrupted by the unrelated 77 and 81. That the order apart from this is correct is shown, I think, by the fact that each successive sonnet seems to bring one closer to the rival, until in 86 he is directly pointed at; the whole series being couched in an ironical or mocking vein. And I suspect that while 77 is an 'occasional' sonnet, for which Thorpe could find no place elsewhere, and perhaps not intended for the Friend at all (see next headnote), number 81 on the other hand, seeming to make a plausible sequel to 80 with its reference to the Poet's being cast away and to his 'decay' (ll. 13–14), was borrowed, I think, from the Death series (71 ff.). For the identity of the Rival see Introd. pp. lxvi ff.

76

Sh. finds himself lagging behind in poetic fashion; he has only one topic and is bound to be monotonous. D. asks, 'Is this an apology for Sh.'s own sonnets—of which his friend begins to weary—in contrast with the verses of the Rival Poet?' I interpret it, as I do the rest of the series, ironically. When alluding satirically to an opponent it was a common practice of Elizabethan writers to speak of him in the plural. Nashe constantly did so. Moreover, when Sh. writes in 83 'Than both your poets can in praise devise', he himself is of course one of the two.

Sh.'s pointed refusal to 'glance aside to new-found methods' and to 'compounds strange' may well refer to the style of a single poet, and if Chapman be the poet aimed at the words describe his style not inaptly.

3. *Why with the time* etc. Cf. 32. 5.

4. *new-found* M.'s hyphen. *compounds* compound words (*O.E.D.*, citing this).

5. *keep...weed* retain my usual poetic style.

7. *tell* (Cap.+M.) Q 'fel'.

8. *where* whence (Sch.).

14. *told* Q 'told,'.

77

Obviously an 'occasional' poem out of place here and maybe not meant for the Friend at all in whom 'wrinkles' (ll. 5–6) would seem odd. But that it is Sh.'s cannot be doubted. Perhaps he is presenting a table-book (cf. 122 and *Ham.* 1. 5. 107), a mirror and a pocket-dial (cf. *A.Y.L.* 2. 7. 20 'he drew a dial from his poke') to another and older friend than the rest of the sonnets were addressed to.

1. *wear* (edd.) Q 'were'.

3. *These* (Cap.+M. conj.) Q 'the'.

4. *this learning* i.e. 'what the glass and the dial have taught thee' (B.)

6. *mouthed* gaping.

7. *shady stealth* stealing shadow (Sch.).

10. *blanks* (Theobald conj.+M.) Q 'blacks'.

11–12. *Those children* etc. 'You will see your thoughts—those children of your brain—nursed, i.e. tended or cared for' (P.).

78

The two references to learning indicate that Sh. has in particular a learned poet in mind, and prob. one who boasts of his own learning and despises Sh. as unlearned. For the ironical tone see head-comment of 76.

3. *alien* belonging to others. *use* habitual practice (of addressing poems to you). Perhaps 'caught my tricks of style' (Ver.).

4. *disperse* publish, put into circulation (*O.E.D.* 4*b*, of books). A hint of what the sonneteers did with their productions. Did Sh. also? *under thee* under your patronage (P.), inspiration (B.).

5. *the dumb* i.e. Sh. *on high* aloud.

6. *heavy ignorance* So *Oth.* 2. 1. 143.

8. *grace...majesty* Qualities of the learned poet.

9. *compile* compose.

10. *influence* An astrol. term. The Friend is spoken of as a star. So=inspiration.

12. *arts* learning, scholarship—includes both scientific and literary scholarship.

13. *advance* raise, lift up.

79

The rival has now become 'thy poet'; the Friend looks favourably upon him; Sh. ridicules his verse.

2. *gentle* refined.

3. *gracious numbers* verses that seemed so attractive to you.

5. *thy lovely argument* the theme of your beauty.
7. *invent* write, compose.
11. *afford* offer.

80

Continuation of 79, but we draw still closer to the rival and are shown him as hostile, deliberately trying 'with all his might' to reduce Sh. to silence. Yet the contrast between the latter's 'saucy bark' and his rival's vessel of 'tall building, and of goodly pride' shows that Sh. is by no means disconcerted despite the ironical opening. And this contrast takes on additional force when we remember that it was drawn by a poet in days when saucy English boats were almost every year engaging, and often sinking, tall-built full-sailed galleons upon the Spanish main. Note too how S. 86 makes use of the same nautical imagery, almost in the same words at times. Yet with opposite effect.

1. *faint* 'feel discouraged' (P.).
2. *a better spirit* 'a greater genius' (P.).
7. *saucy* impudent Cf. *Troil.* 1. 3. 34 ff. for similar nautical image (Steev.).
8. *wilfully* recklessly, coolly.
9. *shallowest* most casual. On. glosses 'without consideration' (citing *2 H. IV*, 4. 2. 118). An obvious quibble.

81

Unrelated to the Rival Poet series, but connected with the Death sequence. In 81 the argument is carried much further: your name will be immortal, whichever of us dies before the other, it will be remembered when my name is utterly forgotten, even as that of the author of these lines, even when every human being now on earth has passed away. In short, as long as there are men to breathe, and eyes to read,

Your monument shall be my gentle verse

Coleridge (*Biog. Lit.* 1817, I. 32 f.) claimed that ll. 5–14 refuted the notion of Pope and others that Sh. was ignorant 'of his own comparative greatness'. But the promise of immortality for one's patron is of age-long antiquity in poetry, esp. with the sonneteers. Cf. Leish. pp. 27–91 ('Poetry as Immortalisation from Pindar to Shakespeare').

1, 2. *Or,..Or* Whether...or. Cf. Abbott, § 136.

3. *From hence*=from these poems (as in line 5) (T.T., P. and Tuck.).

4. *in me each part*=every part of me. 'Each part' is intended to cover 'the better part of me' (74. 8), and so the line means: although the fact that I was the author of this verse is forgotten—and ll. 5–6 emphasize the point by repetition.

7. *common* ordinary, as distinct from a 'monument' for a distinguished person.

8. *entombed in men's eyes* i.e. you will lie within the tomb of men's eyes, because my gentle verse, read as long as the world contains eyes to read, will furnish the tomb.

12. *breathers...world* Cf. *A.Y.L.* 3. 2. 277 'no breather in the world but myself' (M.).

82

Sh. claims no monopoly in the Friend's interest. Yet his sonnets speak the plain truth while his rival's dedications to the Friend are full of 'strained rhetoric' and 'gross painting' which would be more appropriate were paint needed for his cheeks. Yet it is natural the Friend should turn with interest to fresh fashions of poets in these 'time-bettering days'.

2. *without attaint* without disgrace (such as belongs to a cuckold). *o'erlook* peruse.

4. *their fair subject* i.e. you. *blessing every book* i.e. bestowing your blessing upon every book presented to you. This with the reference to 'dedicated words' seems to show that the rival's courtship took the form of dedicatory verses at the beginning of, or accompanying, books (? of learning) he had written.

5. *Thou art as fair* etc. 'You are as clever and wise as you are beautiful' (S.-Smith).

6. *Finding...praise* 'Sh. had celebrated his Friend's beauty (hue); perhaps his learned rival had celebrated the patron's knowledge as well; such excellence reached "a limit past the praise" of Sh., who knew small Latin and less Greek' (D.) Or was he implying, as I think, that the boy's learning was not so extensive after all?

8. *Some fresher stamp* Some more up-to-date style. Lit. some more recently issued currency. *the time-bettering days* Cf. 32. 5 'Compare them [Sh.'s verses] with the bett'ring of the time'. Note variations of sp. in Q. M.'s hyphen.

11. *sympathized* answered to, matched (B.).

12. *true plain...true-telling* Sewell's hyphen; Dyce reads 'true-plain'; Q has no hyphens.

13–14. *used...abused* D. cites *L.L.L.* 2. 1. 225–6:

This civil war of wits were much better used
On Navarre and his book-men, for here 'tis abused.

it is abused is put to wrong purposes, or perh. = is an insult.

83

Develops the theme of 82 but insists that while the Friend is alive his beauty is insulted by any praise a poet can offer it, while in ll. 13–14 he declares himself the better of the *two* poets.

3. (*or thought I found*) The parenthesis gives an air of self-assurance to the tone—as if Sh. were weighing the matter carefully.

4. *The barren tender...debt* i.e. your beauty being beyond all praise, must exceed any praise a poet feels he can pay it. Note Sh.'s sly flattery in the refusal to flatter.

5. *slept in your report* been careless or remiss in writing of you. Ironic. 'Clearly the Friend was not only a prey to flattery but also felt that Sh. himself had not been flattering enough to him. The whole is a subtle rebuke, though perhaps deliberately above the Friend's head' (S.-Smith).

6. *extant* alive (Roll.).

7. *modern* ordinary, commonplace. Cf. *A.Y.L.* 2. 7. 156 'wise saws and modern instances'.

8. *Speaking of worth*=when 'worth' is in question. *grow.* Q 'grow,'.

9. *silence* means, of course, my neglect to flatter you.

11. *impair not* do no harm to.

12. *bring a tomb* B. explains by citing 17. 3:

> [my verse] is but as a tomb
> Which hides your life, and shows not half your parts.

13–14. *There...eyes...devise* Evidence that there is only *one* rival; and if Chapman be the rival, a glance at an earlier debate reflected in S. 21. See the following:

Shakespeare's *Love's Labour's Lost* (first draft *c.* 1593–4) 4. 3. 299 ff.

> From woman's eyes this doctrine I derive—
> They are the ground, the books, the academes,
> From which doth spring the true Promethean fire.
> . . . .
> For where is any author in the world,
> Teaches such beauty as a woman's eyes?

Chapman, *A Coronet for his Mistress Philosophy* (1595), ll. 1–14:

> Muses that sing Love's sensual empery,
> And Lovers kindling your enraged fires
> At Cupid's bonfire burning in the eye,
> Blown with the empty breath of vain desires
> . . . .
> Your eyes were never yet, let in to see
> The majesty and riches of the mind,
> But dwell in darkness; for your God is blind.

And that Sh. well knew the *Coronet* is proved by his parody in S. 21 of Chapman's *Amorous Zodiac* printed in the same volume.

84

Reiterates the theme of 83 but more outspokenly; for the final couplet means: you dote upon praise, and that's why you get offered such bad poetry.

1. *most,* (Q) 'most?' M. Though edd. generally follow M., Percy Simpson (p. 13) insists that Q is correct and 'which' a relative pronoun, a reading P. interprets as follows: 'Who that says most can say more than that you are yourself...?' What could be plainer than the adoring 'You are yourself alone'? Cf. *Ant.* 3. 2. 13 'Would you praise Caesar, say "Caesar": go no further' (Tuck.)

2. *you?* (M.+) Q 'you,'.

3–4. *In whose confine...grew* 'None but yourself can be your parallel; the store which should produce your equal is "Beauty's store", and she hath no exchequer now but yours' [67. 11] (P.).

4. *grew.* (M.+Camb.) Q 'grew,'.

5. *Lean penury...pen* B. citing this and 64. 11, 'Ruin hath taught me thus to ruminate' observes Sh.'s alliteration, so beautiful in 5. 9 ff., 'occasionally almost passes into punning and then offends modern, taste' (Introd. lv).

10. *clear* glorious. Cf. *M.V.* 2. 9. 42.

13. *your beauteous blessings*=the beauty heaven has blessed you with. *a curse* a great evil (*O.E.D.*).

85

'Continues the subject of 84. Sh.'s friend is "fond on praise"; Sh.'s muse is silent while others compile comments of his praise' (D.). But he *thinks* good thoughts.

1. *tongue-tied* Cf. 80. 4. An admission that the rival has succeeded in his design. *in manners* out of politeness (at least).

2. *comments* elaborations.

3. *Reserve* M. glosses 'preserve' and On. agrees, citing *All's*, 3. 5. 63, 'a reservéd honesty'=a carefully guarded chastity; *Cymb.* 1. 1. 87 'always reserved my holy duty'=so far as I may say it without breach of duty. In view of these parallels, emendation is uncalled for. Cf. 32. 7.

3–4. *character* Handwriting; and 'golden quill', 'precious' and 'filed' suggest the notion of creation and writing down a poem in a form which will render it imperishable. The rival would of course, like Sh., promise eternity of fame.

5–6. Roll. cites I Cor. xiv. 16, 'when thou shalt bless with the spirit, how shall he that occupieth the room of the unlearned say Amen at thy giving of thanks'.

7. *that able spirit* the 'better spirit'. Cf. 80. 2.

11–12. *But that...before* Though I cannot find words to rival his, my loving thoughts far outstrip his.

13. *the breath of words* 'words that are mere breath' (Tuck.).

14. *speaking in effect* Cf. 23. 13–14:

> O learn to read what silent love hath writ,
> To hear with eyes belongs to love's fine wit.

86

The last of the Rival Poet series; for, as its final couplet shows, Sh. has come to realize that the Friend has gone over to the enemy. And that being so, he contents himself by giving two reasons why he has been reduced to silence, one genuine (ll. 1–4), the other (ll. 5–12), derisory; and both serving to identify the victorious poet with George Chapman.

A strong case for the identification was cogently set forth a century ago by William Minto, supported by Dowden in 1881, and still further strengthened in 1952 by the arguments of J. A. K. Thomson. See Introd. pp. lxvi ff.

1. *Was it...verse* 'This', P. observes, 'if not ironical, could apply only to Marlowe's verse or Chapman's, and Marlowe died in 1593.' That to Chapman alone it applies is argued out at length in the Introd.

2. *Bound for the prize...you* The piratical galleon 'of tall building, and of goodly pride' spoken of in 80, having put the 'saucy boat' to flight, now has the prize at his mercy. That I take to be Sh.'s answer to

Chapman's gibe about the *Poems* as 'idolatrous plats for riches'. (*all too precious*) Sh. elsewhere uses brackets for emphasis. Cf. *Ham.* 1, 2, 255 'My father's spirit (in arms!) all is not well'.

3–4. *That did...they grew* i.e. My best ideas are still-born. *inhearse* coffin.

4. *Making their tomb the womb* etc. M. compares with *Rom.* 2. 3. 9–10:

> The earth that's nature's mother is her tomb;
> What is her burying grave, that is her womb.

7. *his compeers by night* If this refers to other people besides Homer, they must be ethnics like Virgil, Ovid, or Statius, since the spirits of Christians did not walk by night—unless, as some thought, they came from Purgatory. Marlowe's fearful death and reputation for blasphemy might have qualified him for that part. Prof. K. Muir adds that Chapman implies that Marlowe (perh. his spirit) instructed him to finish his *H. and L.*

8. *astonished* stunned (On.).

9–10. *that affable...intelligence* This I believe is another allusion to Homer, to a false Homer as distinct from the Homer of the *Iliad*, from the study of which, as the world knew, Chapman derived the inspiration for his translation. See Thomson, quoted in Introd., who explains 'affable familiar' spirit as a stock term of the demonologists.

10. *intelligence* lit. a secret agent, a spy. Cf. *K.J.* 4. 2. 116. Prob. another technical term of demonology. Adams cites Ford, *Broken Heart*, III, iv (*Works*, ed. Dyce, 1, 272) 'You have a spirit, sir, have ye? a familiar | That posts i'th'air for your intelligence?' For 'intelligence' as a spirit, see *O.E.D.* 4, and cf. Prospero's Ariel.

13. *countenance* authority, patronage (Sch.). But Roll. notes 'this *could* mean, when your physical beauty became the theme of the rival's poetry'. *filled up* i.e. supplied 'anything that might be lacking in it' (Tuck.).

87–94

The 'Farewell Sonnets'. After 86 a change inevitably takes place in the relations between Poet and Friend: Sh. has admitted that Chapman has a right to the favour the Friend shows him, and though the sonnets continue for a time they are profoundly pessimistic and sometimes bitter. B. describes the group as 'an appeal by the Poet against the Friend's estrangement'. I prefer to call them the Farewell Sonnets.

In my first draft I attempted to expound them as Thorpe gives them; and readers of what I then wrote must have noticed how difficult I found it to explain the sequence of the first half of the eight sonnets. But I can now see that P. is right in regarding 49 as misplaced and by rights a member of this group. Let the reader insert it between 87 and 88 and it will be found to supply what seems otherwise a missing step in Sh.'s bitter account of an anticipated process of gradual estrangement. With this addition the steps become: 87 the Friend had given himself too cheaply and now realizes that the Poet has nothing to give in return; 49 the day comes when he will scarcely recognize the Poet when they meet; 88 he will begin to run him down as he discusses him with acquaintances; 89 he enlarges on his faults to explain why he found it best to drop him; 90 and if it has to come to hatred the unhappy Poet begs him to hate him now when everything else is against him; 91–4 he tries another line of appeal, that of attack.

87

Leishman writes (p. 228): 'Sonnet 87 seems to declare "You have made me feel that in every way I am too much your inferior too much beneath your notice". That it was Sh. who had been made to feel like this rouses disgust with aristocratic pretension which it requires remembrance of such a friend and patron as Beethoven's Archduke Rudolf to counterbalance.'

1. *Farewell! thou* Q 'Farewell thou'. *dear* precious (in both senses); S.-Smith adds 'also grievous, I think doubtfully'.

2. *estimate* value, worth. The line is ironic; cf. *R. II*, 2, 3, 56.

3. *charter* privilege, freedom of action; cf. *Oth.* 1. 3. 245 'Let me find a charter in your voice' (P.). See 58. 9–10.

4. *determinate*=ended, out of date. 'The term is used in legal conveyances' (M.).

5–8. *For how...swerving* 'Based on the legal principle that a contract is unenforceable if it lacks a valuable consideration' (Brooke).

8. *patent* grant of a monopoly (On.). *is swerving* returns to you.

11. *upon misprision growing* 'arising from an oversight' (B.); legal terms again.

12. *on better...making* 'on your forming a better judgment' (Tuck.).

13. *as...flatter* D. cites *Rom.* 5. 1. 1.

88

P. suggests, 'Perhaps a continuation of 49' and Ver. 'Sounds like an echo of sonnet 49; here he does exactly what he there promised to do'.

1. *disposed* (edd.) Q 'dispode'. *set me light* 'value me little, despise me' (P.).

2. *place...scorn* 'Look scornfully upon my merit' (B.).

7. *concealed* secret. *attainted* corrupted.

8. *shalt* (Camb.) Q 'shall'.

12. *double-vantage* M.'s hyphen.

14. *That...wrong* '"That for your good I will bear all evil"; but of course Sh. had admitted his friend's "right" to be forsworn' (P.).

89

Continues the subject of 88. In this Sh. surely reaches the lowest point of self-abnegation.

2. *comment upon* dwell upon, expatiate upon.

3. *Speak of my lameness...halt* i.e. '"Call me lame and I, to make your words good, will pretend to be so." Had he really been lame this would have lost its point' (C. A. Brown).

6. *To set a form upon* to give shape to.

8. *strangle* A favourite metaphor with Sh. Cf. *Tw. Nt.* 5. 1. 146; *Wint.* 4. 4. 47; *H. VIII*, 5. 1. 156; *Troil.* 4. 4. 37; *Ant.* 2. 6. 121.

11. *Lest I* (*too much profane*) Q which M. here follows. Cf. 86. 2 n. and 95. 66.

13. *debate* quarrel.

90

Critics have tried to 'set a form upon' the various woes hinted at. I prefer to quote W. on the sonnet itself. 'I doubt if in all recorded speech such faultless perfection may be found, so sustained through fourteen consecutive lines.' (p. cxxxix).

2. *my deeds* in prose would be 'everything I do' (Tuck.).

3. *spite* See above and cf. 36. 6, 37. 3, 40. 14.

4. *drop in*=call unexpectedly. The earliest ex. in *O.E.D.* *after-loss* (hyphened by Sewell) i.e. 'a future grief' (Sch.) or possibly 'for some less important reason'.

6. *in the rearward* Cf. *Ado* 4. 1. 125 'on the rearward of reproaches' (M.).

8. *linger* protract. Cf. *M.N.D.* 1. 1. 4 'she lingers my desires'.

10. *petty* i.e. in comparison.

11. *shall* (edd.) Q 'stall'.

13. *strains of woe* D. glosses 'inward motions of woe' and cites *Much Ado*, 5. 1. 11–14:

> Measure his woe the length and breadth of mine,
> And let it answer every strain for strain,
> As thus for thus, and such a grief for such,
> In every lineament, branch, shape, and form.

91

'Imagine', Sh. says in 91 to his splendid young gentleman, 'yourself robbed of everything you most value in life: rank, wealth, strength, skill, fine clothes, and how wretched you would be! Your love is worth more to me than any or all of these things, and you would rob me of it!'

Personal as all this appears, Keller (*ap.* Roll.) declares it to be 'obviously inspired by the first Ode of Horace to Maecenas'. A Swedish translator of the sonnets, Mr K. A. Svensson (Lund, 1964) has, however, drawn my attention to a more persuasive, if at first sight astonishing source, viz. Book 1 of Xenophon's *Memorabilia*, embracing his memories of Socrates, and in particular to those passages in which Xenophon defends the great teacher against the charge of having corrupted his pupils Alcibiades and Critias. Svensson details the passages and their Sh. parallels in his note on S. 91, and I here give those from the Greek in a more or less literal translation kindly furnished by Mr D. F. Robinson of the Greek Department at the University of Edinburgh.

What first struck Svensson were the following words of Socrates which Xenophon reports in the *Memorabilia*, I. vi. 14:

> Some delight in good horses or dogs or birds;
> I delight even more in good friends.

And their likeness to what Sh. wrote in ll. 4–5, 8 of 91 is certainly striking:

Some [glory] in their hawks and hounds, some in their horse

. . . .

All these I better in one general best.
Thy love is better

Observe that the parallelism embraces not only words and ideas, but even the very turn of phrase.

Encouraged by this, Svensson thought he could recognize other passages in Xenophon relevant to the argument. For example, the politicians Critias and Alcibiades who brought disaster to Athens were quoted at the trial of Socrates as instances of youths corrupted by him because they had once been his pupils, whereas, as Xenophon points out in *Memorabilia*, I. ii. 24–6, Alcibiades at any rate was well enough behaved while under the influence of Socrates but after that influence was removed his natural arrogance and viciousness asserted itself, so that puffed up like Critias by noble birth and great wealth and himself possessed of such extraordinary beauty that many of the grand ladies ran after him, when the influence of Socrates had been forgotten, what wonder if the bonds of moral discipline grew slack like the training of an athlete who has gained an easy triumph in the games?

Here, if less striking than in the other parallels, are the hints for 'some glory in their birth—some in their wealth', while it is conceivable that the reference to the athletes enjoying an easy triumph might have led Sh. to add 'some in their bodies' force'. As for the point about Alcibiades being run after by the fine ladies because of his beauty, Svensson naturally looks outside S. 91 to 41 and especially ll. 4–8 for a parallel. On the other side he seems to have missed a possible source for Sh.'s scornful

Some in their garments though new-fangled ill

in *Memorabilia*, I. ii. 5 where Xenophon tells us that while Socrates approved of hard physical exercise, he 'disliked foppery and pretentiousness in the fashion of clothes, shoes and behaviour'.

If Svensson be right, Shakespeare made use of the *Memorabilia* as he made use of his other 'sources'; he had read it with interest at some time or other and it was only when he came to write S. 91 that certain points and phrases of Xenophon floated up into his memory to be worked into his art. Was it because he had been thinking of Alcibiades and fearing lest his beloved boy, so similar to him in many ways, might grow up to be the same sort of man? In any case, the sonnet is poetry, original poetry, whatever its remote ingredients might be, not in any sense a translation. A Greek scholar of my acquaintance, for instance, objects to Xenophon's bird (ὄρνιθι) being regarded as the 'source' of Sh.'s 'hawks', protesting the the Greeks knew nothing of falconry and the bird Socrates spoke of was a fighting cock or quail. Sh. knew this and alludes to quail-fighting in *Antony and Cleopatra*. But in S. 91 he is writing about a young Elizabethan gentleman.

My friend Mr Nigel Alexander who has made a special study of English translations from the Classics in the age of Sh. tells me he has not been able to trace the existence of the *Memorabilia* in English at this date, though there were two versions available in Italian. So far no Latin version—which would solve all difficulties—has been discovered. As the *Cyropaedia* of Xenophon was studied at Shrewsbury, it seems at least possible that Sh. may have been put to read the first book of the *Memorabilia* at Stratford. The Greek is not difficult, and what more suitable for schoolboy study than this account of the personality and methods of the greatest of all teachers of the young?

2. *body's* (M.) Q 'bodies'.

4. *horse* Prob. plural.

5. *humour* caprice; lit. personal temperament.

7. *my measure* Cf. *A.Y.L.* 5. 4. 172 'according to the measure of their states'. So 'measure' = lot in life, or (On. 5) 'treatment meted out' (by fate).

9. *better* (M.) Q 'bitter'.

10. *Richer...cost* Steev. cites *Cym.* 3. 3. 23.

12. *of all men's pride* i.e. of having the equivalent of all the things men take a pride in.

92

'This sonnet', writes D., 'argues for the contradictory of of the last two lines [of 91]. No: you cannot make me wretched by taking away your love, for with such a loss, death must come and free me from sorrow'. But l. 14 destroys the whole effect of this conceit. S.-Smith suggests 'It is increasingly evident that while the Friend had tired of Sh., he was seeking some face-saving means of ending the relationship', and again 'There is a strong sense, in this part of the sequence, of being *kept alive*, painfully, by the sheer beauty of the Friend'. I cannot feel all this 'evident'.

2. *For term of life* legal phrase.

5–6. *Then need...hath end* Obscure; interpretations vary. Perhaps the most satisfactory is Stopes: The worst of wrongs is 'to live without his friend's love', the least of them 'to lose his friend and to die at once'.

10. *my life...doth lie* 'i.e. your desertion will kill me' (B.).

11. *a happy title* a title to happiness.

13. *blessed-fair* M.'s hyphen. *blot?* (edd.) Q 'blot,'.

14. *Thou...know it not* 'The third possibility, the state of being deceived' (Stopes).

93

Miserable at his rejection in favour of the rival poet and unable to see the heart behind the seeming face of love, Sh. is also troubled by the fear that, deprived of his guidance, the Friend may now yield to the temptations which his beauty lays him open to. That lovely face is an Eve's apple, an instrument of the Devil which will lead many ladies to hunt him as Alcibiades was hunted. The theme of 93 and its sequel 94 is therefore, as B. notes, self-control: 'take care,' says Sh., 'in ruining others you may ruin yourself'. That the warning also implies a suspicion that the liaison with the Dark Woman is still going on unknown to him, seems more than likely, is indeed hinted broadly in the allusion to 'a deceived husband'. This affords a straightforward explanation.

2. *love's face* the appearance of love. The 'mask of Beauty' (W.).

7. *many's* most people's.

8. *moods* angry casts of countenance (On.).

13. *How like Eve's apple...beauty grow* Cf. 41. 13 'thy beauty tempting her to thee'. It was of course the woman whom the Devil tempted with the apple. And if no *virtue* lay behind thy lovely face, how many women might fall a prey to it!

94

D.'s comment on 94 seems the best: 'In 93 Sh. has described his friend as able to show a sweet face while harbouring false thoughts; the subject is enlarged on in the present sonnet. They who can hold their passions in check, who can seem loving yet keep a cool heart, who move passion in others, yet are cold and unmoved themselves—they rightly inherit from heaven large gifts, for they husband them; whereas passionate intemperate natures squander their endowments; those who can assume this or that semblance as they see reason are the masters and owners of their faces; others have no property in such excellences as they possess, but hold them for the advantage of the prudent self-contained persons. True, these self-contained persons may seem to lack generosity; but then, without making voluntary gifts, they give inevitably, even as the summer's flower is sweet to the summer, though it live and die only to itself. Yet let such an one beware of corruption, which makes odious the sweetest flowers.' A long silence follows, for 95 and 96, if I am right, can only refer to some incident unrelated to either the liaison or the Farewell.

1, 2. Roll. notes the unpleasant repetition of 'do', 'do'.

2. *do show* seem to do (On.).

5. *rightly do inherit* 'possess them as they should be possessed' (P.) or use them as they should be used. *heaven's graces* the favours of heaven.

6. *expense* expenditure and so love (D.).

8. *stewards* i.e. those who spend for the advantage of others.

10. *to it self...die* Cf. 54. 11 (Ver.).

14. *Lilies...weeds* Found again, *ipsissima verba*, in *Edward III* (2. 1. 451; pr. 1596), though proverbial. Cf. Tilley L 297, 'Lily is fair in show but foul in smell'; and *Lucr.* 867 'The sweets we wish for turn to loathèd sours', and 870, 'Unwholesome weeds take root with precious flowers'.

95

This and 96 which goes with it cannot be, as D. argues, a continuation of 93, 94; those warn him not to allow his beauty to become an Eve's apple or the lily of his virtue to fester. Nor can 95, 96 refer to the liaison with the Dark Woman; they clearly deal with a different episode altogether. Line 14 of 96 'Thou being mine, mine is thy good report' strikes a very different note.

Observe, however, that the two friends are not together. The incident referred to is reported to Sh. by a third person, who tells him how the youth is spending his days (95. 5). If the incident alluded to be the Mary Fitton affair, as Leishman once suggested to me,* Sh. might well have heard rumours of it in 1600 shortly after she visited Herbert at night after the wedding festivities of Herbert's cousin on 16 June, an escapade known it appears to all the court, except the Queen herself.† (See T.T. pp. 54 ff.)

3. *thy budding name* Applicable to Herbert who succeeded his father as Earl of Pembroke on 5 February 1601. And if it be so, the sonnet must have been written soon after, since the bud was blasted a few days later. *name!* Q 'name?' Cf. 97. 2.

6. *sport* i.e. with a woman. Amorous dalliance (*O.E.D.*). Q brackets—again for emphasis. Cf. 86. 2 n. and 89. 11.

8. *Naming...report* To connect your name with a scandal is to convert the scandal into commendation (Tuck.).

12. *turns* Q. M. and Camb. unnecessarily read 'turn'. See Abbott, §333.

13. *this large privilege* this unlimited freedom of action.

14. *The hardest knife...edge* Cf. *Ham.* 3. 2. 249 'It would cost you a groaning to take off mine edge'. *Meas.* 1. 4. 60 'But doth rebate and blunt his natural edge'. *ill-used* M.'s hyphen.

96

A pair with 95, and, like that, expressing the anxieties of an indulgent guardian, echoing the ready excuses the world found for his youth and charm. If the Friend be, as l. 11 implies, someone of high rank, the two sonnets

* See Introd. p. ciii. † See Introd. p. lxxxvi.

give us a picture of how the 'sport' of young men of fashion was spoken and thought of by society in general (and was still regarded until modern times). Yet, as Sh. warns him, this attitude will encourage him to impair both his own character and his reputation.

1–4. *Some...resort* 'Some dispraise and some praise, but all agree upon the facts and all agree in loving' (B.).

1. *youth some* G. C. Moore Smith, *T.L.S.* 22 June, 1922, conj. 'youthsome'.

2. *youth and gentle sport* i.e. the sport natural to young gentlemen.

3. *more and less* great and small.

4. *faults...that to thee resort* Cf. 95. 9. Sh. speaks of the 'vices' and 'faults' as evil spirits which make their habitation with or resort to him.

9–12. *How many lambs...state* Sh. asks pity for the women, for the Eves that the apple of beauty would tempt. Eliz. society would have given little thought to them.

10. *translate!* (edd.) Q 'translate.'.

12. *state!* (edd.) Q 'state?'. *thy state* state= social status.

13–14. *But do not so...report* Also the couplet in 36. D. suggests that the sonnet was unfinished in the copy and that Thorpe borrowed from 36 to complete it. S.-Smith thinks it a deliberate repetition on Sh.'s part, 'as an ironic echo from a time when he had not been fully aware of the Friend's character'.

97, 98, 99, [104]

'Sonnets in Absence'. The series begins with the Poet's description of an early and luxuriant autumn that dates back to summer months and is followed by a glorious early spring, peculiarly rich in fruit and flowers, but all 'bleak as December' because the Friend is 'away'. Nearly all critics agree that the tone, though sad, is quite different from that adopted in the preceding sonnets of bitterness and desertion. And I agree with most that the absence spoken of is actual, not metaphorical. But I would stress the following points: (i) that the three sonnets form one of those linked triplets observed by Chambers ((1), pp. 117–18) and were therefore prob. all written at the same time; that (ii) what neither he nor anyone else has noticed is that sonnet 104, a birthday sonnet which, on other grounds, I had convinced myself was certainly misplaced, is linked with Chambers's triplet. Note the rhymes in 97—*been*, *seen*—and 104's *seen*, *green*; and *chide*, *pride*, *dyed* in 99 echoed in the *eyed* and *pride* of 104; while *hand* and *stand* in 99 are repeated in the *hand* and *stand* of 104. It follows that the other three sonnets lead up to S. 104 which (iii) I infer from its first line and the reference to birth in the last, was a birthday sonnet; and this (iv) I suggest explains why 99 was left unfinished. For after writing in 98 about the festive appearance of Saturn in April 1600, he was reminded that that was the season of the Friend's birthday, and so after doodling with the flowers in birthday greetings in 99, he turned to and composed a sonnet which left him with no desire to spoil it by sending the first three of the quartet along with it. For be it noted, in 97–9 he is *remembering* the Friend's beauty; in 104 he is gazing, or had just been gazing, at it.

Finally, I explain the misplacement of the birthday sonnet [104] by supposing it was naturally written on a separate leaf, with nothing on the verso, and that since its contents could afford Thorpe no clue whatever to its true position, he supposed it had gone astray and considered it might well have been intended to follow 103 with its lines 6–14 'Look in your glass...'. On the other hand, omit 104, and 105 follows 103 far better.

97

1. *my absence* i.e. from thee. It is the Friend who is really absent; see 10 n.

2, 3, 4, Q punctuates with a question mark at the end of these lines. As in other similar cases, I replace with an exclamation-mark. Cf. Simpson, p. 85.

5–6. *summer's time, The teeming autumn* This has caused some trouble. The implication is, I take it, that the autumn was particularly fruitful and so early that it had begun in the summer months—in keeping with the *annus mirabilis* which is the theme of the whole triplet. Cf. Richard Levin in *R.E.S.* Nov. 1964, pp. 408–9.

5. *this time removed* i.e. 'the time in which I was remote or absent from thee' (M.). Cf. *Tw. Nt.* 5. 1. 88 'grew a twenty years removed thing'. *teeming* prolific.

6. *increase* offspring, crops.

7. *Bearing the wanton...prime* Giving birth to the heavy burden begotten in the wanton springtime.

8. *lords' decease* (M.) Q 'Lords'.

10. *hope of orphans* 'It was the early autumn, and so the crops and fruit could as yet only be spoken of as a "hope". They would be "orphans" because in the Friend's absence summer seemed dead'. For 'hope of orphans' = unborn orphans, cf. 60. 13, 'times in hope' = 'unborn times' (B.).

14. *winter's* Sewell and M. Q 'winters'.

98

Sonnet 97 was written in early autumn, the Friend having been absent for a whole summer beforehand. More months have now passed; the Friend is still absent next spring and for another summer, a summer once again like winter, because the Friend is still 'away'.

2. *proud-pied* splendidly variegated (*O.E.D.*). M.'s hyphen. (*dressed in all his trim*) in his finest apparel. For brackets, cf. 86. 2 n.

4. *heavy Saturn* i.e. the saturnine planet. That it should seem to laugh at its appearance shows that the April Sh. writes about was one of peculiar splendour as it is hinted in l. 2, and the reference to leaping helped W. to date the sonnet. See Introd. p. lxxxiv.

7. *any summer's story* By 'a summer's story' Sh. seems to have meant some *gay fiction*. On the other hand in *The Winter's Tale* he tells us 'a sad tale's best for winter' (M.). Surely, had summer (=the Friend) not been away, the story it would tell us would have made the flowers sweeter, given the rose a deeper vermilion, etc. But as it was they are but 'figures of delight'.

8. *lap* see in *R. II*, 5. 2. 46–7

Who are the violets now,
That strew the green lap of the new come spring?

9. *lily's* (Capell MS.) Q. 'Lillies', M. 'lilies'.

11. *were* (M.) Q 'weare'. *but sweet* M.'s conj. 'my sweet', would rob the sonnet of most of its meaning. Lettsom's conj. 'but fleeting figures' is more ingenious.

12. *pattern* model.

14. *As..play*=as I amused myself with the flowers so I called up the image of you I carry in my heart. Tuck. cites 27. 10. The line is an introduction to 99 in which he 'plays'.

99

An immediate sequel to 98, having all the appearance of an uncompleted draft. Incidentally it was prob. left unpunctuated, so that the compositor had to supply some; see ll. 2–5 below. After noting that the first line is extrametrical, B. continues: 'It may be conjectured that we have here only a rough draft of the sonnet. The correspondence of line 1 to line 6 shows that the first line was not an afterthought; and the repetition of the reference to "breath" in line 11 suggests that Sh. used a quatrain already written (lines 2 to 5) for his passage about the violet, intending afterwards to reduce it to three lines by limiting the parallel to "complexion"'.

1. *forward violet*=the spring violet. The regular epithet. Cf. *Ham.* I. 3. 7–8 'A violet in the youth of primy nature, | Forward, not permanent'.

2–5. Q punctuates l. 2 without commas, l. 3 with commas after 'breath' and 'pride', l. 4 with question-mark at the end, l. 5 with a comma at the end—clearly compositorial makeshift. My punctuation follows M.

3. *purple pride* Sh. prob. means little more than 'lovely blush'. *purple* (Lat. *purpureus*) 'Used by the poets in the vaguest way' (Ver.). *pride*=magnificence.

6. *for* 'for theft of' (D.) or 'for presuming to emulate' (M.).

7. *buds of marjoram* Compare Suckling's *Tragedy of Brennoralt*, IV. 1:

> Hair curling, and cover'd like buds of marjoram;
> Part tied in negligence, part loosely flowing.

'Dark auburn, I suppose, would be the nearest approach to marjoram in the colour of hair' (D.). B. repeats D. but, noting that in Suckling 'cover'd' must be a misprint for 'coloured', adds that Suckling is of course echoing the line in Sh., and with a bunch of marjoram before him describes the colour of unopened buds as 'that of the pigment known as brown madder' and John (*Flowers of the Field*, ed. 1881, p. 485) describes the buds as 'of a deep-red hue', The plant is 'fragrant and aromatic, and is frequently cultivated as a pot-herb'. No doubt as B. remarks, it is the reddish colour Sh. has chiefly in mind: was he not also thinking of the perfume?

8. *fearfully...stand* Cf. Tilley, T 239 'To sit (stand) upon thorns'—citing this line and *Wint.* 4. 4. 582.

9. *One* (M.) Q 'Our'. *One, blushing shame* punct. Tuck. The red rose embodies 'blushing shame', the white one 'white despair'. *despair* 'At having been found out' (Tuck.). He cites *L.L.L.* 1. 2. 96–99:

> If she be made of white and red,
> Her faults will ne'er be known;
> For blushing cheeks by faults are bred,
> And fears by pale white shown.

and *Lucr.* 1511.

13. *a vengeful canker* Cf. Ven. 656 'This canker that eats up love's tender spring' and *Rom.* 2. 3. 30 'Full soon the canker death eats up that plant' (M.).

100–26

There seems no reason to suppose that these sonnets are not printed in the order in which they were written. For a general discussion of the group see pp. lxxxvi ff. in the Introd.

100

'Written after a cessation from sonnet writing, during which Shakespeare had been engaged in authorship—writing plays for the public, as I suppose, instead of poems for his friend' (D.). And in line 2

> ...that which gives thee all thy might,

followed by line 8

> And gives thy pen both skill and argument

we have the clearest declaration so far that contact with the Friend was the true source of the Poet's inspiration. Had absence taught him to become conscious of what had been unconscious ever since sonnet 18? T.T. cites 78. 13:

> But thou art all my art...

Further, the references to the Friend's 'constancy' (see esp. 101) demonstrate that a complete understanding now exists between them. But the new and most striking note of this final series is one of apology, which begins as apologies for silence, for absence, for poverty of invention (see Tuck. pp. xlvii–xlviii), as if the

Poet engrossed in playwriting could only find time now and then for a sonnet by way of keeping his friendship in repair, to borrow a phrase from Samuel Johnson, but develops from about 109 onwards into confessions of infidelity and petitions for pardon. Above all, Sh. is no longer the elder deeply concerned for a boy's conduct; he now seems to look up for help and guidance. And S.-Smith, noting the increase of confidence and of composure, suggests that one cause of the change might have been 'that he had outgrown his physical passion for the Friend'. I should prefer to put it—'they had both grown up'.

3. *fury* or rage=poetic enthusiasm, 'exaltation of fancy' (Sch.).

4. *light?* (edd.) Q 'light.'.

6. *gentle numbers*=polished verse, i.e. the kind of verse that gentlefolk write (as contrasted with the vulgar blank verse of the common play-houses); cf. 81. 9 and *H. V*, 4. 3. 62–3:

Be he ne'er so vile,
This day shall gentle his condition

i.e. give him the rank of gentleman.

9. *resty*=torpid (Sch.).

11–12. *be a satire...everywhere* 'Devote yourself to poems on the ruins of Time' (Brooke), as, e.g., Ulysses in *Troil.* 3. 3. 145 ff. *satire*=satirist (On.).

14. *prevent'st*=forestal'st.

101

'Continues the address to his Muse, calling on her to sing again the praises of his Friend' (D.).

2. *truth in beauty dyed* Cf. 54. 1–2 and 53. 14 'But you like none, none you for constant heart'. *truth*= fidelity. *dyed* Gild. 'dy'd' Q 'di'd'.

3. *Both truth and beauty on my love depends* 'Perhaps because the Friend is Nature's store of truth and beauty' (P.). *depends* for the usage of 3rd per. sing. indicative as a plural see Abbot §333, Cf. and above, 95. 12.

4. *dignified*=ennobled (like the person the Muse celebrates). One of Sh.'s many assertions that he is a 'true-telling' poet; contrasted with the 'strained touches rhetoric can lend' of other poets, cf. 82. 10–12.

6–8. *Truth needs no colour*... The Muse's answer, given in those quibbling lines, is summarized in the next, 'he needs no praise'. The verbs 'fix' and 'lay' are borrowed from the painter's art. His truth needs no praise or 'colour', because his own beauty or 'colour' sufficiently 'fixes' it. 'His beauty needs no artist's brush to paint and so demonstrate the truth of it' (B.). First printed as a quotation by M.

7. *pencil*=paint brush. *lay* i.e. lay the colour on the canvas or board.

8. *intermixed* i.e. unalloyed (with praise).

11. *a gilded tomb*—that this betokens high birth is borne out by *M.V.* 2. 7. 54–59 in which only a gold casket was worthy for Portia's picture to be 'immured'.

102

'In continuation. An apology for having ceased to sing' (D.).

1. *seeming*, Q 'seeming'.

3. *merchandized* Cf. 21. 14. So in *L.L.L.* 2. 1. 13 ff.:

> my beauty, though but mean,
> Needs not the painted flourish of your praise:
> Beauty is bought by judgement of the eye,
> Not utt'red by base sale of chapmen's tongues.

5. *in the spring* Roll. II, 211 notes 'the emphasis the sonnets give to *spring* (11 times) and *April* (4 times)'. He also notes that Herbert and Sh. were both born in April (Southampton in October).

8. *her* (M.) Q 'his'. But 'her' in l. 10 and elsewhere in Sh. Did he not know that the song bird was masculine? But Philomela was feminine and he probably deliberately followed the classics. On the other hand the bird was English and he well knew that in England it begins singing 'in summer's front' and 'stops her pipe in growth of riper days', i.e. before the end of summer.

9. *Not...now* i.e. 'our love is not less appreciated by me because it is now at a riper stage' (Tuck.).

11. *wild music...bough* alludes to the number of poets now singing the praises of the Friend. *Wild music* perhaps in contrast with the 'gentle verse' of the sonnets. *bough* (Gild.). Q 'bow'.

103

'Continues the same apology' (D.).

1. *poverty* 'poor or inferior matter' (*O.E.D.*, citing this).

3. *The argument all bare*, 'the theme of my verse merely as it is in itself' (D.).

6. *Look in your glass* Cf. 77.

7. *over-goes*=exceeds. *blunt* clumsy, awkward (Sch.).

9–10. Cf. *K. J.*, 4. 2. 28 ff. (Steev). *Lr.* 1. 4. 347 (M.). *well?* (edd.) Q 'well,'.

11. *pass* event, issue (*O.E.D.* citing this).

104 (misplaced)

This sonnet was written immediately after 99 and is linked stylistically with the group 97–9 which it should follow. I have discussed it in the headnote to that group, p. 202. I conclude that it was composed for Herbert's 20th birthday, 8 April 1600, and that the 'three years' it speaks of fix the date of the first meeting of the friends at 8 April 1597, viz. Herbert's 17th birthday—see further my Introd. pp. xcix ff.

The misplacement is also accounted for in the headnote to *Sonnets in Absence* 97, 98, 99 (104) above mentioned.

The 'three years' have naturally provoked much speculation, for which see Roll. II, 59–61. 'The debate over the "dated sonnets"', he concludes 'will probably never end, in spite of its futility'.

4. *shook three summers' pride* Cf. *Rom.* I. 2. 10 'Let two more summers wither in their pride' (Steev.).

7. *perfumes in three hot Junes burned* 'The image seems to be from throwing incense on a fire' (B.).

9. *dial hand* Cf. Tilley, D 321 'To move as does the dial hand, which is not seen to move'.

10. *figure* 'Playing upon the sense of (i) numerical symbol on the dial, (ii) shape, appearance' (Tuck.).

13, 14. *thou...you* 'Ere thou wast' would have been more grammatically consistent, but less euphonious.

105

B., less perceptive than usual, writes: 'This sonnet has no connection with the subject of the previous four sonnets.' On the contrary, it seems to be a reply to 103. In that Sh. complains that his Muse can do nothing but utter the same praise over and over again, as a worshipper in the presence of his god. In this he elaborates his praise by making a trinitarian hymn of it.

1–2. *Let not...show* This states the theme of the sonnet, for Sh. claims that his love *is* idolatry (of a secular type), the worship of one god, by the individual worshipper, and to last for ever. And it is the worship of one god triune in quality, since the deity is fair, kind and true.

9. *Fair, kind, and true...argument* In *N. & Q.* 30 March 1907 (*ap.* Roll.), C. R. Haines drew attention to the following lines in Breton's *Melancholic Humours*, 1600:

Lovely kind, and kindly loving,
Such a mind were worth the moving:
Truly fair, and fairly true,
Where are all these, but in you?

Wisely kind, and kindly wise,
Blessed life, where such love lies:
Wise, and kind, and fair, and true,
Lovely live all these in you.

Sweetly dear, and dearly sweet,
Blessed, where these blessings meet:
Sweet, fair, wise, kind, blessed, true,
Blessed be all these in you.

It is difficult to believe the likeness to the sonnet was accidental, and as Breton is most unlikely to have known the sonnet before 1609, one must suppose that Sh. read Breton in or after 1600 and thought a pretty little conceit might be worked up into a trinitarian sonnet.

It should be added that Ulric Nisbet (*The Onlie Begetter*, 1936, pp. 34 ff.) claims that Breton was an intimate friend of the William Herbert to whom he believes the Sonnets were addressed.

106

This is reminiscent of Ss. 53–4 and is not the only instance in this final group in which Sh.'s 'poverty of invention' leads him to retrospection. Its dating is difficult, for though it has a word promising a definite date this proves on investigation to be frustrating. The word is *blazon* (5) on which B. cites this close parallel from *Tw. Nt.* I. 5. 295 ff.:

> 'I am a gentleman.' I'll be sworn thou art!
> Thy tongue, thy face, thy limbs, actions, and spirit,
> Do give thee five-fold blazon.

Note the use of 'blazon' for the parts or qualities of a person, ll. 5–6.

Chambers ((1), I, 405 ff.) dates it 1600, chiefly on grounds of style, but admits that Manningham's description of a performance at the Middle Temple in 1602, is the first record of its existence; and as Manningham thought it a new play I should conjecture that the performance was that of a fairly complete revision with Armin playing the Clown (see my Note on the Copy for *Tw. Nt.* 1623 in the *New Cambridge Shakespeare*).

On the other hand, there is strong evidence that Sh. was thinking a good deal about 'blazon of arms' between 24 March 1600 and 1 May 1602, so once again the dates leave us in doubt because, though the College of Heralds records a draft made on the first date, for Sh.'s father, allowing him to quarter or impale the arms of his wife Mary Arden together with that allowed to himself in 1596, Sh. may not have seen this draft himself until the death of his father in September 1601 or even before 1 May 1602 when the grant was called up for question at an inquiry into the malpractices of the Garter King of Arms responsible for the original draft. In view of the uncertainties of the records in the Herald's office and the likelihood that Sh. was much engaged with *Twelfth Night* for the revised version that Manningham seems to have seen, the date 1602 is probably that of the sonnet.

8. *master* possess, own (Sch.).

11. *divining* 'as in a glass darkly...not face to face' (P.).

12. *skill* (Tyrwhitt conj. + M) Q 'still'. D. defends, but B. notes: 'If we read "still" there is no noun for "enough" to refer to.'

107

'The Mortal Moon.' 'The most difficult of the sonnets' (B.); though it seems at first sight a simple and natural allusion to a well-known historical event and so seemed to William Minto, one of the earliest and most level-headed critics of the *Sonnets*,* though it is now questioned by critics with a historical axe of their own to grind in keeping with their own identification of the Friend. But B., who is pledged to no special pleading and is only concerned to determine the meaning of the sonnet, line by line and phrase by phrase, gives far the best commentary, most of which must now be quoted.

His first task is to deal with attempts to link the sonnet with those preceding it:

'the "fears" of line 1 seem to point back to the "fear" of 104. 13, and the "prophetic soul of the world" to the "prophecies" of 106. 9; and so D. takes it. He paraphrases: "Not my own fears *that my friend's beauty may be on the wane*, nor the prophetic soul of the world, prophesying in the persons of dead

* See his *Characteristics of English Poetry* (1874), pp. 276, 288.

knights and ladies your perfections, and so *prefiguring your death*, can confine my lease of love to a brief term of years." But there is nothing here, as in 104, about the friend's beauty, and there is nothing in 106 about the friend's death. It is best, therefore, to construe the sonnet without regard to these links of connection which are apparent only. Accordingly, the fears as prophecies (of l. 1) must be interpreted by what follows as fears and auguries of some anticipated future which would be the doom of the poet's love. In the first quatrain the fears are stated in the most general terms as fears for the future; but the second quatrain connects them with some particular crisis, which came without bringing the expected catastrophe. Instead of that it brought a happier era. Apparently the crisis feared was a civil war in which the arts would perish, since "peace" is referred to as its opposite, and the immediate result anticipated by the poet is the survival of his poems.'

Nothing, it will be observed, is assumed in this admirable analysis, no theory or interpretation advanced. A reader who has followed it with care should be in a position to deal with points of particular interpretation recorded in the notes that follow or discussed elsewhere in the Introd.

1. *prophetic* foreboding. Cf. *Ham.* 1. 5. 40 'O, my prophetic soul! My uncle?' (Steev.).

2. *the wide world* the world in general, e.g. Europe, or 'everyone'. *dreaming on*, imagining, conjecturing. Cf. *Ham.* 1. 2. 21 'this dream of his advantage'; 2. 2. 10, 'I cannot dream of'; 2. 2. 555, 'in a fiction, in a dream of passion'. *things to come* what is going to happen.

3. *yet* any longer. *the lease...control*=fix the date when my love must end. 'The metaphor is from a lease which is forfeited at a fixed date' (B.).

4. *confined* limited, as in 105. 7; 110. 12.

5. *The mortal moon...endured* D. believes this points to an actual eclipse, of which there were several at this period. Otherwise, practically all students interpret the line as alluding to Queen Elizabeth, and with few exceptions to her death. The exceptions claim that both 'eclipse' and 'endure' imply a condition of a more temporary nature than death, and they account for the condition in various ways, the best known perhaps being put forward by G. B. Harrison and endorsed by E. K. Chambers, viz. the Queen's Grand Climacteric (i.e. her 63rd year), through which she passed in 1596, a period considered by her physicians and her astrologers as exceedingly dangerous and while it lasted giving rise to great public anxiety. This date is favoured by those who find 1603 too late to suit the youth for whom they claim the honour of being the Friend. But is 'eclipse' really a likely term for a climacteric? E. K. Chambers, who wants 1596 to suit his book, argues for it. But as B. (who has no favourite for W.H.) observes, 'the point must be settled by Sh.'s use of language' and the incontestable fact is that Sh. only uses 'eclipse', in its metaphorical sense, to signify death or annihilation. Here are the passages: *1 H. VI*, 4. 5. 53 'Born to eclipse thy life this afternoon' (Lord Talbot to his son); *Ant.* 3. 13. 153 'Alack, our terrene moon | Is now eclipsed, and it portends alone | The fall of Antony'; and I should add a third: *3 H. VI*, 4. 6. 62 'For, till I see them here, by doubtful fear | My joy of liberty is half eclipsed'. Chambers, misliking these passages, seeks to brush aside the second on the grounds that Cleopatra to whom it refers is not dead and is actually present as Antony speaks the words. This, however, is to misread both B. and Sh. For all the former, who quotes the lines, claims is that 'eclipse' here denotes

'a final not a temporary extinction'. And what Antony refers to, as he talks at her while appearing to ignore her presence, is the total annihilation of the Egyptian fleet which Cleopatra herself led into battle at Actium.

6. *the sad augurs mock...presage* the gloomy prognosticators laugh at their own forecasts. B. notes as a striking illustration of the effect of these presages and of the fears that seized the people of London when it was known that the old Queen was dying without an heir, the following from Donne's sermon on the accession of James I: 'When every one of you in the city were running up and down like ants, with their eggs bigger than themselves, every man with his bags seeking where to hide them safely, Almighty God shed down his spirit of unity and recollecting and reposedness...upon you all.'

7. *Incertainties...assured* The dedication to James by the translators of the 1611 Bible, speaking of his accession, observes: 'Whereas it was the expectation of many, who wished not well unto our Sion, that upon the setting of that bright occidental star Queen Elizabeth... some thick and palpable clouds of darkness would so have overshadowed this land, that men should have been in doubt which way they were to walk, and that it should hardly be known, who was to direct the unsettled state: the appearance of your Majesty, as of the Sun in his strength, instantly dispelled those supposed and surmised mists, and gave unto all that were well affected, exceeding cause of comfort; especially when we beheld the government established in your Highness, and your hopeful seed, by an undoubted Title, and this also accompanied with Peace and tranquillity, at home and abroad.' Such was the voice of the Clergy. How those 'incertainties' affected the citizens is shown in the previous note. Meantime the 'wide world dreaming on

things to come' were reckoning up the names of all those who 'gaped for the throne' because of what was held to be their undoubted titles to it.

8. *olives of endless age* James I, 'the most thoroughgoing pacifist who ever bore rule in Britain' (Trevelyan, *Hist. of Eng.* p. 385) proclaimed himself the Prince of Peace and believed himself inspired by God to bring unity to Christian Europe under one Faith.

9. *this most balmy time* Acc. to Lee (*ap.* B.), 'James came to England in a springtime of rare clemency'. And P. points out that 'if the Friend gained by the accession of James he might aptly be compared to a flower refreshed by rain'.

10. *My love* B. explains 'my affection' not 'my friend'. But D. is doubtful which it means. The Friend is directly addressed as 'thou' in l. 13 which seems to prove B. wrong unless the couplet was added after the rest had been written. *to me subscribes* i.e. 'acknowledges me his superior' (M.). B. thinks this refers to Sh.'s relief at the country escaping a civil war in which the arts would perish, as the stage did forty years later. But it looks like a personal allusion. Was Sh. ever in danger of death like other members of the Essex party, after the attempted rising in February 1601? The company escaped punishment for the performance of *Richard II*; the writer is not alluded to at the trial.

12. *insults o'er* haughtily exults over.

14. *When tyrants' crest* etc. 'Not improbably a veiled reference to the monument that would be erected to the Queen' (B.).

108

P. reads 'cf. 104' and if misplaced here it would make an apt sequel to the birthday sonnet. But D. links this persuasively by paraphrasing it with 107. 10–14 'How can "this poor rhyme" which is to give us both unending life be carried on? Only by saying over again the same old things. But eternal love "in love's fresh case" (an echo of "my love looks fresh", 107. 10) knows no age, and finds what is old still fresh and young.'

1. *character* write.

3. *new...now* (Q); M. 'new...new'; acc. to Landry, p. 437 n. 9, M.'s change is 'unnecessary'.

5. *sweet boy* sweet=mod. coll. 'dear'. Cf. Bartlett 'sweet sir', 'sweet prince', etc.

7–8. *Counting...name* 'Reckoning even old expressions of love as fresh since we are just the same to each other as when I wrote my first poem to you' (B.).

9. *in love's fresh case* in its state of always being fresh.

12. *makes antiquity for aye his page* I suggest= treats the signs of old age with the amused contempt with which a master treats his page. B. sees the image as that of a page walking behind his master.

14. *dead.* Q 'dead,'.

109

During a period when they had not met, the Poet had been devoting himself to other interests; but he protests that he always had his Friend in mind.

4. *in thy breast...lie* M. cites *L.L.L.* 5. 2. 812 'Hence hermit, then—my heart is in thy breast'.

5. *ranged* 'been inconstant' (Sch.).

7. *Just...exchanged* 'Punctual to the time, not altered with the time' (D.).

9. *though* even if.

10. *all kinds of blood* every type of sensuality.

14. *my rose* i.e. the Rose of the world, *Rosa mundi* (Stopes). Cf. I. 2.

110

A natural sequel to 109, giving examples of his errant conduct, l. 2 apologizing, I think, for a particularly notorious, i.e. popular, exhibition of himself on the stage, shown in different noble houses as well as at Blackfriars ('here and there'). D. notes 'This sonnet and the next are commonly taken to express distaste for his life as an actor'. But B., in note on 'motley', asserts 'There is no reference to the poet's profession as player' and Bradley agreed. Yet 'gored mine own thoughts' surely points to play-writing esp. perhaps to *Hamlet*. See Introd. p. lxxxii. Not, as S.-Smith remarks, that it matters greatly, as the sonnet's general application is to his behaviour as a whole.

1. *here and there* see headnote.

2. *a motley to the view* lit. 'a fool in public'. But motley, 'the parti-coloured dress of the professional jester' (On.) might be used symbolically, i.e. a writer for the public stage who is equally at home in either tragedy or comedy.

3. *Gored mine own thoughts...most dear* B. notes that the image is of a bear tied to the stake and baited by dogs in public, citing *Ham.* 5. 2. 248 'To keep my name ungored'; *Troil.* 3. 3. 228 'My reputation is at stake; | My fame is shrewdly gored'; *Tw. Nt.* 3. 1. 119 'Have you not set mine honour at the stake | And baited it?' The line means therefore that Sh. has exposed his most

intimate and sacred thoughts either to the vulgar censure of the populace in the public theatre (that bear-garden, it is perhaps implied) or by acting the jester at social gatherings; and see headnote.

5. *truth* loyalty, fidelty.

6. *Askance and strangely* indifferently and like a stranger to it.

7. *blenches* lit. starts (cf. *Ham.* 2. 2. 601 'If a'do blench'), here=aberrations from rectitude (M.).

7–8. 'the lines seem to mean, these infidelities (by their failure) restored me to my old affection, for they proved the superiority of my old friend' (B.).

8. *love.* (edd.) Q 'love,'.

9. *Now all is done...no end* 'Now all my wanderings and errors are over, take love which has no end' (D.). M. conj. 'save' for 'have', which Landry, p. 438, calls a 'failure of interpretation'.

10. *Mine appetite...grind* The little wanderings from the path had given his 'heart another youth', he tells us in line 7, but that is all over, he will never try to sharpen his appetite again.

13. *my heaven* 'that heaven of mine which is your breast' (Tuck.).

111

The Poet appeals for pity. A continuation of 110 and even more clearly referring to the disabilities of an actor-dramatist's life, though B. tries to play it down. See Introd. pp. li ff. above and M. (1790) 'the author seems here (particularly in l. 4) to lament his being reduced to the necessity of appearing on the stage or writing for the theatre'.

1. *with* (Gild.+) Q 'wish'.

7. *hand:* (M.) Q 'hand,'.

10. *Potions of eisel* Doses of vinegar—a sovereign remedy with the physicians against the plague and various other diseases. Cf. *Ham.* 5. 1. 270. Hamlet mockingly promises to 'drink up eisel' to induce melancholy (see note *ad loc.*). Note that dyers cleansed their hands with vinegar; cf. 'the dyer's hand' (7).

11–12. *No bitterness...correction* 'There is no medicine which I will think too bitter, nor will I refuse a double penance, to punish and more than punish me. "Correct correction" is explained by "double"' (P.).

112

Continues 111. Whatever the 'scandal' (or ill-judged instance of self-exhibition) for which the Poet apologizes in 111, asking pity for the Fate responsible for it, this sonnet (112) shows the Friend's response, and is one of the indications that the young nobleman always accepted the humble status of his player-poet without question and without scorn. Cf. notes to 25.

1–2. *th' impression...stamped upon my brow* Carries on the image of 'brand' (111. 5). *vulgar* public.

4. *o'er-green* The metaphor may be that of (i) covering a bare or worn patch of ground with fresh sward, or (ii) covering up an unsightly building with creeper. But Tuck.'s conj. 'o'er-grain' (=dye afresh) is most attractive since 'dye', or 'colour' often in Sh. implies deception. Cf. *Ham.* 1. 3. 127–8:

> Do not believe his vows, for they are brokers
> Not of that dye which their investments show.

Thus 'o'er-grain my bad'=find specious excuses for something bad, while as *Hamlet* was being written not long before this sonnet, the image in Sh.'s mind was prob. a stain on a garment. *allow* approve (M.).

7–8. *None...wrong.* 'Two sentences are crushed into one, *viz.* For me there are no others in the world than you and I, i.e. none I take into account; and None but you can alter my fixed opinions, whether they are right or wrong, or perhaps, for better or worse' (P.).

8. *wrong.* (edd.) Q 'wrong,'.

10. *my adder's sense*=ears. Cf. *Troil.* 2. 2. 172 and Ps. lviii. 4–5.

12. *how...dispense* How I excuse my indifference to the world's opinion.

13. *so...bred* 'so firmly engrafted into all that I set before me' (Tuck.).

14. *That all the world besides methinks are dead* (M. 1780+Camb. and B.). Q 'That...besides me thinkes y'are dead'. B. writes that W. defends Q 'chiefly on the ground that the obvious emendation, "That all the world besides, me thinks, are dead", is merely a repetition of line 7, and that line 12 is clearly meant to prepare the way for a "startling declaration". "In Q we get one". So we do, but we get a statement which in no way excuses Sh.'s neglect of other critics and flatterers, as it professes to do. And it is not the fact that l. 14 as emended merely repeats l. 7. That said simply, "There is no one alive but you who can move me'; this says "There is no one alive but you"—a climax, and a sufficiently startling "declaration"., In his 1790 ed. M. read 'they are' as an expansion of Q 'y'are'.

113

Another ref. to a period of separation ('Since I left you'). Note that Antony has much the same illusions when he believes he is finally separated from Cleopatra through her desertion to Caesar in *Ant.* 4. 14. We get a comic touch of the same thing at *Ham.* 3. 2. 378 'Do you see yonder cloud', etc.

1. *mine eye...mind* Cf. *Ham.* I. 2. 185 'In my mind's eye'.

2. *to go about* i.e. as I walk about.

3. *doth part* fulfils only part of.

5, 7, 8, 9. *it, his* refers to the eye (Leishman, pencilled note).

5. *heart* same as 'mind' in l. 1 and l. 7 (B.). P. cites *Cor.* 3. 1. 256 'His heart's his mouth'.

6. *latch* (M.) Q 'lack'; latch=catch (sight of) (Tuck.).

7. *quick* 'Not "living" (see l. 11) but "presented in swift succession"' (P.).

10. *sweet favour* (edd.) Q 'sweet-favour'. Delius conj. 'sweet favour'd'. *favour* appearance (On.); countenance (M.).

13. *Incapable* unable to take in more. *of more, replete* (punct. M.) Q 'of more repleat,'. The comp. has misplaced the comma.

14. *untrue*='untruth'. So in *Meas.* 2. 4. 170 'my false o'erweighs your true' (M.). *mine untrue* (Q+ most edd.) M. orig. conj. 'mine eye untrue'.

114

'Continuation of 113, and enquires why and how it is that his eye gives a false report of objects' (D.). 'The question asked in this sonnet is whether the eye deceives the mind by flattery in reporting this fresh beauty in outward nature, or whether love actually has made things more beautiful' (B.).

5. *indigest* shapeless, chaotic. Cf. *K. J.* 5. 7. 26.

9–10. *'tis flattery in my seeing, And my great mind* etc. D. cites *Tw. Nt.* 1. 5. 312 'I...fear to find | Mine eye too great a flatterer for my mind'—a striking parallel.

11. *gust* taste.

13, 14. *If it be poisoned* etc. Referring to the tasters whose duty it was to drink before the King as a precaution against poisoning. Cf. *K.J.* 5. 6. 28. B. paraphrases: If the drink be poisonous, the eye can scarcely 'be blamed for administering to the mind what itself enjoys'.

115

'I once said that my love was at its height. Falsely, but I feared it might be lessened by Time. And why could I not say so truly? Just because love is a child, and my love is still growing' (P.).

2. *Even...dearer* P. asks 'Can this refer to lost sonnets?' And Griffin (*ap.* Roll.) suggests that such sonnets might have followed 85.

4. *My most full flame* Cf. 109. 2 (D.).

4–5. *clearer, But* (Leish.) Q 'clearer. But'—which leaves no verb in the principle sentence, lines 5–12.

6–9. Examples of Time's tyranny.

10. '*Now I love you best*' first printed as a quotation by M.

11–12. *certain...the rest* D. cites 107. 7 'Incertainties now crown themselves assured' for a similar use of the metaphor. *rest?* (edd.) Q 'rest:'.

13–14. *Love...grow.* (Q) M. read 'grow?'—unnecessarily.

116

'Love's not Time's fool'. 'Certain sonnets stand alone....The finest of all [116] with the splendid effect of its unstopped first line, and the masterly ease of its technique, has a universal significance; and it deals with Love as an Absolute' (Alfred Noyes *ap.* Roll. I, 294).

And Tucker Brooke thus analyses the form: '[The sonnet] consists of three separate quatrains, each concluded by a full stop [Q has a colon at l. 12] and a summarizing couplet. The chief pause in sense is after the twelfth line. Seventy-five per cent of the words are monosyllables; only three contain more syllables than two; none belong in any degree to the vocabulary of "poetic" diction. There is nothing recondite, exotic, or metaphysical in the thought. There are three run-on lines, one pair of double-endings. There is nothing to remark about the rhyming except the happy blending of open and closed vowels, and of liquids, nasals, and stops; nothing to say about the harmony except to point out how the fluttering accents in the quatrains give place in the couplet to the emphatic march of the almost unrelieved iambic feet. In short, the poet has employed one hundred and ten of the simplest words in the language and the two simplest rhyme-schemes to produce a poem which has about it no strangeness whatever except the strangeness of perfection.' (Cit. Roll.)

1–2. An echo of the Marriage Service in the Ch. of Eng. B.C.P.: 'If any of you know cause, or just impediment, why these two persons should not be joined together in holy Matrimony, ye are to declare it.' The 'impediments' not admitted are change of circumstance (l. 3) and inconstancy (l. 4).

4. *bends* turns its course. '"To remove" is used in a slightly different sense from "with the remover". Love does not disappear when the loved one is unfaithful. For this sense cf. sonnet 25. 14' (B). It is significant that the expression used then at a crisis in their relations should be recalled here.

5. *ever-fixed mark* sea-mark, beacon. M.'s hyphen. Cf. *Cor.* 5. 3. 74–5:

> Like a great sea-mark, standing every flaw,
> And saving those that eye thee!

7. *It is the star* etc. Cf. *Caes.* 3. 1. 60–61:

> But I am constant as the northern star,
> Of whose true-fixed and resting quality....

'The wandering bark corresponds with "the remover" of l. 4' (B.).

8. *Whose worth's unknown* whose influence (upon affairs) is incalculable by astrological science. *height* the vertical distance from the horizon (P.). Q 'higth'.

9. *Time's fool* 'the sport or mockery of Time' (D.). M. compares Hotspur in *1 H. IV*, 5, 4, 81 'But thought's the slave of life, and life time's fool'—a close parallel.

10. *bending sickle* 'the "crooked knife" of 100. 14' (P.).

12. *bears it out* 'survives' (P.). But the 'it' hints at the 'impediments', so 'endures' is a better gloss. Cf. *All's*, 3. 3. 5:

> We'll strive to bear it for your worthy sake
> To th' extreme edge of hazard

Cf. St Paul's hymn to Charity (Love) I Cor. xiii, which Sh. surely had in mind.

117

It would be difficult to find a greater contrast, contradiction one might say, in the Q text than this and the preceding sonnet. We pass without any connexion from a sublime declaration of perfect concord to a confession of neglecting the Friend for the company of persons of no importance. Some misplacement here cannot be denied (see head note p. 207). And P. refers to 109 in which the tale of the 'wanderings' begins.

1–2. *scanted...repay* 'neglected those offices of friendship by which I should have requited your merits' (P.).

5. *frequent* intimate. *unknown minds* 'people of no interest or importance' (B.).

6. *given to time* 'Given to society, to the world' (D.) *dear-purchased* hyphened by Sewell.

10. *on just...accumulate* 'add a mass of suspicions to the evidence against me' (P.). Q's comma after surmise' is slightly emphatic.

11. *level* the range or the aim. Cf. *L.C.* 309 'not a heart which in his level came' (M.).

11–14. 'If you are levelling at me those accusations, still do not shoot, because...' (B.).

118

See headnote to group 100–26. The physiological imagery of this sonnet which may strike the modern reader as unpoetical if not disgusting, was prob. considered exceedingly ingenious in the age of Donne. Bucknill (*ap.* Roll.) describes Sh. as a 'diligent student of all medical knowledge existing in his time'—knowledge he might easily acquire from Dr Hall, the best-known doctor in the Midlands, who lived in

Stratford and who married Susanna, Sh.'s daughter, in 1607. See Introd. p. lxxvii for the parallels with *Ham.* and *2 H. IV.*

Following 117, the Poet continues to find excuses for his unfaithfulness and now protests it has 'two motives, to make return sweeter, and to prevent satiety' (B.).

2. *eager* bitter. Cf. *Ham.* 1. 5. 69 'curd, like eager droppings into milk' (M.). *eager compounds* 'a description of what to modern ears sounds curiously like a cocktail' (Spurgeon, *ap.* Roll.).

5. *ne'er-cloying* 'the epithet explains why the "policy in love" was mistaken' (B.). M.'s hyphen.

6. *bitter sauces* 'inferior company which he all the time *felt* to be disagreeable' (Tuck.).

7. *sick of welfare* Cf. 'rank of goodness' (l. 12).

10. *The ills that were not,* (Gild.+edd.) Q 'were, not'. 'Satiety, which had not come' (B.).

12. *rank of goodness* B. notes cf. *Ham.* 4. 7. 116 'goodness, growing to a plurisy'. 'Rank' was an epithet used of a state of body which required blood-letting; as in *Caes.* 3. 1. 153 'Who else must be let blood, who else is rank'. D. quotes an excellent parallel from a medical passage in *2 H. IV*, 4. 1. 64, 'To diet rank minds, sick of happiness'.

119

See headnote to group 100–26.

1. *Siren* She 'would seem to be the lady of the sonnets in the Appendix [Section II]. Cf. with l. 2, sonnet 147. 14' (B.).

1–2. *tears Distilled from limbecks* Suggests artificial tears created in a wizard's or witch's laboratory. *limbecks* vessels for distilling. Cf. *Mac.* 1. 7. 67.

4. *Still...win!* 'Either, losing in the very moment of victory, or gaining victories (of other loves than the Friend's) which were indeed but losses' (D.). The contrast of l. 5 with l. 7 shows that the latter is the more probable sense (B.). Q 'win?' Cf. 97. 2 n.

7. *How...fitted* 'How have my eyes started from their hollows in the fever-*fits* of my disease' (D.). We meet in *Ham.* (1. 5. 17) the same image as here, 'Make thy two eyes like stars start from their spheres'. See Introd. p. lxxvii.

8. *In the distraction...fever!* The similarity of this to S. 147 as a whole apart from the medicinal parallels noted above tends to support B.'s thesis at l. 1. Q 'fever?' Cf. l. 4.

11. *ruined love...rebuilt anew* D. notes the reappearance of rebuilt love in later sonnets, and M. quotes the metaphor in *Err.* 3. 2. 4, *Ant.* 3. 2. 29, *Troil.* 4. 2. 103.

14. *ills* (Q) M. and many others altered to 'ill'—perhaps rightly, says D., referring to l. 8. One of M.'s 'unnecessary emendations' (Landry, p. 437, n. 9).

120

Only two critics (Walsh and Porter) seem to have realized that this sonnet refers to what I have called the liaison sonnets (see Roll.). To suppose it does is surely common sense even if not capable of proof. For if 'Siren tears' (119) be, as B. suggests and I believe, a reference to the Dark Woman, it would seem to follow that the Poet has ceased to suspect the Friend of entanglement with her but was by no means free of her himself. S. 147, indeed, seems to belong to the same mood that gave us these physiological apologies for disloyalty.

1. *once unkind* see above. The outline of the liaison story is reflected in this sonnet. See note on l. 6.

3. *Needs...bow* 'I must needs be overwhelmed by the wrong I have done to you, knowing how I myself suffered when you were the offender' (D.).

4. *nerves* sinews (Sch.). Cf. *Ham.* 1. 4. 83 'As hardy as the Nemean lion's nerve'. On. glosses 'esp. pl. = the parts of the body in which the chief strength lies'.

6. *a hell of time* Not related to the mod. coll. expression. M. cites *Oth.* 3. 3. 171–2:

> But, O, what damned minutes tells he o'er
> Who dotes, yet doubts, suspects, yet fondly loves!

and *Lucr.* 1287–8:

> And that deep torture may be called a hell
> Where more is felt than one has power to tell.

One may suspect that the words of Othello come very near to an expression of Sh.'s feelings when he was writing 57, 58 and 61. See Introd. p. lxii.

7, 8. 'I have not put myself in your place, have not taken time to think what I felt when our positions were reversed. "in your crime" = from your offence against me' (P.).

9. *our night of woe* B. conj. 'one' for 'our' (an easy graphical misreading) on the ground that 'our' spoils the antithesis of 'you' and 'me' which runs through the sonnet. But as P. notes 'one' would suggest that joy cometh in the morning, but there is no hint of this. Yet 'our' must *mean* 'one' here; as W. puts it, the phrase refers to some one occasion of great sorrow well known to the Friend and to the Poet which the Friend *once* caused by his 'crime' (l. 8) but for which he *soon*

tendered the fitting salve. Is this not a memory of the incident depicted in 34? Both are in tears in 34 and the Friend offers a 'salve' as in 120. *remembered* reminded. Cf. *R. II*, 3. 4. 14 (M.).

9–10. *remembered...deepest sense* 'reawakened my deepest feeling of pain and made me remember...' (Tuck.).

11–12. *And...fits*! 'Apologised to you as quickly as you to me' (Leishman, pencilled note).

11. *soon...as*=as soon as. Cf. Abbott, §276.

12. *humble salve* Cf. 34. 7 (D.).

13, 14. 'That former trespass of yours against me has become something which I can offer as a payment and ransom for my own offence' (T.T.).

121

A reply to scandal-mongers. This prob. goes with 125, but the point of both remains obscure to most critics, chiefly because they find it open to a variety of possible interpretations, including one which would understand the slander as the attacks on the stage by the Puritans of London. To me, however, it seems natural to associate the sonnet with those immediately preceding. I can see no evidence of any reference to homosexuality, which indeed seems negatived by the sonnet on 'Siren tears' (119). In short I explain the slanders referred to as due to gossip about the philandering of which Sh. had confessed himself guilty in 117–20 and for which he had apologized to the Friend. B. appears to agree.

3. *just* legitimate. *so deemed* deemed vile (B.).

4. *others'* (M.) Q 'others'.

6. *Give salutation to* Cf. *O.E.D.* 'salute'=to affect or act upon; citing *H. VIII* 2. 3. 103 'If this salute my

blood a jot'. B. glosses 'affect, stir, and so infect'. *sportive* amorous, wanton (Sch.). Cf. 95. 6, 96. 2.

8. *in their wills* 'wilfully, or poss. viciously, in their sensual way' (P.).

7. *spies,* (edd.) Q 'spies;'.

9. *I am that I am* Taken out of its context, much has been made of this. Crookback's 'I am myself alone' (*3 H. VI*, 5. 6. 83) and Iago's 'I am not what I am' (*Oth.* 1. 1. 66) have both been quoted. Alden (*ap.* Roll.) comments: 'All Sh. says is, "I have an independent standard of character, and where others do not find theirs fitting it, the crookedness (line 11) may be theirs"'—and that is obviously all it means. *level* Cf. 117. 11.

11. *bevel;* (edd., inc. S.-Smith) Q 'bevel'. *bevel*= crooked. A term used by masons and joiners (Steev.). Sh. was busy with the building and furnishing of New Place about this period. 'Slanting, not upright, as I am' (P.).

12. *rank thoughts* Another indication that 'the charge brought against Sh. involved sensuality in some form or other' (T.T.).

14. *in their badness reign* Cf. Ps. xxxvii. 35 'I have seen the wicked in great power: and spreading himself like a green bay tree'.

122

Beyond the fact that it is apologetic, like most of the sonnets in this final group, there is nothing to give it a place among them. It is an occasional sonnet like 77 though the comparative simplicity of its diction and rhythm suggest an earlier date.

1. *tables* memorandum-book (Sch.). Cf. *Ham.* I. 5. 99 ff. for an account of what young men noted in their 'tables', culminating in 107 'My tables, meet it is I set it down', while at *Ham.* I. 3. 59 Polonius bids Laertes 'character' his advice.

3. *that idle rank* 'that useless series of leaves' (B.).

6. *Have faculty by* are allowed by.

9. *That poor retention* 'i.e. the table-book given him by his friend, incapable of retaining, or rather of containing, so much as the tablet of the brain' (M.).

10. *tallies* sticks on which notches are cut to keep accounts.

11, 12. 'Therefore I ventured to give them away, so as to depend instead on that note-book (*viz.* my memory) which is more fully stored with records of your love' (P.).

12. *more:* (edd.) Q 'more,'.

13. *an adjunct* an attendant.

123

The point of this sonnet is 'that while all things subject to Time are also subject to change; only what is changeless is to be admired' (B.). But here Sh. returns to Ovid's doctrine of 'revolution in Nature' used to a different purpose in 59—'If there be nothing new, but that which is,| Hath been before' (see Lee, pp. 131–2). Even the 'pyramids' discovered, re-erected and rebuilt in Rome a few years before, to the wonder and astonishment of the world, are but the products of Time and are therefore 'nothing novel, nothing strange' to a lover who defies Time and all its works.

No! Time, thou shalt not boast that I do change—develops the theme of 116, 'Love's not Time's fool'.

2. *pyramids* 'Metaphorical; all that Time piles up...all his new stupendous erections are really but "dressings of a former sight"' (D.). But the sense gains much if pyramids be taken (with Hotson) as referring to the obelisks dug up, rebuilt or redressed by Pope Sixtus V in Rome (1585–90). Their erection was one of the wonders of the world and would continue to be so regarded by English visitors to Rome for at least the dozen years that had passed before Sh. here writes of them, rather contemptuously, as to him 'nothing novel, nothing strange'. And it by no means follows, as Hotson argues, that the sonnet must have been contemporaneous with their erection.

5, 6. 'Our lives are brief and so we take for novelty what is really old material re-dressed to look new.'

7. *born...desire* 'specially created for our satisfaction' (D.).

11. *doth lie* tell lies.

124

A difficult sonnet. It is, I believe, agreed that the word 'policy' points to topical conditions or events, and prob. such of which Sh. disapproved, as he always does with politicians. And it is clear that the key to the problem lies in the last two lines. Who then are these 'fools of time' and what is the 'crime' they lived apparently to accomplish? One editor only has offered an answer, B. who is not in any way hampered by predilection for a particular 'Friend'. He explains ll. 13–14 as an allusion to 'the Jesuit conspirators whose object in life was to murder the king, and who when caught posed as martyrs for the faith', and Leishman's pencilled note repeats this interpretation. Such inconstancy of principle would justify the poet in calling them 'the fools of time' and pointing his moral. The moral is that 'Love is the only true policy'. The notes that follow are in the main my paraphrasing based on Beeching's general interpretation.

1. *the child of state* due to or dependent upon public affairs.

2. *Fortune's* Q 'fortunes.' *unfathered* 'without a *true* father' being begotten by Time upon Fortune, and so subject to her caprices. A bastard was 'filius nullius' (B.).

4. *weeds* etc. i.e. 'subject to Time's hate and so plucked up as weed, or subject to Time's love and gathered as a flower' (D.).

5. *builded far from accident* i.e. not subject to the chances and changes of public life. There is prob. an implied contrast with the Houses of Parliament which were *not* so builded.

6. *suffers not in smiling pomp* i.e. it cannot suffer the death prepared for the King, Lords and Commons at the ceremonial opening of Parliament on 5 November 1605.

6–7. *nor falls...discontent* nor fall a prey to sudden disaster at the hands of a party of discontents, held down by penal laws [which the King had repealed but later re-enacted].

8. *Whereto...calls* B. ignores this, D. explains 'When time puts us, who have been in favour, out of fashion', but the text does not speak of 'us' but of 'our fashions' which refers, I take, it to the religion tolerated by the government. I paraphrase: for to such a condition of frustrated restraint does the religious fashion of our time invite men.

9. *Policy*, *that heretic* 'the prudence of self-interest, which is faithless in love. Cf. *Rom.* I. 2. 94 Romeo speaks of eyes unfaithful to the beloved—"Transparent heretics, be burnt for liars"' (D.)

9–10. *It fears not...hours* 'Policy whether in love or in public affairs allows men but a short lease of time; whereas Love is eternal' (B.). Policy (=prudence or self-interest) is thus 'heresy' in love, but the term 'heretic' has prob. a side glance at the religious parallel. *short-numbered* M.'s hyphen.

11. *stands hugely politic* is the supreme self-interest.

12. *That...showers* in as much as it remains unaffected by either sun or shower. The text is suspect, without reason.

13. *witness* 'to the truth that love is the only true policy' (Leishman, pencilled note).

125

This like 121 replies to real or simulated scandal-mongers (see ll. 13–14). D. associates it with 124: 'There Sh. asserted that his love was not subject to Time, as friendships founded in self-interest are; here he asserts that it is not founded on beauty of person, and therefore cannot pass away with the decay of such beauty. It is pure love for love.' And B. thus sums up the argument: 'The poet is repudiating charges laid against him by the [imagined] "informer" of line 13. The charges are of caring too much for his friend's beauty, and laying upon that a basis for eternity. To which he replies in the second quatrain that so far from this being the case his own experience of others has shown him that such conduct leads only to disaster.'

1. *Were't*='Would it be' (B.). *I bore the canopy*= if I carried your canopy, i.e. was one of your most distinguished or most favoured admirers. To carry a person's canopy signified to pay the greatest possible outward honour to him. D. notes that James made his procession through London in 1603–4 under a canopy, and again in Oxford in 1605 with Queen Anne. Only men of great distinction normally acted as bearers but if the King visited Wilton in 1603 (see p. c) Sh. may well have been a canopy-bearer when he entered the house.

2. *extern* outward. B. cites *Oth.* I. I. 62–4:

> For when my outward action doth demonstrate
> The native act and figure of my heart
> In compliment extern.

4. *proves* (Q) M.+Camb. etc., 'prove'. Cf. 101. 3 n.

5. *dwellers...favour* those who make much (or too much) of beauty in form and face.

6. *Lose all, and more* 'cease to love, and through satiety even grow to dislike' (D.). *rent* suggested by 'dwellers', means simply 'regard' or 'attention'.

7. *compound* i.e. the double pleasure they derive from admiring both feature and figure. *simple savour* the taste of that pure happiness which is Love.

8. *Pitiful thrivers...spent?* i.e. to do nothing but gaze in admiration is a poor sort of business. *spent?* (edd.) Q 'spent.'.

9. *obsequious* showing humble devotion.

10. *oblation* A term specially used in religious worship, e.g. in the Communion Service of B.C.P. where it has reference to the bread; and that Sh. wished to remind the Friend of this seems shown by 'not mixed with seconds', 'seconds' being the coarser sort of flour not used for the best white bread. 'I offer,' he says in effect, 'the pure and holy bread of Love'.

13. *suborned informer* 'the false witness, of course imaginary, in the contest between the poet and Time, who brings the charge in lines 1–4' (B.). But P. asks 'Could an imaginary person be "suborned" or exercise control?', and I think rightly believes him to be one of the 'spies' in 121. 7, 8.

126

Unquestionably written as an Envoy to the sonnet series addressed to the Friend. In place of a 14-line sonnet consisting of three quatrains followed by a rhymed couplet, it is a poem of 12 lines wholly composed of rhymed couplets. It carries on and rounds off the theme of the conflict between Love and Time which is that of its immediate predecessors. Finally, though the Friend can still be spoken of as 'my lovely boy', it is clear that the year is not far distant when

Nature will not continue to 'pluck [him] back' with such miraculous skill.

2. *Time's fickle glass his fickle hour:* Cap. conj., *ap.* Roll. Rolfe and Tuck. Q reads 'time's fickle glasse, his sickle, hower'.

3. *by waning grown* i.e. grown more beautiful as you grew older.

4. *Thy lovers withering* 'the growing beauty of the boy shows up the ageing of his friends' (B.). Delius conj. 'lover's' (i.e. Sh.'s) which is attractive.

7–8. *She keeps...kill* 'the skill of Nature in preserving the boy's beauty is a reproach to the power of Time, and may be said to "kill" his "minutes", as it robs them of their influence' (B.).

7. *skill* (edd.) Q 'skill.'—a misprint.

11. *audit* final account Q 'Audite'.

Section II: Sonnets 127–54

The problem of order. Hitherto no one had been able to detect any order in the sonnets of this section, which Mackail described as 'a miscellaneous and disorderly appendix'.* But in a volume entitled *Shakespeare 1564–1964*, ed. by E. A. Bloom, Brown University Press, 1964, Professor Brents Stirling has just published an article which makes an important advance towards determining their correct order and at the same time explaining their present disorder as due to Thorpe or his printer mistaking the order of the leaves upon which the sonnets were written. At the time of writing I had not yet myself been able to see a copy of Professor Bloom's volume. But my friend Professor Kenneth Muir, who has an article of his own in the same book, has generously furnished me with a full account of it, an abstract of which I here set down. In the present edition I must perforce follow the text of 1609 when printing the following sonnets, but with Brents Stirling to guide them readers should be able without difficulty to study the sonnets in the order in which Shakespeare wrote, and will find the results so illuminating as to more than repay the small trouble involved. Indeed, they may if they wish put the matter to the test without further ado, by reading them at once according to the rearrangement for which Stirling argues, viz.: 140, 139, 153, 154, 130, 127, 144, 143 135, 136, 131, 132, 133, 134, 137, 141, 142, 149, 150–2, 147–8, 129, 146, plus three independent sonnets 128, 138, 145.

His list is composed of three groups which he entitles respectively *My Mistress' Eyes* (140, 139, 153, 154,

* J. W. Mackail, *The Approach to Shakespeare* (1930), p. 116.

130, 127); *Poet, Friend and Mistress* (144, 143, 135, 136, 131, 132, 133, 134); *Perjury of Eye and Heart* (137, 141, 142, 149–52, 147–8, 129, 146) and three *Independent* (128, 138, 145). And the evidence for the whole arrangement is based on the fact that most of the sonnets fall into pairs and sequences, a pair being the sonnets functioning together as one (e.g. 135–6, a pair of 'Will' sonnets), and a sequence being two sonnets or two pairs in which the treatment of the subject matter is transitional (e.g. 141–2), while the linking is provided by parallels and repetitions, e.g. 141 qualifies 137 and the word 'plague' occurs in both; 142. 1 takes up the 'sin' of 141. 14; 149. 9–13 has links with 141, 137 and 147; 150 with 141, 149, 137 and 124. The couplet of 147 is a repetition of the couplet in 152; 148 links up with 147 and is rhetorically parallel with 137, the beginning of this series. 129 and 146 express—and conclude—a theme already apparent.

Stirling's theory to account for the displacement of the original order is perhaps the more convincing that it is bibliographical and not stylistic. 'If sonnets were inserted two to a leaf, recto-verso, a leaf accidentally turned over would keep the two sonnets together but transpose the authentic order' (e.g. 140, 139; 144, 143) and 'disruption of sequence would occur by displacement of leaves' (e.g. 149–52, 147–8).

Stirling's theory, in other words, allows for one sonnet on either side of the leaf. Finally, one should note Stirling reckons that Section II contains six 'clear Q pairs' (131–2, 133–4, 135–6, 139–40, 149–50, 153–54); and at the lowest four 'clear Q sequences' 132–3, bridging two of the pairs (see the 'heart'—'groan' link between 131–2 and 133. 1); 141–2 with a last-line first-line link; and 151–2; and perhaps 147–8 should be added. With allowance for overlapping, Stirling claims that these clear pairs and clear sequences account for eighteen out of the twenty-eight sonnets in the series.

It only remains for me to add that while both texts and commentaries of the sonnets will correspond with the order and numbering that Thorpe gave them, their correct position, according to Brents Stirling, will be indicated at the beginning of each commentary so as to facilitate readers who wish to follow the mind and heart of Shakespeare. To do so gives me, at any rate, a very different impression of the attitude of the Poet to his Mistress from that previously entertained. For one thing it underlines his admission to the Friend (42. 2) 'I loved her dearly'.

What the sonnets tell us when restored to order. See Introd. pp. xxviii ff.

* * * * *

127

B.S.: Sixth of *My Mistress' Eyes* series.

1–14. *In the...look so.* Steev. writes, 'The reader will find almost all that is said here on the subject of complexion is repeated in *Love's Labour's Lost* 4. 3. 255 ff.:

> O, if in black my lady's brows be decked,
> It mourns that painting and usurping hair
> Should ravish doters with a false aspect;
> And therefore is she born to make black fair.'

D. compares S. 7 of Sidney's *Astrophel and Stella* (perhaps following the Germans, Conrad, 1879, and

Krauss, 1881). Sh.'s debt to Sidney's sonnet seems clear from lines like

> When nature made her chief work, Stella's eyes,
> In colour black, why wrapt she beams so bright?
>
> . . . .
>
> Or would she her miraculous power show,
> That whereas black seems Beauty's contrary,
> She even in black doth make all beauties flow.

1. *In the old age* formerly (P.). *fair* lovely (with a pun on 'fair') = of fair complexion.

3. *successive heir* 'heir by order of succession, as in *2 H. VI*, 3. 1. 49' (D.). This leads on to 'bastard'. P. explains 3–4 *But now* etc. 'now it is painted so as to look beautiful and succeeds to Beauty's empire, though not the rightful heir, while Beauty has the discredit of being its reputed parent'. Cf. Ss. 67, 68 and notes above, together with Bassanio's speech, *M.V.* 3.2. 88 ff. Sh. seems to have cosmetics and false hair much in mind at this lawsuit period. About 1604, he was lodging with the 'tire-maker' Christopher Montjoy in London and made a deposition in a lawsuit between Montjoy and his son-in-law. (See Maunde Thompson, *Shakespeare's Handwriting*, 1916, p. 4.)

7. *bower* Not apparently an arbour; but *O.E.D.* (citing this) 'A vague poetical word for an idealized abode, not realized in any actual dwelling'.

9. *eyes* (Q) M. follows Q and, Landry says, 'resists a temptation' to emend 'eyes' to 'hairs' or 'brows' as Staunton and others have done.

10. *so suited* Either 'of the same colour as those of the raven' (M.) or 'so clad' (D.). *and* (Q) Dyce conj. 'as', perhaps rightly.

10–12. *they...esteem* 'they seem to mourn that those who are not born fair, are yet possessed of an artificial beauty, by which they pass for what they are not, and thus dishonour nature by their imperfect imitation and false pretensions' (M.).

13. *becoming of* gracing (D.).

128

B.S.: One of three independent sonnets: 128, 138, 145.

Mackail (*ap.* Roll.) found 128 and 145 'trivial in substance and undistinguished in style'—and perhaps not by Shakespeare. P. also notes 'un-Shakespearean in sound and rhythm. Compare 8.' But it echoes 8 and tells us that both Mistress and Friend had a lovely voice.

Steev. describes a virginal as 'a small kind of spinet' and quotes Lording Barry's *Ram Alley*, 1611, 'Where be these rascals that skip up and down faster than virginal jacks?' Add to the smallness of the instrument the fact that both the keys and the jacks were of wood, the former 'not being plated with ivory' (Tuck.) as the keys of the later harpsichord were, and we have all that one requires for the understanding of the sonnet, which depicts a woman seated at her little box-like instrument, playing and perhaps singing. As she plays, she has at times to press down with the 'tender inward' of one hand 'saucy jacks' that leap too high and so become stuck or she fears may become loose, and it is these the Poet envies rather than the fingers which move along the keys. Shakespeare does *not* confuse 'jack' with 'key' as many have supposed, even *O.E.D.* ('jack' sb.). An article in *English Language Notes* (1 September, 1963) by James Brophy on 'Shakespeare's Saucy Jacks' written, I gather, independently of Naylor though quoting him from Rollins, does not I think add anything to Naylor's explanation (*Poets and Music*, 1928, p. 92) which runs: 'The lady [in this sonnet] had been "tinkering" the virginals....The plectrums or their neat little carriages...are always going wrong in some way; and in this case the lady, having removed the rail which ordinarily stops the "jacks" from jumping right out of the instrument when the keys are struck, was leaning over her work, testing it by striking the defective note, and holding the "tender inward" of her hand over the jack to prevent it from flying to the other end of the room.' I do not believe the sonnet describes all this, though it is worth quoting for the information it gives about the instrument.

1. *my music* He addresses the Friend in similar language in 8. 1 'Music to hear'. *thou, my music,* (edd.) No commas in Q.

3. *sway'st* Q 'swayst,'.

9. *state* Q 'state,'.

11. *thy* (Gild.) Q 'their'. See Introd. p. xxvi.

14. *thy* (Gild.) Q 'their'.

129

B.S. Tenth in *Perjury* series.

'66 and 129 unlike the rest of the sonnets are not written in quatrains, though the rhymes are so arranged' (B.). Lee writes 'This noble sonnet may have owed its whole existence to Sir P. Sidney's sonnet on "Desire"'; and also 'The ravages of lust is a favourite topic with sonneteers' (cited Roll.).

1. *The expense of spirit* 'a technical term in medicine' (B.), meaning 'the expenditure of the vital spirits', supposed to be the vehicle of the life force.

Here Sh. means this, while implying something far more. *in a waste* by a shameful waste of one's soul, with an obvious pun.

4. *rude* brutal. *not to trust* treacherous (P.).

9. *Mad* (Gild. & M.) Q 'Made'—a not unusual misprint in the plays. Landry (p. 438) defends Q unconvincingly.

10. *Had...extreme* Laura Riding and Graves (*ap.* Roll.) defend the Q punctuation (here followed): [this] 'comprises all the different stages of lust: the after-lust period (*Had*), the actual experience of lust (*having*), and the anticipation of lust (*in quest*), and that the extremes of lust are felt in all these stages (*to have extreme*)'.

11. *proved, a very woe* (M. & Camb.) Q 'proud and very'.

12. *Before...dream* Cf. *Lucr.* 211 ff. 'What win I if I gain the thing I seek? | A dream, a breath, a froth of fleeting joy' (Tuck.). *dream.* (edd.) Q 'dream,'.

13. *well...well* used in two senses.

130

B.S.: Fifth of *My Mistress' Eyes* series.

'A less pleasant variation of the *motif* of sonnet 21' (B.). This sonnet is often completely misunderstood, even by justly famous writers like Brandes ('Sh. has made it abundantly clear...that the lady was no beauty'), or Bernard Shaw whose play 'The Dark Lady of the Sonnets' is largely based upon the Mary Fitton theory and an absurd misinterpretation of this sonnet (see the Preface to the play in his *Misalliance* volume, 1914, pp. 118–19). No less misconceived is the notion (first propounded by Jordan in 1881 but recently revived) that a mistress mocked in such repulsive fashion must be a negress! Yet what the sonnet tells us, as no one who pauses to consider the final couplet can fail to see, is that none of the ladies that Petrarch and the conventional sonneteers sing can compare with Sh.'s lady for beauty. And incidentally, if not primarily, it is a parody of their love-poetry. Indeed, as Cruttwell points out (*The Shakespearean Moment*, 1954, pp. 18–19), Sh. seems to have had specially in mind the preposterous 'Passion' of Thomas Watson; see Introduction, p. cx.

2. *lips* (Q), 'M. 'lips''.

131

B.S.: Fifth of *Poet, Friend and Mistress* series.

2. *whose...cruel* who are made cruel through pride of their beauty.

3. *dear* fond, loving (*O.E.D.*).

9. *swear,* (edd.) Q 'swear'.

11. *One...neck* 'in quick succession'; cf. *1 H. IV*, 4. 3. 90–2:

> In short time after he deposed the king,
> Soon after that deprived him of his life,
> And in the neck of that tasked the whole state.

14. *this slander* i.e. that of ll. 6–7.

132

B.S.: Sixth of *Poet, Friend and Mistress* series. His Mistress' eyes mourn for him, though she disdains him in her heart. Light badinage.

2. *torment* (Q) Many edd., including D., B. and P. follow Q 1640 'torments'. But 'torment' is infinitive—the eyes pity, knowing the heart to torment me with disdain.

9. *mourning eyes* (most edd.) But Q's 'morning

eyes' is poss. to stress the quibble (D.) who compares *Shr.* 4. 5. 31–32:

> What stars do spangle heaven with such beauty,
> As those two eyes become that heavenly face?

12. *suit* B. notes 'Prob. not "clothe" [D.] but "adapt", "fit"'. But P. glosses 'Let your heart too pity me and wear mourning'.

133

B.S.: Seventh of *Poet, Friend and Mistress* series.

The poet expostulates with the Mistress for her pursuit of his friend and pleads for him.

1. *groan* 2. *wound* 3. *torture* 5. *cruel* Conventional language of the sonneteers.

4. *to slavery* i.e. to a slave. *be?* Q 'be.'.

6. *next* nearest. *harder...engrossed* P. explains 'Have captured and hold even more securely'. *engrossed*=taken the whole of (Sch.) monopolized (On.).

8. *crossed,* debarred, cut off.

9. *Prison...steel...ward* steel ward=bolts or chain for securing an offender in a prison cell.

11. *keeps*=imprisons. *guard*=guard-house, or the house at which a distinguished person is consigned for custody. Cf. *O.E.D.* 'guard' sb. 17*a* and *Lr.* 5. 3. 47–8 'To send the old and miserable King | To some retention and appointed guard' (Tuck.).

12. *Thou canst not then* etc.=so long as my friend's heart has no harsher prison that 'the gentle closure of my breast' (48. 11), you can use no 'rigour' in your own gaoling of myself.

13–14. *And yet thou wilt...in me*. An elaborate conceit, which it is difficult to take seriously, as one cannot but take 42, the close parallel of this sonnet and written, one must believe, at the same time. Tuck. glosses: 'In imprisoning me, you are imprisoning all that is *in* me, and he is in my heart; therefore whatever harshness you show to *me* affects him also, and I shall feel for *him* any rigour which I should not feel for myself.'

134

B.S.: Eighth in *Poet, Friend and Mistress* series.

Direct sequel to 133. The legal phraseology of this sonnet conveys, Tucker notes, 'a humorous vein of double meaning. The woman has compelled both men to render carnal service to her beauty. She insists upon having in that relation the friend as well as the poet, whose service does not satisfy her claim. He playfully pleads that his friend has merely acted for him (cf. 40. 5–6) and that he is quite willing to take the whole burden upon himself, if she will give up the friend. But neither she nor the friend is so inclined.'

2. *mortgaged to thy will* pledged to do thee service. *will*=(i) wish, (ii) sexual appetite. Poss. a play upon the name Will also.

3. *that other mine* 'my alter ego' (D.).

4. *my comfort* Cf. 144. 'Two loves I have', etc. Was he already speaking of him to others as 'his comfort'?

6. *covetous* Does this mean sexually greedy or imply that she receives a fee for his visits like a courtesan? Cf. next note.

7. 'This suggests that the friend came under the fascination of the poet's mistress in discharging some office of kindness or civility to her on the poet's behalf' (W.). If Sh. was absent from London, such a mission would be the more likely. See my note on 59.

9. *statute* legal phrase for 'a security or obligation for money' (M.), i.e. she sold her beauty.

10. *Thou usurer...use* 'All' is stressed. She will not lend a penny (of her beauty) except on 'use' (i.e. at interest). 'The line is a parenthetical exclamation' (Tuck.). For this sense of 'use' cf. 'thy love's use' (20. 14).

12. *my unkind abuse* this unkind ill-treatment of me (B.).

135

B.S.: Third of *Poet, Friend and Mistress* series.

This is the third of the 'Will' sonnets, which B.S. arranges as 143 (Lo as a careful huswif), 135, and 136 (If thy soul check thee). But Thorpe having ordained otherwise, it will, I think, not seem entirely preposterous to explain the whole matter here, as I can best do by quoting B.'s little essay on the matter (pp. xxxvi ff.), to which I can see no possible reply except to deny, as the Southamptonists do, that in these sonnets Shakespeare refers to anybody called William but himself, which is on the face of it absurd. But see note on 143 where I think B. wrong. B. begins with 143, which B.S. has now shown to be the earliest of the three, and continues:

In this sonnet the 'dark lady', pursuing the poet's friend while the poet pursues her, is compared to a housewife chasing a chicken and followed by her own crying child. It concludes:

So run'st thou after that which flies from thee,
Whilst I thy babe chase thee afar behind,
But if thou catch thy hope, turn back to me:
And play the mother's part, kiss me, be kind:
So I will pray that thou mayst have thy Will,
If thou turn back and my loud crying still.

The word 'Will' is printed here in the original text in italics, and the pun is in Shakespeare's manner. Sonnet 135 opens:

> Whoever hath her wish, thou hast thy will,
> And 'Will' to boot, and 'Will' in overplus,
> More than enough am I that vex thee still,
> To thy sweet will making addition thus.

The third Will here must be Shakespeare, because '*Will* in overplus' corresponds to 'more than enough am *I*'; and few critics with the 143rd sonnet also in mind would hesitate to refer the second Will to Shakespeare's friend, for whom the 'dark lady' had been laying snares. But the Southamptonites, who cannot allow that the friend's name was Will, are constrained to deny that there is any pun at all in 143, and to refer that in 135 to the distinction between 'will' in its ordinary sense and 'will' in the sense of 'desire'. But the balance of the line makes it almost necessary that, as 'Will in overplus' must be a proper name, 'Will to boot' should be a proper name also. And that there are more Wills than one concerned in the matter is made more evident still by other passages, where the poet jocosely limits his claim on the lady's favour to the fact that his Christian name is Will, acknowledging that not a few other people have as good a claim as he:

> Shall will in others seem right gracious,
> And in my will no fair acceptance shine?

and again,

> Let no unkind, no fair beseechers kill,
> Think all but one, and me in that one 'Will'.

1. *will* (rom M+), Q *Will*. B. evidently takes it for a misprint, as it prob. is influenced by the two *Will*'s in l. 2, but he does not say so, and prints it as a common noun in his text, though he seems to imply it in his note which runs here: 'For the jingle between "wish" and "will" cf. *Gent*. 1. 3. 63: "My will is something sorted

with his wish". For "will" in the sense of carnal desire, to which there seems a reference in line 5, cf. *Lear* 4. 6. 268, "O indistinguished space of woman's will!" [a parallel which explains the point of "large and spacious" here (J.D.W.)]. D. suggests that *Will* in l. 1 may refer to the lady's husband; the Q prints it in italics, like the 'Will' in l. 2, and it has been conjectured from 136. 2 that the husband's name was 'Will'. But if 'Will' in l. 1 were a proper name we should expect in line 4 'thy sweet Will*s*'.

6. *thine?* Q '*thine,*'.

8. *shine?* Q 'shine:'.

9. *The sea...rain* Cf. *Tw. Nt.* 2. 4. 103; and 1. 1. 11 'Thy (=Love's) capacity receiveth as the sea' (D.).

13. *Let no unkind...kill* D. conj. 'Let no unkind "no"'=let no unkind refusal kill fair beseechers. B. calls this 'ingenious' but adds '"Think *all* but one" seems to require no fair beseechers'.

136

B.S.: Fourth in the *Poet, Friend and Mistress* series and third of the 'Will' sonnets.

1. *check* rebuke, chide (Sch.). *come so near* touch to the quick (Tuck.)—a fencing term. For interpretation, doctors differ; e.g. Brooke paraphrases 'if this bold address cause your conscience to upbraid you', and Adams asks 'Why not "come so near to your bed"?'

2. *blind* 'Proleptic=let it shut its eyes and then swear to it' (Tuck.). Q prints *Will*.

3. *And will...there* Adams interprets this 'will' as 'her husband called Will'. No evidence for a husband of this name; and B., says the word means 'carnal desire' here and in l. 5. In l. 5 Q prints *Will*.

6. *Ay, fill* (M.+edd.) Q 'I fill'.

7. *things of great receipt* when dealing with a large number of items, as in accounts.

8. *Among a number...none* Cf. *Rom.* 1. 2. 32–3:

> Which on more view, of many mine being one
> May stand in number, though in reckoning none.

B. comments, 'the poet need not be counted, but must be reckoned with'. D.: 'You need not count me when merely counting the number of those who hold you dear, but when estimating the *worth* of your possessions, you must have regard to me.'

10. *store's account* the inventory of your property (P.).

137

B.S.: First in the *Perjury of Eye and Heart* series.

'This sonnet accuses Love of perverting first the eyes and then the judgment' (B.).

1. *Love* Q 'love'

2. *see?* (edd.) Q 'see:'.

4. *Yet what...to be* 'Take the worst for the best; suppose his lady to be beautiful and loving' (P.).

6. *Be anchored* Cf. *Meas.* 2. 4. 4 'My invention... anchors on Isabel'; and *Cymb.* 5. 5. 393. *where all men ride*=the wide world's common place (l. 10) but with obvious equivocation.

9. *that* Emphatic: =that place (that woman). *several* 'a "several" was that part of common land which was allotted to individuals. Compare Maria's quip in *L. L. L.*, 2. 1. 222: "My lips are no common, though several they be"; to which Boyet replies "Belonging to whom?"' (B., after Johnson.).

12. *face?* (edd.) Q 'face,'.

13–14. *In things...transferred.* P. writes: 'This may mean, My heart and eyes have in the past judged truth to be a liar and now judge falsehood to be truth. "False plague" seems to mean "plague of falseness". They are given over to a disease which renders them incapable of distinguishing.'

138

B.S. ranks this as an 'independent' sonnet. The version in *The Passionate Pilgrim* runs as follows:

When my love swears that she is made of truth,
I do believe her, though I know she lies,
That she might think me some untutored youth,
Unskilful in the world's false *forgeries.*
Thus vainly thinking that she thinks me young,
Although *I know* my *years be* past the best,
I smiling credit her ſalse-speaking tongue,
Outfacing faults in love with love's ill rest.
But wherefore says *my love that she is young?*
And wherefore say not I that I am old?
O, love's best habit is *a soothing tongue,*
And age, in love, loves not to have years told.
  Therefore *I'll* lie with *love,* and *love* with me,
  Since that our faults in love thus smothered be.

B. comments on the variants which he underlines: 'It is interesting to have so clear an example of Shakespeare's rewriting. It will be noted that the amended copy gets rid of the difficult conclusion to line 8, and also of the new idea in line 9, which interferes with the statement of the two faults in the octave; viz. the woman's inconstancy and the man's pretence of youth and innocence.'

Blair Leishman's pencilling against this sonnet in B.'s ed. reads 'Very interesting variations from the version in The Passionate Pilgrim'.

1. *truth*=fidelity: see 54. 2.

7. *simply*=unconditionally, absolutely (Sch.). P. adds 'in my assumed simplicity'. *false-speaking* M.'s hyphen.

9. *unjust*=unfaithful, false (On.).

139

B.S.: Second in the *My Mistress' Eyes* series. Sh. knows his mistress is often unchaste.

3. *Wound me...tongue* Cf. *Rom.* 2. 4. 14 'Stabbed with a white wench's black eye' (M. and Steev.). Tuck. explains *with thine eye*, 'by glancing it aside (l. 6).'

4. *Use power...art* P. paraphrases: 'Use your power energetically, reject me in plain words instead of wounding me as it were by strategy, as you do when you let me see by your looks that you are in love with someone else.' *Use power with power*='in a strong and open way; and do not slay me by indirect and artful means' (Tuck.).

7. *What*=why.

8. *o'erpressed defence* efforts at defence, too hard-pressed by the assailant (D.).

14. *rid* make an end of.

140

B.S.: First of the *My Mistress' Eyes* series, i.e. the first series of Section II.

2. *tongue-tied* cf. 85. 1 n.

4. *pity-wanting*=unpitied (Sch.). Hyphened by Gild.

5. *wit*=wisdom.

6. *to tell me so* 'to tell me, thou *dost* love me' (M.).

11. *ill-wresting* 'misinterpreting to disadvantage' (Sch.). M.'s hyphen.

13. *so* i.e. so believed. *belied.* (Gild.) Q 'be lyed.'

14. *Bear...wide* 'That is, as it is expressed in a former sonnet (93): "Thy looks with me, *thy heart in other place*"' (M.). Loane (*T.L.S.* 19 March, 1925, p. 200) notes: 'Looks like an inversion of the well-known Italian proverb, "I pensieri stretti e il viso sciolto"' (cited Roll.).

141

B.S.: Second in the *Perjury of Eye and Heart* series.

The Poet does not really see a 'thousand faults' in his mistress' person, still less refuse to enjoy the 'sensual feast' she offers him; he protests all this in order to emphasize the fact that his heart has been so cruelly imprisoned in the hard steel of hers that it has ceased to rule his body and left it to become her abject 'slave and vassal wretch'.

4. *Who*=which, as in l. 11. *of view* i.e. of what it sees, as in 148. 11 (P.).

5. *tune*=tone, for the sound of the voice (*O.E.D.*).

6. *feeling* (Q) Most edd. 'feeling,' B. 'The poet says that his delicate feeling is not "prone to base touches", not that it is'. *base touches* Euphemistically —sexual commerce (Sch.).

8. *To any...alone* Tuck compares *Ven.* 445 ff.:

> But O, what banquet wert thou to the taste,
> Being nurse and feeder of the other four!

9. *But...nor*=But neither...nor. Cf. 86. 9. *five wits* a common expression, by analogy with the five senses (Tuck).

10. *serving* Cf. servant=lover.

11. *who* i.e. the heart. 'The heart by ceasing to rule leaves the man a mere "likeness'" (B.).

13. *Only* Sch. takes this with 'thus far'; Roll. prefers to take it as meaning 'but'.

14. *pain* punishment. Cf. *Rom.* 1. 5. 94.

142

B.S.: Third in the *Perjury of Eye and Heart* series.

In a manner an explanation of 141, since it clearly paints the situation underlying both sonnets.

1. *dear* inmost, vital (Sch.); especial (Brooke).

2. *Hate...loving* 'You hate my love, not because it is sinful, but because you love, sinfully, elsewhere' (W.)

6. *scarlet ornaments* B. writes: 'The same expression is found in *King Edward III* (pub. 1596) ... The parallel would suggest that this is an early sonnet, and the writing confirms this suggestion.' But the parallel does not prove that the sonnet was written before *King Edward*; and l. 7 shows that sealing wax is also meant Cf. 94. 14 n.

7. *And sealed...love* Cf. *Meas.* 4. 1. 5

> But my kisses bring again,
> Seals of love, but sealed in vain

and *Ven.* 51-2.

8. *Robbed others' beds'...rents* T.T. thinks this implies that the lady had received the attentions of other *married* men.

10. *hide* suppress, keep secret (Sch.).

14. *self-example* M.'s hyphen.

143

B.S.: Second of the *Poet, Friend and Mistress* series. First of the 'Will' sonnets, and like the others, 'intended to be only half serious' (B.), the fact that both Poet and Friend are called Will affording an opportunity for jesting of which the former takes full advantage. In this sonnet however the primary meaning of 'Will' (l. 13) is the meaning it bears in 135. 5, viz. 'desire'. Thus ll. 13–14 may be paraphrased: 'If you stop running after that other Will and turn back to make love with me I will see that you get all you desire from one who is after all Will too.' B. appears on pp. xxxvi–xxxvii to deny that Sh. can be including himself here.

1. *huswife* (Q) B. alone follows Q since it preserves the Eliz. pronunciation (hussif).

8. *Not prizing* disregarding (B.).

12. *part, kiss* (edd.) Q 'part kiss'.

13. *So...Will* Q prints *Will.*

144

B.S.: First of the *Poet, Friend and Mistress* series. But it might well serve as an introduction to both Sections I and II, since it is the theme of the whole collection.

This sonnet has another version in *The Passionate Pilgrim*, which runs as follows:

Two loves I have, of comfort and despair,
That like two spirits, do suggest me still:
My better angel, is a man (right fair)
My worser spirit a woman (coloured ill.)
To win me soon to hell, my female evil
Tempteth my better angel from my side:

And would corrupt my saint to be a devil,
Wooing his purity with her fair pride.
And whether that my angel be turned fiend,
Suspect I may (yet not directly tell)
For being both to me: both, to each friend,
I guess one angel in another's hell:
  The truth I shall not know, but live in doubt,
  Till my bad angel fire my good one out.

2. *suggest* whisper advice, whether good or bad (B.). *still*, ever.

6. *side* (M.+S.-Smith.) Q 'sight'. *P.P.* 'side'.

8. *foul* *P.P.* 'fair', the only important variation (B.). *pride*, cf. 151. 10.

9. *fiend* (M.) Q 'finde'.

14. *Till my...out.* 'To fire out' = orig. 'to smoke a fox out of its den', but Roll. notes the meaning of 'communicate a venereal disease'.

145

B.S.: Third 'independent' sonnet.

'An occasional sonnet, having no connexion with the series. It is in octosyllabic measure. There is no reason to doubt its Shakespearean authorship' (B.)—but P. and Mackail do. M. quotes *Lucr.* 1534–40.

I have replaced M.'s italics by quotation-marks.

146

B.S.: Final sonnet in the *Perjury of Eye and Heart* series.

But note it has no direct reference to the Mistress; though 'rebel powers' may be taken as implying the 'worser spirit'. Ostensibly it is religious in character;

one may call it a meditation. Unfortunately it has been condemned as corrupt, without due cause, and so has lacked proper recognition.

1. *centre* Cf. *Rom.* 2. 1. 2 'Turn back, dull earth, and find thy centre out'. Acc. to the old physiology, man's soul was during life 'grossly closed in' by this 'muddy vesture of decay', the body.

2. *My sinful earth...array* (Massey+W.+T Tuck.) Q 'My sinfull earth these rebell powers that thee array'. M. and most edd. have explained the obvious misprinting of Q by assuming that the printer inadvertently repeated the last three words of l. 1 at the beginning of l. 2, and thus created a gap which must be filled by some emendation or other. But Massey, etc., rightly decided, I think, to look for the corruption at the other end of the line, and it is clear that if 'that thee' be omitted we are left with a line both metrically satisfactory and pregnant in meaning, inasmuch as the word 'array' is now seen to carry the double sense of (i) 'defile' in reference to 'sinful earth' (see *O.E.D.* 'array' vb. 10), and (ii) 'clothe', referring to the 'costly gay' garments. 'Rebel powers' mean of course the fleshly lusts while 'these' may be rendered 'that everyone knows about' (cf. Sch. p. 1212). And for 'rebel powers' one may compare '*Shylock* My flesh and blood to rebel! *Sol.* Out upon it, old carrion, rebels it at these years?' *M.V.* 3. 1. 32 ff. Finally, l. 2 is what Tuck. calls a kind of 'parenthetical development' common in Sh. but, appearing to be incomplete to Thorpe or the printer, was supplied with 'that thee' to make sense.

4. *outward walls* 'W. quotes from *Macbeth* 5. 5. 1 "Hang out our banners on the outward walls"; and there seems reason to suppose that this idea was in the poet's mind, but that he modified the expression in order to suit the human body rather than the castle

with which he was comparing it; and also to prepare for what was coming' (B.). Cf. *R. II*, 3. 2. 169 'And with a little pin|Bores through his castle wall'.

10. *that* the body. *pine* starve. *aggravate* 'make heavier; Cf. Daniel (*Civil Wars*, II, 16): "To aggravate thine own affliction's store"' (B.). *aggravate thy store* refers to the body; 'let your servant, the body, suffer want rather than its master, the soul' (P.).

11. *terms*, in the legal and academic sense: long periods of time.

14. *And death...then*. Cf. St Paul I Cor. xv. 54–5 'So when this corruptible shall have put on incorruption....O grave, where is thy victory?'

147

B.S.: Eighth in the *Perjury of Eye and Heart* series.

Bucknill (p. 287) writes: 'This sonnet is entirely medical, and so graphic, that explanation is needless.'

1–2. *My love...disease* Cf. Sidney's *Arcadia* (1593), Bk. III (1922 ed. II, 9) 'Sick to the death, still loving my disease'.

5–7. *My reason...left me* Cf. *M.W.W.* 2. 1. 5 ff.: 'Though Love use Reason for his precisian [?physician], he admits him not for his councillor.'

9. *Past cure...past care* Cf. Tilley, C 921, who quotes *1 H. VI*, 3. 3. 3; *L.L.L.* 5. 2. 28; *R. II*, 2. 3. 171; *Ham.* 1. 2. 106; *Mac.* 3. 2. 11.

10. *frantic-mad* M.'s hyphen.

148

B.S.: Ninth in the *Perjury of Eye and Heart* series, and he writes: 'This sonnet is rhetorically parallel with the beginning sonnet 137. And it finally answers the question that 137 asks.'

4. *censures* judges (B.), estimates (M.).

8. *Love's eye...:no,* Lettsom's notion that 'Sh. seems to intend a pun on *eye* and *ay*' has beguiled some, but 'If so, it is impossible to make it evident in reading, for the pun requires two inconsistent punctuations'. (B.) W. regards Q's as 'a piece of punctuation so exquisite as to affirm an author's hand'.

14. *Well-seeing* M.'s hyphen.

149

B.S.: Probably Fourth in the *Perjury of Eye and Heart* series.

Alternatively, he suggests that this and 150 might follow 148, owing to their carrying on the theme of blindness.

2. *partake?* edd. Q 'pertake:' take part. 'A *partaker* was in Shakespeare's time the term for an *associate* or *confederate* in any business' (M.). B. quotes *1 H. VI*, 2. 4. 100.

4. *all-tyrant,* (B.). Q 'all tyrant'. This is the general view of most; 'that is, "for the sake of thee, thou tyrant"' (M.). W. interprets 'all tyrant' as 'tyrant to myself', but as B. notes, 'all' has no force if applied to the Poet.

12. *eyes?* (edd.) Q 'eyes.'.

150

B.S.: Probably Fifth in the *Perjury of Eye and Heart* series.

But see note on 149. B.S. also writes: 'Sonnets 137,

141, and 150 are plainly meant to function together. Their wide separation in Q prevents this; the restored sequence permits it and also retains the three sonnets in necessary logical order (141 following from 137 and 150 from 141.)'

2. *with insufficiency* notwithstanding, or even by virtue of, defects. See 149. 11 (B.).

5. *becoming* grace. M. cites *Ant.* 1. 1. 49, 1. 3. 96, 2. 2. 238-9. Ver. explains 'the faculty of making things ill look well'.

7. *warrantise* Cf. *Ham.* 5. 1. 221 (B.). *skill* sagacity (Sch.).

10. *hate?* Q 'hate,'.

151

B.S.: Sixth in *Perjury of Eye and Heart* series (but see note on 149).

To the objectors to this sonnet, Roll. writes: 'One might reply that the woman in question is represented as a prostitute, who presumably enjoyed grossness.'

1. *conscience* 'There is a play upon senses of "conscience," namely (1) moral sense and understanding, (2) guilty "knowing"'. (Tuck.).

2. *love?* (edd.) Q 'love,'.

3. *cheater* Ver. glosses 'rogue'. On. suggests a double meaning (i) mod. deceiver, (ii) decoy duck (cf. *2 H. IV*, 2. 4. 92) or tame animal.

7. *may,* Q's comma is rhythmical (Simpson, p. 26).

8. *reason* = talk.

10. *pride* sexual desire, 'heat' esp. in female animals (*O.E.D.* 11).

11. *be,* (edd.) Q 'be'.

152

B.S.: Seventh in *Perjury of Eye and Heart* series (see note on 149); and he writes: '152 makes dominant the "perjury" note begun in 142, and, like 150, joins it (lines 11–14) with the "eye" theme of previous sonnets.'

1. *I am forsworn* 'presumably towards his own wife' (Tuck.).

3. *thy bed-vow broke* This proves she was a married woman (as Mary Fitton was not at this stage). *new faith torn* 'The breach of "new faith" is in vowing "new hate" to the poet. There is no reference (as W.) to breaking off the intrigue with the friend' (B.).

6. *twenty?* (edd.) Q 'twenty:'.

7. *misuse* 'If "my vows" are the "deep oaths" of lines 9 and 10, "misuse" will mean "misrepresent", *sc.* by swearing that you are beautiful' (P.).

11–12. *to enlighten...see* 'To make thee appear "bright" (147. 13) I gave my own eyes to blindness, or at any rate made them forswear themselves' (B.).

13. *I*, (Sewell+edd.) Q 'eye'.

153, 154

B.S. thinks these a 'pair', and part of the series *My Mistress' Eyes*. But I feel doubtful and prefer to believe that they are early essays, if indeed they are Sh.'s at all. 'This and the following sonnet are composed of the very same thoughts differently versified. They seem to have been early essays of the poet, who perhaps had not determined which he should prefer' (M.).

153

The orig. source of the sonnet appears to be an epigram in the Greek Anthology. Controversy has raged over Sh.'s source (see Roll. for a full account). But Tuck. observes, 'A number of Latin translations from the Anthology existed in the 16th cent., nor was it necessary that Sh. should have had access even to these. Their contents were not kept literary secrets.'

1. *his brand* i.e. Cupid's torch.

2. *A maid of Dian's* i.e. one of the chaste nymphs of Diana, goddess of Chastity.

4. *that ground* that region.

5. *Love* Q 'love'.

6. *lively* living.

7. *seething* boiling (Sch.).

8. *strange* (edd.)<Q 'strang'—prob. a Shn spelling.

9. *Love's* Q 'love's' *new-fired* M.'s hyphen.

11. *bath* '"Query, whether we shall read *Bath* (i.e. the city of that name). The following words seem to authorise it" Steev. There is undoubtedly a reference to the Bath waters, for the Greek original says nothing about curative powers' (B.).

12. *distempered* diseased, bodily or mentally deranged (Sch.).

14. *eyes* (edd.), Q 'eye'.

154

2. *heart-inflaming* M.'s hyphen.

10 *Love's* Q has no cap.

LIST OF THE SONNETS IN CONJECTURED ORDER OF WRITING

SECTION I. TO THE FRIEND

Marriage Sonnets

1. From fairest creatures we desire increase,
2. When forty winters shall besiege thy brow,
3. Look in thy glass and tell the face thou viewest,
4. Unthrifty loveliness why dost thou spend,
5. Those hours that with gentle work did frame
6. Then let not winter's raggéd hand deface,
7. Lo in the orient when the gracious light
8. Music to hear, why hear'st thou music sadly?
9. Is it for fear to wet a widow's eye,
10. For shame deny that thou bear'st love to any
11. As fast as thou shalt wane so fast thou grow'st,
12. When I do count the clock that tells the time,
13. O that you were your self, but love you are
14. Not from the stars do I my judgement pluck,
15. When I consider every thing that grows
16. But wherefore do not you a mightier way
17. Who will believe my verse in time to come,

A Glorious Morning

18. Shall I compare thee to a summer's day?
19. Devouring Time blunt thou the lion's paws,
20. A woman's face with nature's own hand painted,
21. So is it not with me as with that muse,
22. My glass shall not persuade me I am old,
23. As an imperfect actor on the stage,
24. Mine eye hath played the painter and hath stelled,

The Poet goes on a Journey

25. Let those who are in favour with their stars,
36. Let me confess that we two must be twain,
37. As a decrepit father takes delight,
38. How can my muse want subject to invent
39. O how thy worth with manners may I sing,
26. Lord of my love, to whom in vassalage
27. Weary with toil, I haste me to my bed,
28. How can I then return in happy plight
29. When in disgrace with Fortune and men's eyes,
30. When to the sessions of sweet silent thought,
31. Thy bosom is endearéd with all hearts,
32. If thou survive my well-contented day,
43. When most I wink then do mine eyes best see,
44. If the dull substance of my flesh were thought,
45. The other two, slight air, and purging fire,
46. Mine eye and heart are at a mortal war,
47. Betwixt mine eye and heart a league is took,
50. How heavy do I journey on the way,
51. Thus can my love excuse the slow offence,
52. So am I as the rich whose blesséd key,
53. What is your substance, whereof are you made,
54. O how much more doth beauty beauteous seem,
55. (Ovid) Not marble, nor the gilded monuments
56. Sweet love renew thy force, be it not said
59. (Ovid) If there be nothing new, but that which is,
60. „ Like as the waves make towards the pebbled shore,
62. „ Sin of self-love possesseth all mine eye,
63. „ Against my love shall be as I am now
64. „ When I have seen by Time's fell hand defaced
65. „ Since brass, nor stone, nor earth, nor boundless sea,

66. (Ovid) Tired with all these for restful death I cry,
67. „ Ah wherefore with infection should he live,
68. „ Thus is his cheek the map of days outworn,
69. — Those parts of thee that the world's eye doth view,
70. — That thou art blamed shall not be thy defect,
71. (Ovid) No longer mourn for me when I am dead,
72. „ O lest the world should task you to recite,
73. „ That time of year thou mayst in me behold,
74. „ But be contented when that fell arrest,
75. — So are you to my thoughts as food to life,
81. (Ovid) Or I shall live your epitaph to make,

Liaison Sonnets

48. How careful was I when I took my way,
57. Being your slave what should I do but tend,
58. That god forbid, that made me first your slave,
61. Is it thy will, thy image should keep open
40. Take all my loves, my love, yea take them all,
41. Those pretty wrongs that liberty commits,
42. That thou hast her it is not all my grief,
33. Full many a glorious morning have I seen,
34. Why didst thou promise such a beautious day,
35. No more be grieved at that which thou hast done,

(Not to the Friend?)

77. Thy glass will show thee how thy beauties wear,

The Rival Poet

76. Why is my verse so barren of new pride?
78. So oft have I invoked thee for my muse,
79. Whilst I alone did call upon thy aid,

80. O how I faint when I of you do write,
82. I grant thou wert not married to my muse,
83. I never saw that you did painting need,
84. Who is it that says most, which can say more,
85. My tongue-tied muse in manners holds her still,
86. Was it the proud full sail of his great verse,

Farewell Sonnets

49. Against that time (if ever that time come)
87. Farewell! thou art too dear for my possessing,
88. When thou shalt be disposed to set me light,
89. Say that thou didst forsake me for some fault,
90. Then hate me when thou wilt, if ever, now,
91. Some glory in their birth, some in their skill,
92. (Poss. also liaison) But do thy worst to steal thy self away,
93. " " " So shall I live, supposing thou art true,
94. They that have power to hurt, and will do none,
95. (Poss. Fitton affair) How sweet and lovely dost thou make the shame,
96. " " " Some say thy fault is youth, some wantonness,
97. (Sonnets while absent) How like a winter hath my absence been
98. " " " From you have I been absent in the spring,
99. " " " The forward violet thus did I chide,
104. To me fair friend you never can be old,

---

100. Where art thou Muse that thou forget'st so long,
101. O truant Muse what shall be thy amends,
102. My love is strengthened though more weak in seeming,

103. Alack what poverty my muse brings forth,
105. Let not my love be called idolatry,
106. When in the chronicle of wasted time,
107. Not mine own fears, nor the prophetic soul,
108. What's in the brain that ink may character,
109. O never say that I was false of heart,
110. Alas 'tis true, I have gone here and there,
111. O for my sake do you with Fortune chide,
112. Your love and pity doth th' impression fill,
113. Since I left you, mine eye is in my mind,
114. Or whether doth my mind being crowned with you
115. Those lines that I before have writ do lie,
116. Let me not to the marriage of true minds
117. Accuse me thus, that I have scanted all,
118. Like as to make our appetite more keen
119. What potions have I drunk of Siren tears
120. That you were once unkind befriends me now,
121. 'Tis better to be vile than vile esteemed,
122. Thy gift, thy tables, are within my brain
123. No! Time, thou shalt not boast that I do change,
124. If my dear love were but the child of state,
125. Were't aught to me I bore the canopy,
126. O thou my lovely boy who in thy power,

SECTION II. TO THE DARK WOMAN

I. *My Mistress' Eyes*

A. 140. Be wise as thou art cruel, do not press
139. O call not me to justify the wrong,
B. 153. Cupid laid by his brand and fell asleep,
154. The little Love-god lying once asleep,
C. 130. My mistress' eyes are nothing like the sun,
127. In the old age black was not counted fair,

II. *Poet, Friend, and Mistress*

144. Two loves I have of comfort and despair,
143. Lo as a careful huswife runs to catch,
135. Whoever hath her wish, thou hast thy will,
136. If thy soul check thee that I come so near,
131. Thou art as tyrannous, so as thou art,
132. Thine eyes I love, and they as pitying me,
133. Beshrew that heart that makes my heart to groan,
134. So now I have confessed that he is thine,

III. *Perjury of Eye and Heart*

137. Thou blind fool Love, what dost thou to mine eyes,
141. In faith I do not love thee with mine eyes,
142. Love is my sin, and thy dear virtue hate,
149. Canst thou O cruel, say I love thee not,
150. O from what power hast thou this powerful might,
151. Love is too young to know what conscience is,
152. In loving thee thou know'st I am forsworn,
147. My love is as a fever longing still,
148. O me! what eyes hath love put in my head,
129. Th' expense of spirit in a waste of shame
146. Poor soul the centre of my sinful earth,

Independent Sonnets

128. How oft when thou, my music, music play'st,
138. When my love swears that she is made of truth,
145. Those lips that Love's own hand did make,